Instructor's Manual

to Accompany

Experiencing the World's Religions
Tradition, Challenge, and Change
Second Edition

Michael Molloy
University of Hawai`i
Kapi`olani Community College

with Lecture Supplements by
Brett Greider
University of Wisconsin
Eau Claire

and

Jeffrey C. Ruff
University of California
Santa Barbara

Boston   Burr Ridge, IL   Dubuque, IA   Madison, WI   New York   San Francisco   St. Louis
Bangkok   Bogotá   Caracas   Kuala Lumpur   Lisbon   London   Madrid   Mexico City
Milan   Montreal   New Delhi   Santiago   Seoul   Singapore   Sydney   Taipei   Toronto

McGraw-Hill Higher Education

A Division of The **McGraw-Hill** *Companies*

encounter

1 2 3 4 5 6 7 8 9 0 QPD/QPD 0 9 8 7 6 5 4 3 2 1

ISBN: 0-7674-2045-4

This book is printed on acid-free paper.

www.mhhe.com

CONTENTS

Preface   v

Part I: Concepts and Strategies for Teaching World Religions   1

    Introduction   1
    Goals of the Course   1
    Teaching and Learning Techniques   2
        Lecture   2
        Writing in the Classroom   2
        Writing Outside the Classroom   2
        Drawing   3
        Group Discussion   3
        Student Presentations   3
        Audiovisual Presentations   4
        Guest Lecturers   4
        Religious Sites in the Community   4
    Teaching Issues   4
        Giving Credit   4
        Students with Learning Disabilities   4
        Difficult Students   5
    Organizing the Course   5
        The Order of Presenting World Religions   5
        The Use of Additional Texts   6
        Sample Course Description   6
        Semester-System Syllabus   7
        Quarter-System Syllabus   7

Part II: Individual Chapter Resources for *Experiencing the World's Religions*   8

        Chapter 1   Understanding Religion   8
        Chapter 2   Oral Religions   19
        Chapter 3   Hinduism   28
        Chapter 4   Buddhism   40
        Chapter 5   Jainism and Sikhism   51
        Chapter 6   Taoism and Confucianism   59
        Chapter 7   Shinto   68
        Chapter 8   Judaism   75
        Chapter 9   Christianity   86
        Chapter 10   Islam   101
        Chapter 11   Alternative Paths   110
        Chapter 12   The Religious Search in the Modern World   120

Part III: Transparency Masters   128

PREFACE

A world religions course is potentially one of the most interesting courses that a student can take. In such a course, teachers are able to offer something for every type of student. For the thoughtful, the course offers philosophy. For those with a feeling for beauty, it offers art, music, and architecture. For those who find people fascinating, it offers the full spectrum of human behavior. For those who love books, it offers texts to investigate. For the physically active, it allows direct physical experience of local sites and the possibility of future travel. For those who love the past, it offers ancient cultures and wonderful old languages. And for those who love the modern world, it offers the fascination of exploring our burgeoning contemporary culture with new eyes.

What is true for students is also true for teachers. The course, while covering a specific core of religions, allows a multitude of approaches. Since people teach best what they love, I think that teachers should, to some extent, let their own enthusiasms shape and color their courses. Their enthusiasm will ignite similar appreciation in their students. I encourage all teachers of a world religions course to give individual form to their course, as they discover through experience what brings them and their students the greatest satisfaction. The course should be a success with students, but it should also bring joy to teachers. It will bring joy to everyone if teachers refuse to be simply teaching machines (doing work better done by a computer) and instsead inject into their teaching their own personality, interests, and humanity.

Teachers, I think, should also encourage humor. It seems to me that humor is a form of insight, and when kind, it is always an addition to a classroom. Both textbooks and teachers' manuals, I have sadly learned, are expected to be free of humor. (As one reviewer of Chapter 6 commented, in cutting out my reference to the Flintstones and their love of rocks: "*I* am the humorist in my classes.") Humor, however, need not be missing from a class. Teachers should shamelessly add their own—to lectures, quizzes, and commentary. A good course should have some of the dynamism of a game of volleyball or tennis, with a give-and-take between both sides. (This is difficult in large lecture sections, but not impossible.) Humor helps free the energy that students can bring to a course, encouraging them to contribute their own insights. It also adds joy.

The material in this instructor's manual is, of course, only a compilation of suggestions. Every teacher will want to supplement what is offered here. Teachers should draw from it only what they think might be useful, and they are invited to experiment with the offerings and pass on their own suggestions to the author.

This instructor's manual is divided into three parts:

Part I gives general ideas that I have found helpful in teaching the course effectively. Among the topics are

- an overall approach to teaching the course.

- teaching and learning techniques (including ideas for lectures, writing in the classroom, writing outside the classroom, drawing, group discussion, student presentations, audiovisual presentations, guest lecturers, and visits to religious sites in the community).

- teaching issues (including giving credit and dealing with students who have learning disabilities and working with difficult students).

- organization of the course (including the order of presenting world religions, the use of additional texts, sample course description, and semester-system and quarter-system syllabi).

Part II gives specific material for each chapter:

Learning Objectives

Chapter Outline

Lecture Supplements

Notes on *For Fuller Understanding*

Lists and Descriptions of Useful Video Resources

Current Internet Resources

Multiple-Choice Questions

Essay Topics

The lecture supplements (by Brett Greider and Jeffrey Ruff) offer summaries of recent books and articles that teachers can use to present additional material to an interested class or as a research project for an individual student. The suggested videos include both old classics (such as those by Huston Smith and Alan Watts) and many recent works. One of the pleasures of teaching a world religions course is the availability of good videos that can illustrate important points, take viewers in their imaginations to foreign lands, and add a visual dimension to a well-organized verbal presentation. (Not all of a video need be used—just the best part—and instructors can use the mute button and do their own narration when they want.) The Web sites given here are only a small sample. The Internet has thousands of interconnected Web sites, some with complex illustrations. Students and teachers will be amazed at the amount of wonderfully presented material available to them there.

Regarding the test questions, I recommend occasionally adding a humorous option to the multiple-choice answers, to keep the students attentive and to lower the level of test-taking anxiety. The essay questions can be useful not only for tests but also for in-class student writing, for group discussions, for written and oral responses to videos, and for homework assignments.

Part III provides essential terms and concepts formatted for use as overhead transparencies orstudent handouts. I use at least three or four overheads per class period, uncovering the appropriate line of material as I am speaking about the topic. This allows control over classroom discussion (student discussion tends to stop when a new group of words appears on an overhead projection). Overhead projections also show students the correct spelling of unfamiliar terms, present essential ideas for their notes, help prepare them for tests, and generally keep them alert and active. Other teachers may prefer to give such information as handouts on which students can take notes.

Part I
Concepts and Strategies for Teaching World Religions

Introduction

A course in world religions is a wonderful course to teach. Many students have a keen interest in the topic, and those who don't—those who think the course will be boring—often end up being intrigued. The study of world religions naturally intersects with many other fascinating disciplines that students are studying concurrently—art, music, history, literature, philosophy, and psychology. The course can be enriched, too, in many ways. In the classroom, the teacher can enhance the course with guest speakers (who are usually happy to speak, and to do so for free), videos, and music. Outside the classroom, students can visit museums and experience concerts, lectures, films, art exhibits, and religious sites.

At the end of the course, the students will have a much greater understanding of the world and of themselves, and the teacher will have the joy of having contributed to cultural understanding, to tolerance, and to enjoyment of life. At the end of a world religions course that has been effectively taught, students frequently write, "This is a course that every college student should take."

Another satisfaction for instructors is that the course invites creativity and even artistry on the part of the teacher. It can be a course that is deadly dull—a lifeless recital of names, dates, and movements—or a course that is full of intellectual satisfaction, which opens innumerable windows and doors for its students. The effectiveness will lie to a great extent in the hands of the teacher. Luckily, good teaching can be taught. It is largely a matter of technique. Used regularly, effective teaching techniques will help bring about excellent learning experiences. This teacher's guide is meant to bring about just such a response.

Goals of the Course

I consider the basic principles and goals of effective teaching of world religions to be

1. *Blending objective and subjective.* The ideal course seeks to guarantee that students know all the essential elements of major religions—the history, significant scriptures and doctrines, important thinkers, major art and architecture, and location. At the same time, the ideal course will make every effort to tie these facts to the current knowledge, interest, and needs of the students.

2. *Understanding other people and other cultures.* A course in world religions is valuable in that it brings greater understanding of people in one's own culture who hold different beliefs and values and it brings appreciation for the great cultural variety among human beings. It is a significant contribution to multicultural awareness.

3. *Understanding oneself.* Most students will study this course in college, and the majority will be in their late teens and early twenties. For many students, the college period is a time of intense and necessary clarification of their own beliefs and values. A course in world religions can be very helpful in this important personal endeavor.

4. *Reinforcing other disciplines.* Religions express themselves in art, music, architecture, poetry, and story and may be studied from the vantage points of many disciplines. To study religion is automatically multidisciplinary and helps integrate the student's study of other disciplines.

5. *Learning actively.* The most effective kind of learning involves activity on the part of the student. An example of this is that students often cannot remember the details of lectures in a course, but they remember well the paper they wrote for the course. While the backbone of a religion course will generally be lectures, that method must be complemented by methods and assignments in which the students are more than passive listeners. Among these methods are writing assignments in and out of class, group discussions, response questions to videos, and student presentations. An effective class may be given over half to lecture and the other half to other teaching and learning techniques. An inventive teacher will find as many ways as possible to supplement lectures with techniques that make the student active.

6. *Learning visually.* We have often heard the old saying that "one picture is worth a thousand words," and many students remember far better what they see than what they hear. A world religions course allows teachers to

teach not only verbally but also visually. They are able both to show and to tell. This can be done through videos, religious objects brought to class, and students' drawing of religious art that they see in museums and at religious sites.

7. *Learning through experience.* The involvement of many senses, of movement, and of travel enriches and strengthens the learning experience. The study of the religions of the world really begins to mean something when a person goes out to explore the world. The dead facts of religion come alive when they make everyday experience meaningful.

Teaching and Learning Techniques
Lecture

Lecturing is a valuable way to distill and convey information. It also allows teachers to present their own understanding of material and to talk about their own experiences, which is important if the material is to be humanized. Lecturing will probably remain the primary technique of teaching world religions, but it must be employed with sensitivity.

World religions are filled with a daunting number of foreign terms, the names of gods and goddesses, dates, and the names of leaders and movements. Students can drown in these details. The teacher must decide a standard by which to judge whether to introduce foreign terms or simply to translate them, to include names of movements and leaders or to exclude them, and so on. The standard that I use regularly is that of "the educated person." Everything that I include in my courses is tested by this criterion. Typical questions I ask myself are the following. Would an ordinary person eager to be well educated want to know about this? Would we expect an educated layperson to know this? If the answer is no, I save the material for an upper-level course that specializes in a single religion. The study of world religions is so full of profound ideas and interesting people that it seems necessary to carefully choose details that will cast light on these ideas and people rather than to allow details to cloud them.

Overhead projections (either via transparencies or computer) are useful in giving essential information, outlines of important topics, and correct spellings. Using overhead projections is much faster and clearer than writing on the blackboard. Projections also enhance the lecture experience with a visual component.

Writing in the Classroom

Writing is increasingly being recognized as an important technique of active learning. It may be done in the classroom as well as at home. While students often balk at writing at home, they usually enjoy writing in the classroom, and their enjoyment of in-class writing can be utilized by teachers.

In-class writing will be short and informal. It is usually what is often called "focused freewriting," but can include a wide variety of types, such as letters, dialogue, and even poetry. (For example, when Zen is covered in the course, students can write haiku.) Writing can be used at the beginning of a class to prepare students for a discussion, in the middle of class to focus attention, and at the end of class to summarize. Writing is also quite appropriate at the end of a video presentation or before a group discussion. Typically, the teacher will present two or three questions or prompts on an overhead projection or write them on the board and then give students about five to ten minutes to write. Students can read to each other in groups. Their in-class writing may be collected by the teacher or not, as seems appropriate. A teacher can use some typical questions or prompts such as "The main point so far has been . . ." "The biggest question in my mind is . . ." "What are the main messages of the video we just saw?"

Writing Outside the Classroom

The traditional assignment of a term paper is still a useful technique, but the teacher has to be careful to make assignments that cannot be taken from the Internet or bought from a term paper service. It's best to choose topics that the students really would like to explore and ones that demand a certain amount of creativity and a personal touch. It is also helpful to give a selection of options. Here are some possibilities: description of one's own personal religious ideas and practice and how they were arrived at; creation of a new religion; description of attendance at a religious service that is different from the religion in which the student was raised; description of one's religious upbringing; an imaginary pilgrimage to ten religious sites anywhere in the world; a short story in which religion plays an important role; or an interview with a local religious leader. (It is good to request that the term paper be typed and technically perfect, as this is a valuable professional exercise for the student.)

In place of (or in addition to) a term paper, short semiformal papers can be required. Good topics are comparisons of religions, solutions of problems raised by a religious teaching, summaries of main points of a chapter of text, and responses to a reading assignment. These papers can be the basis for discussion in later classes.

Another possibility is to write short response papers to sights and events outside the classroom. Students appreciate being told of upcoming concerts, art exhibits, movies, plays, and talks that relate to religion, both on and off campus. Credit can be given for short response papers. (These papers can be informal and written by hand and do not need to be returned. They can also be collected in a portfolio turned in at the end of the course.)

Drawing

Drawing is an important way to learn. Because drawing takes time to do, it is a particularly good technique for contemplating something of beauty. Having students draw also indirectly teaches the importance of nonverbal response. The present-day emphasis on writing is healthy, but nonverbal aesthetic response has to be valued, too. Drawing can be used alone or in conjunction with a written response, as the teacher desires.

Drawing is particularly appropriate for student viewing of religious artworks in museums and exhibitions and for student visits to examples of beautiful religious architecture in the region. Students will often say "I can't draw," and I always respond "You are just the person who will benefit from this exercise. This exercise is not meant for people who are already excellent artists." I then explain that the drawings only need to be simple and in pencil (museums ordinarily forbid drawing in pen in their galleries). Students will sometimes ask to photograph instead of draw. Photography is certainly a legitimate artistic response that I do not want to discourage, but I always ask that the students also do drawings in addition to their photographs. Drawings, of course, are not graded on ability but are given a certain number of points when they are turned in.

Students generally find that they love to draw—after they actually do it. Each person's drawing is highly unique, and the subjects can also be unique. I usually ask students simply to find something interesting at the religious site or exhibit of religious art and to draw what interests them. One student, I recall, did drawings of door locks and hinges at several churches—small but complex artworks and truly fascinating. A pleasant by-product of drawing exercises is that they are a delight for a teacher to look at because they are so different. Often students who are quiet in class or whose native language is not English will produce extraordinary drawings, which offer insight into their ways of seeing the world. Students enjoy sharing their drawings, too, which can be done in groups at the end of a course.

Group Discussion

Students can be broken up into groups of two to five, depending on the purpose and the amount of time available. Questions can be proposed by the teacher, and groups can elect a recorder to write down their conclusions, which will then be available for full-class discussion. (Group discussion is particularly appropriate after a video, possibly in conjunction with a written response.) Individuals in groups can also read their writing to one another and comment on it. Group discussion has important social benefits, too, in that it promotes intellectual dialogue—surely a goal of the college experience. It also counteracts the isolation and loneliness that college students can experience in a new environment. Students who are shy about speaking to a whole class will often have no difficulty talking in a small group.

In my own experience, I have found it useful in the first weeks of a course to break students into groups with their geographical neighbors in the classroom. This allows them to get to know the people sitting around them. Only after about a month do I mix up the groups, which is done by giving each student a number (e.g., from 1 to 8) and then having students of the same numbers form groups. I also generally save group discussion until the last part of the class period, so that students can leave the classroom talking with their classmates.

Student Presentations

Very short oral presentations by students are a good way to begin a class. In my classes I invite all students to be looking for newspaper and magazine articles on religion, books of interest (especially those full of photos), and religious objects that they have at home, and I often ask for volunteers who will be looking for things to bring to class. Students bring these things to class, introduce themselves, and then speak in a few sentences about what they have brought. Then we pass the news article or object around. Students who bring in something write their names on a credit sheet at the end of the class for eventual credit. This is a good way to begin a class since it generates friendly feelings, helps students to get to know each other's names, and allows time for late students to arrive. The teacher can also bring in newspaper articles and books to be passed around at this time. (In my office I keep a collection of books with large photos about religions. I bring these to class to pass around among students.) Five or ten minutes is the usual amount of time spent on these. More formal student presentations are also possible, particularly in smaller classes, honors classes, writing-intensive classes, and seminars.

Audiovisual Presentations

Ours is a highly visual age, and students expect to see as well as to hear whatever is described. Luckily, many good videotapes are available. The best length for a videotape is twenty to twenty-five minutes. Longer than that, and some students lose interest. If a videotape is longer than thirty minutes, the teacher should consider showing just part of the video or showing it in consecutive classes. It is possible to personalize the presentation by fast-forwarding through unimportant parts and by using the mute button when the teacher wants to add an appropriate comment. Slides and CDs may also be used if the classroom is properly equipped to do so. Students sometimes offer to show videotapes or play music on CDs. Videos may also be taped from television. A good teacher will make a collection of videos for classroom use.

Guest Lecturers

Guest lecturers abound. Most religious groups are eager to be heard and understood and are quite approachable. Some, such as the ISKCON (Hare Krishna) followers, even ask to be invited into the classroom. Ministers, nuns, priests, rabbis, and even monks are often accustomed to public speaking and do an excellent job when they come into the classroom. An honorarium is always welcome, but they do not expect it.

Because religion ties in closely with other disciplines, it is possible to share guest speakers with teachers of anthropology, history, art, and other related subjects. Instead of having a guest speaker come to a classroom, an auditorium can be reserved, and students from several classes that meet at the same time can attend the talk. Students enjoy the break from their usual routine. Teachers can request that their students write a short response paper for credit.

Religious Sites in the Community

Almost every community has several religious buildings of architectural interest or a museum where religious art may be found. There may also be a site of native religion nearby. Students enjoy visiting these places for credit. I hand out maps and worksheets and ask students to do a simple drawing of something religiously significant at each site (as explained elsewhere). Worksheets contain the address and phone number for the site, hours that the site is open, and often a simple map and bus directions. Drawings can be done on the back of the worksheet. I have students hand in these worksheets in portfolios with their term papers at the end of the course.

Teaching Issues
Giving Credit

Credit should be given for anything that a teacher wishes a student to do. This means that a course should be structured in such a way that an appropriate number of points be given for tests, papers, oral presentations, drawings, response papers, and the like. Some elements will be graded and scored. Other elements will receive points simply for being performed. In my own classes, I typically have a scale of approximately 400 points. Three exams, each worth 100 points, are given. Another 100 points comes from all other sources—term paper (30 points maximum), drawings of religious sites and artworks (10 points each), short response papers to events (5 points each), and oral presentations (1 point each). Teachers can experiment and tailor this approach as they see fit, but my experience has shown that students have to be rewarded with points or some form of credit for whatever they do for the course. It also gives them a greater sense of control over their activities and their grade. Giving a variety of things to do for credit recognizes that students have varied interests and that there is much difference in the amount of time that individual students have for class projects.

Students with Learning Disabilities

In these days of mainstreaming, teachers must expect every kind of learning disability among their students. Some students are unable to see, hear, walk, or write. Others present more complex problems: dyslexia, epilepsy, bipolar disorders, emotional imbalances. Working with counselors is important. Counseling centers often try to alert teachers to the problems of their students and give advice about dealing with them properly. They also will coordinate notetakers, tape-recording of books and lectures, and special desks for students in wheelchairs. They can help if a teacher encounters unexpected problems in dealing with such students.

A generous teacher, however, can often turn these difficulties into benefits. It is quite touching to see the courage of physically and mentally challenged students working in class. For example, students who cannot hear can nonetheless often make oral presentations or speak in sign language that is then translated aloud by an interpreter. Students who have no learning disabilities gain a great deal from these courageous students, and the entire group of students in a class can feel much closer to each other as a result.

Difficult Students

Difficult students can destroy the effectiveness of a class and end the pleasure a teacher can feel in teaching it. Religion classes pose a special problem because they sometimes attract people with strong religious convictions who want to find converts, people who have been hurt by religion and have become strongly antireligious, and people with religious obsessions. The difficulty of such students, however, just "comes with the territory" and is counterbalanced by the pleasure of working with the many delightful students who make up most religion classes. Dealing properly with difficult individuals is essential for the smooth functioning of a classroom. Since teachers "set the weather" in the classroom, those who cannot deal patiently with difficult students should not be teaching religion. But knowing what to expect and having a few techniques for dealing with difficult individuals can create the difference between a course that is an enjoyable success and one that is a painful failure.

I apply five basic principles for dealing with difficult students in my classroom:

1. Never embarrass a student publicly. A teacher can always speak to a student after class about change in behavior. Public humiliation of a student will alienate all the students of a class.
2. Work to make difficult students into friends, not enemies.
3. Allow students of strong opinions to make contributions to the class, if at all possible.
4. Figure out ways to channel the energies of difficult students so that their contributions do not undermine the teacher's control of the classroom or the learning of other students. This can be done in several ways. For example, a teacher can limit the amount of time that any student can speak. Also, when a student becomes difficult, it is easy to shift gears. Have students write or break into discussion groups, show a video, or present notes on an overhead projection that have to be copied. Sometimes it is necessary to end a difficult student's oral contribution in class somewhat abruptly, but it must be done without anyone's losing patience.
5. Work with the counselors. They can give advice about handling difficult students and can help if (in a rare situation) an intractable student needs to be removed from a course.

Difficult students offer a special challenge to teachers, but if their energies can be properly channeled, they bring color and spice to a classroom. And they are always memorable.

Organizing the Course
The Order of Presenting World Religions

Almost all world religion textbooks introduce Hinduism and Buddhism before other major religions and then end with the Abrahamic religions. Perhaps this is done because Hinduism, having no founder, seems to be among the most ancient of living religions. Some instructors like this order because it immediately introduces religious concepts that seem exotic and colorful for students raised in the Abrahamic traditions.

It is possible, however, to present the major religions in a different order. Some teachers like to take up the Abrahamic religions early, because their students are most familiar with the concepts and terminology. This order allows students to wade into the sea of religion rather effortlessly. This also sets up a strong model to use for contrast with certain elements of Hinduism and Buddhism. Teachers might try both orders of presentation to see which is more successful.

Additional variation is also possible in the presentation of native religions and Shinto, which may be grouped together and taught at the beginning or end of a course.

The Use of Additional Texts

Some teachers use only a textbook or complement it with handouts. Others like to have students read primary texts in addition to a textbook. A few teachers use no textbook but have students rely on the teacher's notes and read only primary texts. I have found that a textbook helps give students necessary guidance in the essentials of the major religions and helps keep them from feeling lost. It also allows them to read additional material at home that cannot be covered in the lectures. My lectures are confined to what I think is the most essential information, and I underscore that by using overhead projections that give important terms, historical facts, and concepts in outline form. (These can be found in Part III of this instructor's manual.) In addition to the textbook, however, I always use supplementary texts. (Currently I use the Bible, the Tao Te Ching, and *Siddhartha,* which students always enjoy.) During the study of Hinduism and Buddhism, I have found it useful to assign one of these books: the Bhagavad Gita, Hesse's *Siddhartha,* or the Dhammapada. In the section on Chinese and Japanese religions, these have proven useful: the Tao Te Ching or a basic book on Zen. In the section on the Abrahamic religions, one can use a paperback version of the Christian Bible or the Qur'an. It is also possible to use an anthology of scriptures from world religions. It helps the students when the teacher and students read together in class from the supplementary books and then discuss their meaning.

Sample Course Description

World Religions   E-mail address
Office   Office telephone
Name of instructor   Office hours

• COURSE OBJECTIVES

This course is designed to introduce you to the major religions of the world—Hinduism, Buddhism, Taoism, Confucianism, Shinto, Judaism, Christianity, and Islam. At the end of the course, you will have increased your awareness of the important elements of the major religions—their myth, symbols, ritual, doctrine, moral codes, and artistic expression. You will recognize the differences among the religious traditions. You will better understand the religious issues and conflicts in the modern world. You will have a deepened appreciation of your own religious background and that of the community in which you live.

• TEXT(S)

[Here give list of required and recommended texts.]

• REQUIREMENTS

This course is divided into thirds; and there will be three examinations, one at the end of each third of the course. The examinations are noncumulative. Please be present for the examinations. The first third of the course, after presenting oral religions, will take up the religions that developed in India: Hinduism and basic Buddhism. The second third of the course will focus on the religions of China and Japan: Taoism, Confucianism, Shinto, and special schools of Buddhism, including Zen. The final third of the course will discuss the Abrahamic religions: Judaism, Christianity, and Islam.

A term project is required. This may be fulfilled by any *one* of the following possibilities: (1) attending a church/temple service of a religion different from the one in which you were raised, (2) creating on paper a new religion, (3) planning an imaginary pilgrimage that involves visiting at least ten religious sites, or (4) designing your own project of similar difficulty. If you choose to do the attendance at a service, you are expected to write a response paper that will include a description of the building, details of the service, and specifics about the congregation. If you choose to create a new religion, you are expected to write a paper that is divided into separate sections, such as Commandments, Sacred Places, Beliefs, Ceremonies, Sacred Book, and so on. The more detail you include, the better. If you plan an imaginary pilgrimage to religious sites, please give your basic itinerary and details of the ten religious sites you would like to visit. If none of these projects appeals to you, please plan a creative or research project of your own and ask the instructor for approval.

All term papers are to be typed and double-spaced and on $8^{1}/_{2}$" x 11" white paper. *All term papers must be perfect in spelling, punctuation, and grammar.*

Your final grade will be determined by the total number of points you accumulate in the course. Each test will be worth 100 points (and make up seventy-five percent of the grade). The term project is worth 30 points maximum. You may make visits on your own to places of local religious interest that the instructor will recommend (the instructor will hand out assignment sheets), and these visits will be worth 10 points each. Additional points can be gained by short oral presentations (1 point each) and from attending off-campus concerts and lectures as indicated by the instructor (5 points each). Approximately 360 points are needed for an A; about 320 for a B; and 280 for a C.

Tentative test dates are _____, _____, and _____. Enjoy the course!

Semester-System Syllabus

Week 1	Introduction and oral religions
Week 2	Hinduism: Vedic religion, caste system, and the Upanishads
Week 3	Hinduism: Bhagavad Gita, Yogas, popular religion
Week 4	Buddhism: life of the Buddha, basic teachings
Week 5	Buddhism: Theravada and Mahayana, Jainism
Test I	
Week 6	Taoism and early Chinese religion
Week 7	Confucianism
Week 8	Chinese Mahayana
Week 9	Tibetan Vajrayana
Week 10	Japanese Buddhism, Zen, Shinto
Test II	
Week 11	Judaism: origins, Hebrew scriptures, rabbinical Judaism, Reform
Week 12	Christianity: Jesus, Paul, monasticism, Orthodoxy
Week 13	Christianity: medieval, Reformation, modern Christianity
Week 14	Islam: Muhammad, Qur'an, Five Pillars, Sufism, modern Islam
Week 15	New religious movements
Week 16	Religion and the future: modern challenges
Test III	

Quarter-System Syllabus

Week 1	Introduction, oral religions
Week 2	Hinduism: Vedas, Upanishads, Bhagavad Gita, popular religion
Week 3	Buddhism: life of Buddha, Theravada/Mahayana division, Jainism
Test I	
Week 4	Chinese religion: Taoism, Confucianism, and Buddhist schools
Week 5	Japanese religion: Shinto, Buddhist schools, Zen
Test II	
Week 6	Judaism: origins, Hebrew scriptures, rabbinical Judaism, Reform
Week 7	Christianity: Jesus, Paul, Orthodoxy, medieval Catholicism, Protestantism, modern challenges
Week 8	Islam: Muhammad, Five Pillars, Sufism, development
Week 9	New religious movements
Week 10	Religion and the future: modern challenges, contemporary directions
Test III	

Part II
Individual Chapter Resources for
Experiencing the World's Religions

Note: For each chapter of the textbook, the following materials are included:
Learning Objectives
Chapter Outline
Lecture Supplements
Notes on *For Fuller Understanding*
Video Resources
Internet Resources
Multiple-Choice Questions
Essay Topics

Chapter 1   Understanding Religion

Learning Objectives

After reading this chapter, the student should be able to
- discuss the role and function of religion in human life.
- describe theories of the origin of religion.
- describe the series of characteristics used to identify a religion.
- discuss conceptions of the sacred.
- discuss the importance of symbolism in religion.
- explain the three patterns for comparing and contrasting religions.
- know the value and benefits of studying religion.

Chapter Outline

First Encounter
Why Is There Religion?
    Speculations on the Sources of Religion
    Key Characteristics of Religion
    The Sacred
    Religious Symbolism
Patterns among Religions
    First Pattern: Focus of Beliefs and Practices
    Second Pattern: Religious Views of the World and Life
    Third Pattern: Religious Views of Male and Female
Multidisciplinary Approaches to the Study of Religion
Key Critical Questions
Why Study the Major Religions of the World?
The Pilgrimage
Religion beyond the Classroom
For Fuller Understanding
Related Readings
Key Terms

Lecture Supplements

Molloy's text introduces students to ways of "experiencing the world's religions" through cultural contexts. Categories such as sacred arts, symbolism, relationship to nature, and gender issues make this text particularly rich with human experience. Using personal "encounters," Molloy introduces religions through travel and cultural diversity that may immerse students in the worlds of "others" for the first time. Beginning with oral traditions of indigenous and regional religions, students can begin to appreciate the role of the "senses" in "sensing the sacred" through religious practices. The orientation to nature through natural landscape settings or "sacred sites" is a very down-to-earth way to introduce diverse religions. Teaching of the introductory course on world religions has undergone significant transformations in recent years. Mark Juergensmeyer, ed., in *Teaching the Introductory Course in Religion* (Atlanta, GA: Scholars Press, 1991) brings together the insights of numerous teachers of world religions. This book is the result of several institutes supported by the National Endowment for the Humanities and broke new ground for the contemporary direction that Molloy's text represents. In this book, Mark Juergensmeyer gives a thorough presentation of basic fundamentals of teaching an introductory religions course. He provides sample rhetorical questions to classify course objectives and to target specific areas of study. With that classification set, he presents discussions on three different course options. These options are "World Religions," "Introduction to Religion," and "Introduction to Religious Studies." This book includes chapters on pedagogical approaches to teaching various world religions and essays explaining how scholar teachers approach the course. As a complement to the Molloy text, this book covers the full range of pedagogical approaches to course material, including syllabi.

In "Meditation and Masks, Drums and Dramas: Experiential and Participatory Exercises in the Comparative Religions Classroom" (*Teaching Theology and Religion* 2, no. 3 [1999]: 169–172), G. William Barnard discusses a number of experiential pedagogical techniques to get students engaged in the material of religious studies. He discusses the difficulties of teaching students who may hold specific or narrow religious views and how to overcome some of the barriers to learning. Many of his suggestions are very practical and are applicable to the limits of short classroom periods and large classes. The issue of experiments in learning by multisensory methods (whether visual, sonic, olfactory, or other sensory approaches) adds a dimension that enhances the cultural approach and examples employed in Molloy's text. On a more theoretical level, the essays in *A Magic Still Dwells: Comparative Religion in the Postmodern Age,* edited by Kimberley Patton and Benjamin Ray (Berkeley: University of California Press, 2000), chart a course toward a broader vision of comparative religion's methodologies, assessing the current critical approaches with a view to addressing the problems raised by structuralism and deconstruction, cultural anthropology and phenomenology, as well as questioning whether comparisons are justified. A range of views are represented, from Huston Smith to Jonathan Z. Smith, to very current assessments within the discipline of teaching Judaism, Buddhism, African, pluralistic American, and ancient cultures religious studies. While this text is not meant to be a guide for teachers, scholars of religion using Molloy's text will be stimulated by the critical assessment of our discipline.

The following resources are useful for scholars who want a conceptual orientation to the study of religion through comparative and culturally oriented methods, including Molloy's emphasis on the arts and on nature. None of these texts is of particular use to introductory students, yet they will be quite helpful for instructors who want to provide a methodological background to these issues. Russell McCutcheon, *The Insider/Outsider Problem in the Study of Religion: A Reader* (Controversies in the Study of Religion) (New York and London: Cassell, 1998), offers the first in a new series confronting the study of religion, facing questions such as, How can a nonparticipant describe or understand the causes of religious beliefs, social structures, and behaviors of "other" people? This anthology uses anthropological methodologies, linguistics, and philosophy to confront questions raised by the study of religion. Also from Cassell is the *Guide to the Study of Religion* by Willi Braun and Russell McCutcheon, eds. (New York and London: Cassell, 2000). This substantial (462+ pages) and excellent volume is a very current guide to studying religion with contemporary methodologies, explaining various approaches such as cognition, gender, ritual studies, sociocultural studies, postmodernism, postcolonialism, ideological studies, ethnic cultural issues, and so on.

A. (Key questions: What is religion? What is the sacred? How is religion studied?)

Students may often have preconceived "text"-oriented definitions of religion. One way to open the first classes is with the questions about defining *religion* and the *sacred* with various methodological approaches. Two books may provide a background to comparative approaches. Eric J. Sharpe, *Comparative Religion: A History*, 2nd ed. (La Salle, IL: Open Court, 1991), provides a historical context for the development of the field. It also provides sketches of many of the important thinkers in chronological order.

John Lyden, in *Enduring Issues in Religion* (San Diego: Greenhaven Press, 1995), brings together a survey of several short excerpts from theologians and religious insiders and from skeptics and scholars commenting from outside the various religions. Chapter 1 includes definitions of religion from Otto, Freud, Marx, and Tillich (as well as others). Feelings of total dependence, awe and mystery, and ultimate concern are contrasted with reductionist theories such as religion as the opium of the people or as psychological projection. Definitions of the sacred include the perspectives of monotheistic traditions, stressing God's revelation, the triune God revealed through Christ, and Allah as the one God. The true reality of Brahman is presented from Vedantic Hinduism. Emptiness and the Tao are discussed from Buddhist and Taoist positions. The way of heaven as the basis for moral harmony is emphasized for Confucianism. The Native American position (from the Sioux perspective) finds the sacred as present throughout the world. With each selection spanning fewer than ten pages, Lyden's book provides a useful introduction for students who want to do further reading on a variety of world religion topics and methodological perspectives. Likewise, it provides the instructor with brief historical notes and "thumb-note" summaries of theoretical perspectives. Each selection includes questions that work well for either discussion or short writing assignments.

Ninian Smart, in *Dimensions of the Sacred: An Anatomy of the World's Beliefs* (Berkeley: University of California Press, 1996), offers a contemporary attempt to present a phenomenological discussion of trends, dimensions, and types of religious expression. It provides an extensive glossary of important scholarly and traditional religious terms across several religions. Although its organization is not likely to be easily understood by beginning students, lecturers should find it straightforward. It is particularly useful for considering categories across several traditions. For example, the ritual dimension is discussed in terms of several different religions. Other dimensions include doctrine, myth, ethics, politics, and society. It provides several clues that facilitate class discussion; for example, How do ethical categories compare across traditions, such as Buddhism, Christianity, and Islam? For an assessment of the field of religious studies, a special issue of the *Journal of the American Academy of Religion,* "Settled Issues and Neglected Questions in the Study of Religion," 62, no. 4 (Winter, 1994), may assist the teacher seeking a scholarly overview of specific key issues in particular religions. This issue offers scholarly questions, significant figures in the profession, and bibliographies, although rapid new developments since its publication have occurred. *A Magic Still Dwells* (see above) complements this collection of essays.

B. (Key words: Tylor, Frazer, Freud, Durkheim, Eliade, theories of religions, evolutionism)

A very useful book for sorting out methodologies for students by introducing pivotal thinkers is Daniel L. Pals's *Seven Theories of Religion* (New York: Oxford University Press, 1996). Although this book does not offer a general overview of the dozens of theorists of religion, it thoroughly considers a selected few. Its short introduction provides a summary of the history of the study of religion and an annotated bibliography. Pals begins with E. B. Tylor and J. G. Frazer's intellectualist theories of the source of religion. Tylor's beginning point was that religion is belief in spiritual beings, for which he used the term *animism.* Tylor argued that beliefs are based on reasoning and observation but are simplistic because they arise at a low level of cultural development. According to his theory, cultural and religious beliefs evolve into more developed states. Eventually, animistic ideas develop into ideas of gods, then to one god, and eventually a scientific worldview replaces belief in spirits and gods. Frazer, through a comparison of the world's mythologies, continues Tylor's evolutionary method by positing that "primitive" conceptions develop from ideas of magic in religion and ultimately are disregarded in the face of scientific development. His theory is based on the assumption that magic is a pseudoscientific attempt to confront and control natural forces. As intellectual sophistication develops, magic is discovered to fail. Religious conceptions replace magic. Religion is based on humans entreating gods for help in their encounters with nature, life, and death. Ultimately, rational scientific thinking replaces these previous conceptions when people finally understand the laws of nature.

Tylor and Frazer desired a scientific view of religion. They found this by borrowing evolutionist theories from natural sciences. Their theories are intellectualist because they focus on religion as a matter of belief and intellectual orientation to the world. Most aspects of these two theories have been rejected by modern theorists, yet they are still important because they provided a starting point for much of the subsequent inquiry into both religion and culture.

Freud's contributions to the study of religion are important, not for their specific details, but because of their pervasiveness. Freud suggested that religion must be understood as more than just the surface manifestation of beliefs and behavior. Deep, hidden motivations and personality traits shape religion in ways that must be examined and understood. Freud also continued the trend of viewing religion in terms of evolution, predicting that it would disappear as the world embraced scientific rationalism. Although Freud generally rejected any legitimate role for religion in the modern world, his theories have contributed much to understanding symbolism and hidden elements of human behavior. C. G. Jung was an early associate of Freud. Although they parted ways, Jung's ideas about symbols and about religion developed from the intellectual environment that owes much to Freud. Jung was not as antagonistic toward religion, and thus his and Freud's theories together offer a good starting point for theories of religion and personality.

The remainder of Pals's book is devoted to considering the significant contributions of Emile Durkheim, Karl Marx, Mircea Eliade, E. E. Evans-Pritchard, and Clifford Geertz. Durkheim and Marx are considered (like Freud) in terms of their explanatory functionalism stressing society and economics, respectively. Eliade is considered as a distinct departure from the explanatory (reductionist) theories of the social sciences, preferring a more sympathetic and subjective approach. Evans-Pritchard and Geertz are included for their more recent roles in attempting to overcome the division between more and less reductive approaches. They are both interested in overcoming the polarization of interpretation versus explanation. Interpretation seeks to understand religion in its own context in a more subjective fashion. Explanation (often associated with reductionism) attempts objectivity and scientific orientation.

All chapters are relatively short and straightforward. Explicit in these selected theorists are both outlines of some speculations on the why and what of religion and key characteristics. Belief systems, community, ethics, emotions, ritual, and sacredness are key terms that in some cases were originally defined by the above theorists. The difference between the use of the term *sacred* in Durkheim and Eliade is one case. Instructors will find this reference useful for summaries of these theories and for the section of criticisms of each approach. This work is less appropriate for class discussions but can be helpful for students desiring more information or working on short research projects. Pals's book demonstrates how the study of religion is a mixture of many different approaches.

C. (Key words: religion, categories and definitions of religion)

In "The Category 'Religion' in Recent Publications: A Critical Survey" (*Numen* 42, no. 3 [1995]: 284–309), Russell T. McCutcheon presents an essay on the issues involved in using the term *religion*. He states, "What counts as religion and, more importantly, who gets to decide? How useful is this category, given its clearly European and largely Christian-influenced heritage? What is the role of the scholar of religion in attempting to determine a normative definition? And what is at stake in the long-standing debate over whether religion is sociopolitically autonomous—in a word, *sui generis*—or simply a scholarly, taxonomic category used for but one aspect of the continuum of human, historical practices?" After making this statement, McCutcheon reviews several books and conference proceedings.

This article is most helpful in its delineations of the different approaches to definition and analysis. Under the section concerning key characteristics, Molloy briefly raises the issue of the use of the term *religion* and suggests *spiritual path* as one possible alternative. McCutcheon's article does well to briefly summarize the debate concerning this very issue. Since students who attempt understanding of the world's traditions will undoubtedly encounter this issue, an instructor can use this article as a summary source for the issues and for its relatively current bibliography. Specialists in non-European, non-Christian traditions tend to have the most difficulties with the terminology. It is helpful for students to become aware of the difficulties of translating terms and ideas across linguistic and cultural boundaries. Additionally, the question of "Who gets to decide?" provides a forum for assessing the political nature of scholarly research.

There are extreme views on both ends of this theoretical question. It is helpful to address the use of the term *religion,* so that students remain continually aware of the provisional nature of analytical categories. Categories make useful understanding possible but should not be sewn as intellectual straitjackets.

Key issues: All the various attempts at understanding and explaining religious behavior take a position on the category of religion. Some view religion as an autonomous category, an expression of some type of sacred reality, that needs interpretation. Others tend to see religion as an artificially constructed research heuristic that is employed to select particular human behaviors for further examination and explanation. Students will encounter both of these perspectives and the various syntheses of these two polarities of analytical thought. By describing the place and orientation of different theories and ideas along this continuum from interpretation to explanation, students can comprehend how religion has been and can be understood.

D. (Key words: art, religion, material culture)

The natural world is often interpreted through symbolism and sacred arts such as masks, paintings or other images, architecture, carvings, chants, dance, and other "multisensory" methods of interpreting religious experience. One emphasis that students might begin with is that "culture texts" are not always written in alphabetic texts but may use visual scriptures and other forms of sacred texts. This direction in religious studies incorporates anthropological methodologies with other disciplines of "participant observation" such as on-site observation of ceremonial arts and symbols. When viewed first through oral traditions and Asian religions, the approach to Christianity, Judaism, and Islam later in the course may be more culturally based in the methods students have acquired. Examining the arts as sacred texts then makes more "sense" to students, who can appreciate Western traditions in fresh and culturally sophisticated ways, rather than limiting the lens to the written texts of scholarly European traditions.

Until recently, most introductions to the world religions were entirely in alphabetic texts without pictures. John Cort, in "Art, Religion, and Material Culture: Some Reflections on Method" (*Journal of the American Academy of Religion* 64, no. 3 [Fall, 1996]), discusses how the "focus on written texts in the study of religion is due . . . in part to the nature of the Euro-American academy itself" (p. 614). He remarks that "even when visual materials are brought into the classroom, most teachers of religion use them to supplement texts, and implicitly or even explicitly view the visual data as secondary to the textual data. Intellectual culture in Euro-American society is, and has been for many centuries, primarily concerned with explication, interpretation and furtherance of the written word" (p. 614). Molloy illustrates how the study of religion has turned in a new direction emphasizing a "textuality" of culture in the varieties of religious expression through art and social organization.

Nadine Penz Frantz in "Material Culture, Understanding and Meaning: Writing and Picturing" (*Journal of the American Academy of Religion* 66, no. 4 [Winter, 1998]), further explains the methodologies of material culture studies in religion that view how a tradition transmits and adapts as a response to change, and is therefore "a constitutive part of the construction of a culture's worldview" (p. 793). She develops an excellent way of knowing through our bodies, the senses, how to read the symbolism of architecture, dance, song, and other culture texts. "The question of representation through material culture becomes one of interpretation, performance and re-presentation" (p. 794). This essay provides a much needed understanding that cultures are not static or frozen in abstract texts but are dynamically adapting to change and cultural evolution through varieties of human expression and interpretation. This will be a revelation for students who struggle with romanticized or stereotyped perspectives on other cultures and will open their eyes to other avenues of discourse through material artifacts and social contexts. The article above by Barnard will assist teachers with techniques.

Notes on *For Fuller Understanding*

1. *Explore the insights of Freud or Jung about religion, and use those insights to examine the religious tradition with which you are most familiar. How would Freud or Jung understand that religion?*

   Freud's book *The Future of an Illusion*, being both short and challenging, is a good introduction to his thought on religion and would be useful for this exercise. For an introduction to Jung, an anthology or theme-oriented selection from his writings on religion may be valuable (for example, *Mandala Symbolism* or *Four Archetypes*). Videos of the lives and thought of these two thinkers are also available.

2. *Can you add to the list of human needs, given in this chapter, that religion might sometimes fulfill?*

   Students are quite likely to know several people who take one or another religion seriously. One way to approach this task is to suggest that they list such persons with pseudonyms and describe the needs a particular religion or religious practice satisfies for each.

   Another approach is to do a Web search on *religion* or *religious*. Students are likely to be quite amazed at the various needs that religions on the Web are positioned to fulfill.

3. *In this book we will be using architecture and travel as ways of studying religions. You might begin to make a list of interesting religious buildings and travel destinations in your area.*

   Teachers can be especially helpful in this regard, because they will have a greater familiarity with their region than will most students. They can help students discover, visit, and learn more about significant temples, churches, and sites sacred to native religions. Local libraries and reference librarians can also be of help to students. This exercise would be especially valuable as a group project, since each student will bring some knowledge of the region to the project.

4. *Begin keeping a notebook or journal of references to religion that you see in newspapers and on television. What patterns do you see there? What issues recur?*

   Newspapers frequently have a regular section on religion in their Saturday editions. On television, religion is often mentioned not only in news but also in documentaries and travel programs. The mention of religion is more sporadic in television sitcoms but is a valuable topic for investigation.

   Lyrics to popular songs and themes in films should also be investigated. Some instructors have students create a scrapbook or chapbook of religiously inspired or tinged "texts"—from radio advertisements through song lyrics and movie titles. If you do this, you may also want to provide class time occasionally for students to share their personal compilations.

Video Resources

The descriptions of these videos are drawn from the companies' brochures.

C. G. Jung: The World Within
This video takes a fascinating look at the philosophy and personal life of Carl Gustav Jung. It offers a glimpse into Jung's "Red Book," in which he recorded images from his unconscious. Jung discusses his work on dreams, archetypal figures, ritual, and fantasy. (60 minutes) [Insight]

The Forbidden Goddess
Christians, Jews, and Muslims alike have for millennia believed in a solitary male God known by his Hebrew name, Yahweh. However, recent work in the heart of the Holy Land is revealing a different story: one of a dual partnership between Yahweh and his wife, the Canaanite goddess Asherah. (28 minutes) [Religion]

A Hero's Journey
A portrait of Joseph Campbell, best known for *The Power of Myth* series he did with Bill Moyers. Here we see Campbell on his own personal quest as he talks about his boyhood interest in American Indians, which led him to understand that myths were more than fanciful tales. As he studied Hinduism and Buddhism as a young man, read *Ulysses,* and was introduced to the work of Carl Jung, he formulated his belief that myths are symbolic stories alive with meaning to guide us in our lives. Campbell is also seen teaching classes, where we get to watch the master storyteller at work. Full of ideas to live by, this is an engaging, thoughtful, lively biography. (58 minutes) [Palisades]

Jung on Film
This seminal film interview with Carl Gustav Jung represents a record of an original genius. The pioneering analytical psychologist tells us about his collaboration with Sigmund Freud, about the insights he gained from listening to his patients' dreams, and about the turns his own life has taken. Dr. Richard I. Evans, a Presidential Medal of Freedom nominee, interviews Jung, giving us a rare glimpse into the life and career of this important historical figure. (77 minutes) [Palisades]

Religion
Using examples from several major religions, this program explores the various functions of religion and shows how religion reflects a society's values. Religion is analyzed as a social structure, and the ways in which it changes to meet the needs of a society are detailed. The video also examines religiosity in the United States and contemporary trends in religion. (30 minutes) [Insights]

Who Am I, Why Am I Here?
In this public television special, best-selling author Thomas Moore (*Care of the Soul* and *Soul Mates*) shows how the great spiritual traditions try to answer the timeless question of *Who Am I, Why Am I Here?* (60 minutes) [Hartley]

The Wisdom of the Dream: The World of C. G. Jung
Enter the world of dreams and the unconscious with this three-part series on the life and work of Carl Jung. A wonderful introduction to Jung, this program also offers a new depth of understanding to those who are familiar with his work. Interviews with Jung's followers illuminate his "user-friendly" psychological approach to life. *The Wisdom of the Dream* captures the essential spirit of Jung, a gentle man who was a psychiatrist and a scholar, a painter and a traveler, but above all, a healer and a dreamer. This production won the Gold Medal at the 1989 New York International Film & TV Festival. (each volume 53 minutes) [Palisades]

The Wisdom of Faith
In the first four programs of this five-part series, Huston Smith talks with Bill Moyers about his experiences with the world's great religions: Hinduism, Buddhism, Confucianism, Islam, Christianity, and Judaism. In the final part, Smith discusses his philosophy of religion, born of both his scholarship and his faith, and shows how all "wisdom traditions" share fundamental truths. (each program 58 minutes) [Religion]

Internet Resources

Academic Info on Religion
http://www.academicinfo.net/religindex.html

AllFaiths Press®
http://allfaithspress.com

American Academy of Religion: Other Online Resources
http://www.aar-site.org/other

The American Religion Experience
http://are.as.wvu.edu

Electronic Texts
http://www.acs.ucalgary.ca/~lipton/texts.html

Exploring Religions
http://august.uwyo.edu/Religionet/er/DEFAULT.HTM

McGill FRS Guide to Religious Studies Resources on the Internet
http://www.mcgill.ca/religion/subject.htm

Religious and Sacred Texts
http://davidwiley.com/religion.html

Religious Studies Web Guide
http://www.acs.ucalgary.ca/~lipton/images.html

Internet Resources for World Art

American Visions
http://www.pbs.org/wnet/americanvisions

Asian Art Museum of San Francisco
http://www.asianart.org

Centre Georges Pompidou
http://www.cnac-gp.fr/

Fine Arts Museum of San Francisco
http://www.thinker.org/index.shtml

Florence Art Guide
http://www.mega.it/eng/egui/hogui.htm

Giverny (Monet's gardens)
http://www.giverny.org/index.htm

Guggenheim Museum in Bilbao
http://www.bm30.es/homegug_uk.html

Hellenic Ministry of Culture's Guide to Athens
http://www.culture.gr/maps/sterea/attiki/athens.html

Kyoto National Museum
http://www.kyohaku.go.jp

The Louvre
http://www.louvre.fr

Museum of Modern Art
http://www.moma.org/

The Smithsonian
http://www.si.edu

Uffizi Gallery
http://www.uffizi.firenze.it/welcomeE.html

Vatican Museum
http://www.christusrex.org/www1/vaticano/O-Musei.html

World Wide Web Virtual Library/Museums
http://vlmp.museophile.com

Multiple-Choice Questions

1. Literally, the word *religion* means
    a. meditate on.
    b. worship.
    *c. connect again.
    d. rise above.

2. A common element often found in religions is
    a. respect for sculpture.
    *b. feelings of wonder.
    c. rules governing meditation.
    d. use of permanent places of worship.

3. The prophetic orientation in religion emphasizes
    a. ceremonies.
    b. feelings of oneness with the universe.
    c. traditions.
    *d. beliefs and moral codes.

4. The early anthropologist who saw religion as rooted in a belief in spirits and worship of them was
    a. E. B. Tylor.
    *b. James Frazer.
    c. Sigmund Freud.
    d. Carl Jung.

5. Sigmund Freud, when analyzing the origin of religion, emphasized
    *a. the human need for psychological security.
    b. the certainty of an afterlife.
    c. his belief that religions were essential to psychological health.
    d. the valuable role that religions play in assisting people to find meaning in their lives.

6. The disciple of Freud who ultimately rebelled against him was
    *a. Carl Jung.
    b. Wilhelm Schmidt.
    c. Rudolf Otto.
    d. Clifford Geertz.

7. Wilhelm Schmidt, an Austrian philologist, argued that human beings originally believed in
    *a. one God.
    b. two gods of equal importance.
    c. multiple gods of nature.
    d. no God.

8. Belief in many gods is called
    *a. polytheism.
    b. monotheism.
    c. agnosticism.
    d. atheism.

9. Belief in one God is called
    *a. monotheism.
    b. polytheism.
    c. atheism.
    d. agnosticism.

10. A mystical orientation in religion is characterized by
    a. an emphasis on mysterious happenings.
    *b. seeking union with something greater than oneself.
    c. extensive use of holy water and statues.
    d. a belief in alien origins of life forms.

11. A sacramental orientation in religion is characterized by
    a. daily prayer.
    b. use of silent meditation.
    c. extensive use of bells and powders.
    *d. a belief that certain rituals and ceremonies help one achieve salvation.

12. Anthropology typically studies religions as
    *a. cultural creations with multiple aspects.
    b. clusters of sacred buildings, rivers, and mountains.
    c. systems of philosophical explanation of the universe.
    d. artifacts of superior beings.

13. A universal religious symbol that is circular, or that blends a circle and a square, is called a
    *a. mandala.
    b. mudra.
    c. mantra.
    d. megalith.

14. The prophetic orientation in religion is particularly strong in
    *a. Protestant Christianity.
    b. Tibetan Buddhism.
    c. Vedic Hinduism.
    d. Taoism.

15. Pantheism is the belief
    *a. that all reality is divine.
    b. in the ancient Greek religion that the god Pan was the source of cosmic order.
    c. in endless reincarnation.
    d. in a timeless realm of happiness at the top of the universe.

16. One religion that particularly values and makes use of silence is
    a. Shinto.
    b. Judaism.
    *c. Zen Buddhism.
    d. Islam.

17. One name of an early female deity was
    a. Wotan.
    b. Mercury.
    *c. Astarte.
    d. Izanagi.

18. In religious studies, the word *myth* means
    a. a story that is historically true.
    b. a story that is historically untrue.
    *c. a story that is psychologically meaningful and may be either historically true or not.
    d. a story that is found in similar form in many religions.

19. Literally, *philosophy* in Greek means
    a. great system.
    b. world study.
    c. careful analysis.
    *d. love of wisdom.

20. A major French artist created a large painting with the title of *Where Do We Come From? What Are We? Where Are We Going?* The artist's name was
   a. Pierre Bonnard.
*b. Paul Gauguin.
   c. Rosa Bonheur.
   d. Claude Monet.

21. Among many reasons, religions exist to help people
*a. deal with the certainty of death.
   b. find ways to express themselves in art.
   c. select careers that are socially redeeming.
   d. have valuable texts to study.

22. The Scottish anthropologist who was the author of the multivolume study of mythology called *The Golden Bough* was
*a. James Frazer.
   b. C. G. Jung.
   c. Sigmund Freud.
   d. E. B. Tylor.

23. The German theologian who held that religions originate in human response to the mysterious side of reality was
*a. Rudolf Otto.
   b. Carl Jung.
   c. Karl Rahner.
   d. Dietrich Bonhoeffer.

24. The American thinker who argued that religion brought a new vitality to people's lives was
   a. James Frazer.
*b. William James.
   c. E. B. Tylor.
   d. Carl Jung.

25. Literally, *psychology* means
   a. study of nature.
   b. internal structure.
*c. study of the soul.
   d. procession of images.

26. What psychologist saw religion as a way for people to find their fulfillment as unique individuals, a process he called "individuation"?
   a. Rudolf Otto
   b. E. B. Tylor
   c. Sigmund Freud
*d. Carl Jung

27. Female imagery in religions may be seen in
   a. lightning bolts.
*b. spirals and eggs.
   c. rocks.
   d. mountains.

28. The approach that especially makes use of reason to find answers to religious questions is
   a. psychology.
   b. mythology.
*c. philosophy.
   d. anthropology.

29. The conception of time that is found in religions that emphasize a creation and a cosmic purpose is usually
     a. cyclical.
    *b. linear.
     c. repetitive
     d. psychological.

30. That area of investigation that looks for and interprets religious evidence in ancient sites, buildings, and objects is
     a. anthropology
     b. mythology
     c. sociology
    *d. archeology

Essay Topics

Note: I have phrased the following as if they were to be used as parts of an examination; hence I often specify a quantity of items or a specific approach. If I were to use the questions instead to prompt exploratory thinking—for journal entries, personal essays, or even group discussion—I would make the questions more open-ended.

1. Why do religions exist? Please give at least three possible reasons, and defend them with good arguments (and, when appropriate, references to others who offer similar reasons).

2. List, and briefly describe, five characteristics that are typically associated with a "religion."

3. Explain the difference between transcendent and immanent notions of sacredness. What emphases might we expect in a religion that acknowledges a transcendent god or gods? What emphases might we expect in a religion that emphasizes sacredness that is immanent?

4. Could we use the term *religion* for a belief system of only one person? Please explain your answer.

5. Religions often speak of the sacred or treat people or places as sacred. Is there anything objectively "sacred," or is this just an imaginative human projection? Please defend your answer.

6. List four symbols typically thought of as religious and explain meanings with which each is typically associated.

7. Explain the distinctions among sacramental, prophetic, and mystical orientations of religions.

8. Describe the range of attitudes among religions toward words and special texts.

9. Explain how a continuum with "exclusivity" at one end and "inclusivity" at the other can be used to describe religious views.

10. How do we typically distinguish between religion and philosophy?

11. Offer, with evidence, an explanation for why males and male imagery came to dominate many of the religions of the past few thousand years.

12. Describe at least three contemporary examples of religious devotion to female deities or religious use of female imagery.

13. Describe three different discipline-based approaches to the study of religions, and explain the particular emphasis of each.

14. The term *religion* seems literally to mean "connect again." What elements do you see being connected by a religion?

Chapter 2   Oral Religions

Learning Objectives

After reading this chapter, the student should be able to

- describe the three patterns shared by oral religions.
- explain the view of reality held by oral religions.
- describe the importance of ritual in the practice of oral religion.
- discuss rite of passage ceremonies.
- define the function of taboos.
- describe the role of the shaman.

Chapter Outline

First Encounter
Discovering Oral Religions
    Past Obstacles to the Appreciation of Oral Religions
    The Modern Recovery of Oral Religions
Studying Oral Religions: Learning from Patterns
    Human Relationships with the Natural World
    Sacred Time and Sacred Space
    Respect for Origins, Gods, and Ancestors
Sacred Practices in Oral Religions
    Life-Cycle Ceremonies
    Taboo and Sacrifice
    Shamanism, Trance, and Magic
    Artifacts and Artistic Expression in Oral Religions
Personal Experience: Gods in Hawai`i
Oral Religions Today
Religion beyond the Classroom
For Fuller Understanding
Related Readings
Key Terms

Lecture Supplements

The study of oral religions is emerging in contemporary religious studies in the light of new methodologies as a challenging new field, and Molloy incorporates many of these exciting approaches. Students can gain from this chapter a foundation for understanding the rest of the religions in the text with an appreciation of sacred material culture and environmental relationships in religious experience. It can break the ground open for planting new approaches to religion and critiquing the framework that dominates the academic text-based religious studies traditions. When they are introduced to the serious appreciation and interpretation of sacred arts, for example, students can understand that by prioritizing alphabetic texts in the Western academy, the oral religions and indigenous people of our world have not been studied on their own terms of religious expression. Clearly, anthropology of religion (see resources below) has contributed most to this new horizon, but emerging syntheses of disciplines within a "postcolonial" critical dialectic is transforming the field. Native American scholars, such as Alfonso Ortiz and Vine Deloria, Jr., for example, have trained critical perspectives of indigenous thinking and corrective polemical views upon the academy's "Orientalist" and colonial categories. They caution students to approach indigenous peoples on their own terms with respect for the critical voices of indigenous leaders and religious traditions.

Molloy's text is well illustrated with images that convey visual information for students. Rather than being simply secondary and subordinate to the text, many of these images demonstrate the way sacred arts convey "meaning" through symbolism and their integral context of ceremony or ritual. Using the text's illustrations as forms of visual texts is a way to open students to the varieties of "culture texts" that may often communicate as much information as any written alphabetic text. Not only are the oral religions distinguished by their emphasis on sacred arts, they also function to transmit profound levels of meaning as "sensory-scriptures" equivalent to "literate religions" in their own way. As Molloy points out in the section titled "Artifacts and Artistic Expression in Oral Religions," "Sacred objects and images in native religions are not separate endeavors but an essential part of the religious expression itself." In addition to the visual information provided in the text, additional media should be incorporated to emphasize this dimension of oral religions. One written text combining a CD of diverse "sonic texts" that could be useful is *Shaman, Jhankri & Nele: Music Healers of Indigenous Cultures* by Pat Moffitt Cook (New York: Ellipsis Arts, 1997). In this ethnomusicology of oral religion in specific cultural traditions, eighteen recordings are accompanied by a ninety-six-page text describing the ways of healing and transforming religious states of consciousness through music.

The forms of culture and cosmological orientation appropriate to bioregional cultures are dynamic and adaptable, not as romantically imagined and portrayed in popular culture images, nor as tragically left behind by globalization and institutional religions. Molloy discusses the vitality and recovery of indigenous people by introducing current revitalization movements such as Hawaiian sovereignty and Native American struggles, as well as discussing the many threats to oral cultures. Students should learn from this section of the course how indigenous cultures in resurgence for the last decade of the twentieth century made courageous religious statements on contemporary issues. The topics of environmental destruction and ecological vision, social justice and human rights, land rights and traditional ceremonial sites, repatriation of artifacts and sacred arts, and respect for their languages and religions in a postcolonial world are challenges to the way we study religion today.

A. (Key words: oral religions, indigenous, native, aboriginal, tribal, traditional, nonliterate, bioregional)

Defining oral religions may be "problematized" by discussing openly in class how many of the world's original religions were "earth based" in a bioregional way, and how cosmologies (orientation to the cosmos and explanations of human relationship to the world) were expressed in ecological correspondence to the "sacred land" through ceremonies. The survival of cultures and their adaptation to their environment often shape their symbol systems, so the "material culture" of sacred arts often reflects the response to their place in nature. It is important for students to understand that indigenous religions are not "past tense," as many preconceptions of modern students may perpetuate the marginalization of these cultures to a "precontact" romantic view of the past. In fact, today many indigenous people not only struggle to survive, but we are also seeing a resurgence and revitalization of some of these religions around the world. Adaptation to the twenty-first century includes political resistance movements (such as the Hawaiian example and the Mayan uprisings in Mexico and Guatemala) and use of international communications media and the World Wide Web (the Inuit use laptops and cell phones for fishing information and contact over distances; the Chiapas Mayan uprising was broadcast on the Web; solidarity networks exchange environmental and political information). Films like *Surviving Columbus* raise awareness of international indigenous issues; newspapers, radio stations, and Web sites counter the stereotypes of isolation and disempowerment; traditional sacred arts are interpreted in modern contexts. Rather than having only nonliterate and merely "oral" cultures, indigenous people are expressing themselves in various "textualities" as sophisticated cultures using many forms of expression to convey sacred meaning.

B. (Key words: anthropology, shamanism, taboo and sacrifice, ceremonies)

In recent years, anthropologists have applied more study to oral peoples than scholars within religious studies have done. A general reference for the overlap between religious studies and anthropology is found in Clinton Bennett's *In Search of the Sacred: Anthropology and the Study of Religions* (London and New York: Cassell, 1996). This book traces the history and development of anthropology and the study of religion. Bennett teaches and works in the field of religion but has engaged in fieldwork. He argues that anthropological awareness by students of religion is necessary because field research and methods have been most developed in anthropological schools. Appropriate to Molloy's introduction, Bennett considers the fields' common roots and founding scholars, including Tylor, Durkheim, Lévi-Strauss, Douglas, Eliade, and others. Bennett discusses the shift from considering native specialists and conversationalists as informants to seeing them as consultants. This book offers a helpful bridge between anthropological study of oral peoples and the traditions of religious studies scholarship that have focused more on texts and large-scale societies. A. C. Lehmann and J. E. Myers, in *Magic, Witchcraft, and Religion: An Anthropological Study of the Supernatural* (Mountain View, CA: Mayfield, 1997 [1985]), provide an anthology of scholarly articles that are useful source material on many of the oral religions of the world. Selections from this work provide specific case studies across the spectrum of oral religion that could be lifted out for further reading or research projects in a world religions class.

Both of the above texts illustrate the trend in study of oral religions away from general theories to culturally specific case studies. Yet they also demonstrate that the subject can be addressed in terms of patterns and family resemblances found across these traditions. Two of the following three sections are of a specific nature, yet they resonate with the important patterns identified by Molloy.

C. (Key words: shaman, trance, healing, dance, storytelling, folklore)

Assessments of shamans and shamanism have followed two trends in scholarship. Critical psychological approaches have often labeled and diagnosed shamans as madmen, neurotics, and charlatans, whereas popular views have beatified shamans, lumping them often uncritically with mystics, yogins, and saints. Roger Walsh, in "The Psychological Health of Shamans: A Reevaluation" (*Journal of the American Academy of Religion* 55, no. 1 [Spring, 1997]: 101–124), examines the pathological assessments of shamans. He offers this definition of shamanism: "Shamanism is a family of traditions whose practitioners focus on voluntarily entering altered states of consciousness in which they experience themselves, or their spirit(s), traveling to other realms at will and interacting with other entities in order to serve their community." He also assumes that shamans do not form a homogeneous group, and that the category shaman is applied to several types of tribal healers and religious figures. Walsh carefully addresses several different biases that have caused some researchers to view shamans in terms of illness and psychopathology. Psychological schools have tended to interpret unusual experiences, especially those of a mystical nature, as pathological. Epilepsy, hysteria, and schizophrenia are some of the common diagnoses. Walsh analyzes each of these in turn and demonstrates how none of them is appropriate for explanation of shamans and shamanic behaviors. He discusses initiation crisis and how it is more often a prelude to healthy growth and development than a sign of pathology. He concludes that it is not analytically sound or appropriate to use pathology as a guide for understanding shamanism. He states, "Something much richer, more complex, and more beneficial seems to be going on and deserves open-minded research."

D. (Key words: American Indians, Western Apache, relationship between places and religion)

Native American studies has been transformed by the scholarship of American Indian scholars, and religion has become one of the keys to cultural revitalization. A helpful and well-illustrated scholarly general overview is *Native North America*, by Larry Zimerman and Brian Leigh Molyneaux (Norman: University of Oklahoma Press, 1996). This text surveys a range of issues: colonial encounter, geography and region, life of the spirit, sacred arts and sites, sacred history and mythology, ceremonial practices, contemporary revitalization and survival, and application to social issues and scholarship. It is lavishly illustrated, including maps, and would provide a helpful supplement to Molloy's text. Hawaiian sovereignty is another very stimulating discussion topic in class raised by Molloy in the text. The following resources will be helpful in bringing these issues out in the classroom.

The Western Apache are one among numerous groups and tribes of American Indians, or Native Americans. *Wisdom Sits in Places: Landscape and Language among the Western Apache* (Albuquerque: University of New Mexico Press, 1996) by Keith H. Basso demonstrates the intimate connection between location or place and social and religious self-identity. After many years of collaboration with Western Apaches in the Cibecue community on the Fort Apache Indian Reservation (Arizona), Basso followed an elder's suggestion that he make a map of the region based on Apache places and names. From this project and its accompanying research, Basso began to understand the profound nature of the meaning of places and their impact on Apache self-identity. According to this work, the land itself and the people's historical relationship with the land assert considerable influence on morality, identity, and community. The relationship of words, names, and stories to specific places is powerful and sacred. Basso states that "places and place-names provide Apache people with symbolic reference points for the moral imagination and its practical bearing on the actualities of their lives—the landscape in which the people dwell can be said to dwell in them" (p. 102). Sacredness and power as important qualities of land and people are addressed in terms of language, social organization, and landscape. What is repeatedly apparent throughout the book is that the Apache genuinely understand and experience land and nature as sacred. Likewise, morality and community are defined in terms of placement on the land of the community's ancestors and history.

This work is not an imaginary or romantic portrayal of native peoples. By making a detailed and cultural-specific examination of language, community, and place, Basso offers an example of a particular people who are genuinely and indivisibly tied to land in a form of land-to-people kinship. It speaks strongly in favor of the view that specific native peoples possess environmental and ecologically complex connections to their traditional lands. This work illustrates the sacredness of the Apache relationship to the natural world; if considered in the context of native peoples in general, the work also demonstrates the potentially devastating effects that forced relocation and external land management have had on the indigenous peoples of the world. Although this work addresses a particular group, specialists in other fields are finding the work to be revealing for considerations of land-based religions far beyond one reservation in Arizona.

Instructors will find this book useful on several levels. Each of the four chapters was written as an independent essay and thus can be managed by undergraduates doing research, or by professors who want to flesh out their lecture notes. Additionally, each essay is centered on the sense of place of a particular Apache individual. This type of focus illustrates that although all peoples are informed by local bodies of knowledge, it is individuals (not cultures) who possess a sense of space. While all chapters offer unique insights, Chapter 4 (which bears the same title as the book) is particularly helpful in its connection between local forms of wisdom and knowledge and their connections to the local landscape. This work would also be useful if consulted in connection with Molloy's conclusion. Its applicability to contemporary views of nature, environment, and ecology are self-evident from even a summary glance.

E. (Key words: colonialism, conscientization, revitalization, cosmovision, transmodernity)

Latin American scholars frequently use the Spanish term *cosmovision* (worldview) to describe the sociocultural worlds of indigenous peoples as "holistic" and integrated or "organic" cultural systems whose elements all have religious meaning. Rather than simply a "worldview" that implies a mental construct, this is an integral contextually sophisticated "spiritual" relationship with all aspects of one's world, cultural and natural. Enrique Dussel is a major religious scholar living in Mexico proposing an "Indoamerican" cosmovision that critiques the postmodern Euro-American academic worldview with a postcolonial analysis of globalization and materialism (see *The Invention of the Americas* for his overview). Modernity is problematized beyond Eurocentric definitions of religion, reason, and progress, as he proposes a contemporary vision toward a pluralistic *transmodernity* that includes the validity of diverse indigenous worldviews countering the globalization that threatens them. Capitalism is analyzed as a historical system of global reach, with a dynamic full of historical contradictions and coloniality, and he proposes a framework for inclusive cultural relations in the modern world. Dussel's work is widely studied in Latin America and abroad, and provides a framework for the confrontation between indigenous people and the effects of globalization. Set alongside the intellectual proponents of indigenous revitalization movements (such as Hawaiian, Mayan, and Native American cultural activists) and international environmental issues, these new directions demonstrate that indigenous religious worldviews are very relevant to the modern study of religion. Integral indigenous worldviews may offer a way to move beyond the conundrum of modern alienation and destruction of our planet toward a way of reenvisioning an approach to the sacred experience of nature through ecological spirituality and respect for the Earth in an embodied religious sensibility.

Notes on *For Fuller Understanding*

1. *Your area now has, or once was home to, native peoples. Make a list of their traditional religious sites, beliefs, and practices. Visit the sites with friends or classmates and make a report to your class.*

   Often the best sources of information are native elders and teachers, tribal councils, and offices of indigenous people's affairs. These will frequently be mentioned in local news accounts. Information can also be found on the Internet, at local libraries, and at the departments of religion, history, and anthropology of local colleges and universities. Reference librarians can be consulted at local libraries.

2. *Are there any museums or galleries in your area that house special examples of native religious objects? Visit one and do a drawing of a single object. Explain in writing its background, use, and maker as well as you can.*

   Drawing can create a connection with a religious object and is an excellent way to contemplate it, bringing questions about its maker and its use. Students can also describe in words what they learned in the process of doing the drawing.

   Traditional religious objects have been the inspiration for modern art done by contemporary native artists. Art galleries in some regions also sell modern artworks by native artists that are frequently based on traditional religious designs. These galleries should be visited, too.

3. *Investigate the festival of Kwanzaa. Who created it, and why? What are its rituals? How would you compare it with an established folk celebration, such as Thanksgiving, Christmas, or New Year?*

   Almost every urban area has Kwanzaa celebrations. Those that are public are arranged by community leaders, who are happy to share their knowledge and interest. One of these leaders may also be glad to visit a class to explain Kwanzaa, show slides, or even do a demonstration. Students can also look on the Internet for information.

Internet Resources

African Traditional Religion
http://isizoh.net/afrel

ATA Catalog
http://eleusis.ucsf.edu/african/AfricanTribal/afrtribal.html

Dreamtime Art
http://www.aborigine.com/

Earth Prayer & the Sunset
http://www.indians.org/welker/blackelk.htm

Foundation Course in African Dance Drumming
http://www.cnmat.berkeley.edu/~ladzekpo/Foundation.html

Hawai`i - Independent & Sovereign Nation-State
http://www.hawaii-nation.org/index.html

Links to American Indian Resources
http://greatspirit.earth.com/links.html

Lonely Planet—Destination Australia
http://www.lonelyplanet.com/destinations/australasia/australia

Myths and Legends
http://pubpages.unh.edu/~cbsiren/myth.html

A New Look at Juju
http://afgen.com/juju.html

Spirits of the Land Foundation Home Page
(Native American Indian Resource for Culture, History, Law, Treaties and Traditions of Tribes,

Bands and Nations)
http://greatspirit.earth.com/

The Zuni Connection Homepage
http://www.keshi.com/

Multiple-Choice Questions

1. The goddess Pele is associated with
   a. childbirth.
   *b. volcanoes and fire.
   c. Brazil.
   d. the Haida.

2. Which of the following has been of special value in the new appreciation for and understanding of oral religions?
   a. the study of newly discovered sacred texts
   b. use of electricity and battery power
   *c. ready availability of cameras and recorders
   d. the worldwide spread of television

3. The transmission of oral religions is made more difficult by the fact that teachings are often conveyed in ways that are
   *a. relatively impermanent.
   b. passed on in symbolic language.
   c. known only to initiates.
   d. written in unknown languages.

4. The teachings of oral religions are typically conveyed by all of the following *except*
   a. sand paintings.
   *b. sacred scripture.
   c. masks and dance.
   d. memorized chants.

5. *Biophilia* refers to
   a. the study of biology.
   *b. a love of all forms of life.
   c. a method for studying oral religions.
   d. a kind of hula.

6. African tribal masks influenced the art of
   *a. Pablo Picasso.
   b. Claude Monet.
   c. Ralph Vaughan Williams.
   d. ethnomusicology.

7. In a holistic culture,
   a. written manuscripts have a special place.
   b. children play a prominent role in ritual.
   c. religions express truths through symbolism.
   *d. virtually every object and act may have religious meaning.

8. Compared with oral religions, today's dominant religions are
   *a. much younger.
   b. much older.
   - c. much more difficult to transmit.
   d. more holistic.

9. Animism holds that
   a. animal sacrifice is necessary for ritual purity.
   b. mountains are often at the end of sacred paths.
   c. animal nature must be subservient to human beings.
   *d. the life force exists in every part of the universe.

10. Hehaka Sapa, also known as Black Elk, saw the circle as
    *a. a form in which many elements of nature arrange themselves and show similar origin.
    b. a special form of the calumet.
    c. evidence that man must dominate nature.
    d. taboo for the people of Easter Island.

11. In Hawai`i, during the celebration of *Makahiki*
    a. the gods were believed to take on human forms.
    b. touching volcanic rock was *kapu.*
    c. people received food from the nobles.
    *d. war and heavy work were forbidden.

12. The concept of *sacred space* is evident in all of the the following *except*
    a. Uluru (Ayers Rock).
    b. the pyramids of Teotihuacán.
    *c. Lono.
    d. Mount Kilimanjaro.

13. Many African religions tell how the High God created the world and then
    *a. abandoned it.
    b. went to Uluru.
    c. became the mother of the Pueblo.
    d. joined the spirits of the dead.

14. Circumcision is a rite often associated with
    *a. entry into adulthood.
    b.   the vision quest.
    c.   the final passing from this life.
    d.   taboo and sacrifice.

15. The sacrifice of an animal may occur
    *a. in order to placate a spirit after a taboo has been broken.
    b.   to celebrate the arrival of menarche.
    c.   as an alternative to polygamy.
    d.   as an essential part of the ritual using *Amanita muscaria.*

16. A libation involves
    *a. the pouring of a liquid on the ground as an offering.
    b.   the shaman's ability to fly through the air.
    c.   the forbidding of incest and marriage among close relatives.
    d.   vivid dreams and visions.

17. A special ability to know or even enter the spirit world is associated with
    *a. the shaman.
    b.   the Lakota Bible.
    c.   John Mbiti.
    d.   animism.

18. Divination is employed to
    a.   compensate for violation of a taboo.
    b.   restore a woman to the social order after childbirth.
    *c. read the past or look into the future.
    d.   ensure that peyote will be protected by the Supreme Court.

19. Dancers often wear masks
    a.   that complement the flowers making up the lei.
    b.   because they have great memories for oral texts.
    c.   because birds are often assumed to have protective powers.
    *d. in order to become the spirit represented by the mask.

20. Christmas, though a Christian holy day, began as a celebration of
    a.   the old English goddess of dawn.
    *b. the winter solstice.
    c.   Samhain in Ireland.
    d.   the return of ancestral spirits to the world.

21. Oral religions today are especially threatened by
    *a. destruction of habitat.
    b.   ecotourism.
    c.   resistance to the spread of television.
    d.   the weakness of the logging industry.

22. Maori religion is part of the cultural rebirth in
    *a. New Zealand.
    b.   New Mexico.
    c.   New Guinea.
    d.   Australia.

23. The calumet is a
    *a. pipe.
    b.   drum.
    c.   mask.
    d.   sand painting.

24. Until recently, oral religions were looked at as
    a. too involved with symbolism.
    *b. primitive and undeveloped.
    c. overly complex.
    d. a peak of religious early insight.

25. Sacred time tends to focus on the
    a. distant future.
    b. immediate future.
    c. present.
    *d. distant past.

26. Sacred space is often constituted by
    *a. a great mountain or tree.
    b. the construction of a skyscraper.
    c. the command of a ruler.
    d. the veneration of a sacred book.

27. The vision quest in Native American religions
    a. has often been associated with marriage ceremonies.
    *b. is frequently undergone at the time of adolescence.
    c. always makes use of hallucinatory herbs.
    d. is a part of preparing for death.

28. Important times in the development of the individual are often marked in oral religions by ceremonies. These are commonly called
    a. initiatory ceremonies.
    b. circumambulations.
    c. scarification.
    *d. rites of passage.

29. The belief that all elements of the world are inhabited by spirits or spirit is called
    a. divination.
    b. naturalism.
    c. spiritualism.
    *d. animism.

30. Oral religions
    *a. frequently make little or no distinction between a god and an ancestor.
    b. make clear distinctions between natural and supernatural.
    c. frequently value androgyny.
    d. almost always mark marriage with public religious ceremonies.

Essay Topics

1. Explain why oral religions are no longer called *primitive* religions but instead are called *primal* religions. What is the difference of meaning in the two terms?

2. Offer two reasons why oral religions in the past received less scholarly attention than the dominant religions.

3. Describe three developments that have promoted renewed interest in oral religions.

4. What do we mean when we describe a culture as *holistic?*

5. Describe the relationship of human beings with the rest of nature that is typical of several North American native religions.

6. Describe briefly two examples of *sacred time* and two of *sacred space.*

7. Explain the notion of the High God in oral religions.

8. Describe three typical life-cycle ceremonies and give an example of each from a specific oral religion.

9. Explain the notion of taboo. Describe two specific religion-based examples, and speculate on how or why each arose.

10. What roles does the shaman typically perform in oral religions? List three contemporary professions that involve work that might be undertaken by a shaman.

11. Describe the trance state as practiced by a specific religion. What is the goal of the practice?

12. Describe the special roles played by the arts in oral religions—roles often taken by texts in book-centered religions. Offer two specific examples.

13. Describe two specific trends that today threaten the existence of oral religions.

14. Describe one specific example of oral religion existing within elements of a religion that apparently absorbed it.

Chapter 3   Hinduism

Learning Objectives

After reading this chapter, the student should be able to

- describe the origins of Hinduism.
- explain a monistic worldview.
- discuss concepts of karma, rebirth, and liberation.
- discuss aspects of social life, such as caste and stages of life.
- explain the practices and goals of the four religious paths.
- describe features of devotional Hinduism practiced by the majority of Hindus.
- recall the names and characteristics of Hinduism's most popular gods.

Chapter Outline

First Encounter
The Origins of Hinduism
    The Earliest Stage of Indian Religion
    The Aryans and Their Religion
    The Vedas
The Upanishads and the Axis Age
    The Origin of the Upanishads
    Important Concepts of the Upanishads
        Brahman and Atman
        Maya
        Karma
        Samsara
        Moksha
Living Spiritually in the Everyday World
    The Bhagavad Gita
    The Caste System
    The Stages of Life
    The Goals of Life
    The Yogas
        Jnana Yoga
        Karma Yoga
        Bhakti Yoga
        Raja Yoga
        Hatha Yoga
Devotional Hinduism
    The Trimurti: Brahma, Vishnu, and Shiva
    Worship of the Divine Feminine: Devi
    The Guru as Object of Devotion
    Devotion to Animals
    Other Forms of Religious Devotion
    Personal Experience: Gazing into the Mother's Eyes
Hinduism and the Arts
Hinduism: Modern Challenges
    Mohandas Gandhi
    Hindu Influence beyond India
Religion beyond the Classroom
For Fuller Understanding
Related Readings
Key Terms

Lecture Supplements

There is a panorama of possible directions in which to go in the study of Hinduism, and even defining "it" (Sanantana Dharma) is a lively subject of debate. This is a field still searching for a paradigm, and our students are provided a working framework by Molloy; only when they have gotten their minds around it might you consider introducing further complexity. Once they grasp the term as an umbrella covering a diverse range of religious phenomena and after studying this chapter of the text, they might be ready for a more sophisticated understanding of religions. The academic field of South Asian studies, Indologists, and specialists in Hinduism is immense and ranges in spectrum from classicists to specialists in contemporary popular religion, from Sanskritists to vernacular communities, from historians of religion to anthropological participant observers making pilgrimage to gurus. The field of Hinduism expands to consider other religions of India, which might even further confuse the issues. Molloy's approach brings a huge topic within manageable grasp of our students.

Further background for teaching Molloy's text depends on the directions one chooses to investigate. Students might select short research topics, for example, and report on them briefly in class to demonstrate various aspects. The following suggestions approach some of the current trends in the field, including women's issues, renewed interest in goddesses, saints and sadhus, yoga and Tantric studies, popular religion and sects, and Vedic traditions in ritual and sacrifice. New religious movements always comprise a dynamic element surrounding each religious field, and of course in Hinduism one could run in many directions to stimulate student interests. Teaching with material culture, such as the sacred arts and temple architectures, music, and poetry is always a rich multisensory way to engage students on this cultural level of sensuous spirituality. Diana Eck's *Darsan: Seeing the Divine Image in India,* 3rd ed. (New York: Columbia University Press, 1998) is still a classic for introducing this sensory approach to Hinduism. Music and mantras might be used to demonstrate the level of religious experience in chants and ragas, such as Ravi Shankar's collection *Chants of India* (CD produced by George Harrison, Angel, 1997). Berendt Joachim-Ernst's *The World Is Sound: Nada Brahma, The Music and Landscape of Consciousness* (Rochester, VT: Inner Traditions International, Ltd., 1991) gives a deeper treatment of music in India for stimulating learning, especially the section "India and Jazz" (pp. 200ff) showing the way music in India has a socioreligious impact. The following selected scholarship will support Molloy's approaches to Hinduism with plenty of foundational background.

A. (Key words: saints, poetry, hymns, popular religion, sacrifice, modernity)

The current study of Hinduism is particularly stimulating for the cultural fieldwork exemplified by the scholarship of Doniger, Hiltebeitel, Inden, Marriott, Hawley, K. M. Brown, Juergensmeyer, Heesterman, B. K. Smith, and Diana Eck, just to name a few. Especially noteworthy for introducing our students to the poetry of the great saints of India who are revered across the entire spectrum of society is Jack Hawley and Mark Juergensmeyer's *Songs of the Saints of India* (New York: Oxford University Press, 1988). These eminent scholars of South Asian studies present the poetry of Ravidas, Kabir, Nanak, Surdas, Mirabai, and Tulsidas with selected verses in original translations, and a biographical and interpretive essay on each. Not only do these poems have great universal Hindu themes, but also they are part of the hagiographical traditions of India at every level and are even revered in films and comic books of India—two genres in which popular religion abounds. In his fascinating exploration of saints in modern India at a more specialized level, Juergensmeyer's *Radhasoami Reality* (Princeton, NJ: Princeton University Press, 1995) explores these topics in detail, examining how the teachings of medieval saints are applied by today's businessmen, computer programmers, office workers, and intellectuals, demonstrating the complexity of modern Hinduism. Juergensmeyer is a leading scholar in the field of contemporary South Asian popular religion and politics and is also the authority to study on the issue of violence and religion (see *Terror in the Mind of God: The Global Rise of Religious Violence* in the *Comparative Studies in Religion and Society* series; Berkeley: University of California Press, 2000). If the direction of discussing violence in India is pursued, Juergensmeyer's work is seminal.

For a scholar of issues in the ancient Vedic traditions in the development of contemporary Hinduism, one should read the foundational material by J. C. Heesterman, such as *The Broken Wheel of Sacrifice* (Chicago: University of Chicago Press, 1993). The subjects of sacrifice and ritual are put in the context of India's classic literature, Vedism and Brahmanism, as well as examining the impact on modern religion and violence. Heesterman gives the study of Hinduism a substantial foundation for exploration of the big issues in religious studies, and may give any teacher the insights to connect how we compare and research world religions. Key issues in ancient vedic practices of sacrifice, warriorship, fire offerings, and self-sacrifice (asceticism) continue to emerge in perplexing ways of life in *The Broken Wheel of Sacrifice,* even as modernization has transformed the ancient ways to more contemporary individual religious aspirations and practices.

B. (Key words: ritual, ancient India, sacrifice, Vedas)

Much important work has been devoted to the study of the early period of Indian religious history as demonstrated in the Vedas and the Vedic corpus of Brahmanas and in accompanying literatures. English-speaking scholars have only recently gained access to an important collection of essays exploring different aspects of Vedic culture and practice. Charles Malamoud's *Cooking the World: Ritual & Thought in Ancient India* (Delhi: Oxford University Press, 1996; translated from French version [1989] by David G. White) contains a series of essays that seek to explore the intense speculations by Vedic authors that were focused on ritual action. Several of the observations in the work arise from the Vedic definition of man as sacrificed and sacrificer. Reflections on man's dual role, as potential sacrificial victim and as the only creature who can perform sacrifice, provide a basis for understanding ancient Indian rituals and ritual speculation. *(Man,* as opposed to *human,* is the appropriate word choice in this case because women were usually denied an active role in Vedic sacrificial ritual.)

Malamoud discusses several connected issues. Molloy's text outlines Vedic culture and rightly connects speculations about the cosmos and the sacrifice as the source of the later Vedic speculations connected with the Aranyakas and the Upanishads. Malamoud's essays on the ideology of village and forest and his discussion of the theology of debt provide useful insight into later Indian religious developments. The village was the place of sacrifice and the source of appropriate sacrificial victims. The forest was understood as a wild and chaotic place, disconnected from the ordered world of humans. As a world outside human control, it was the place of wild animals, monsters, and gods. It is specifically this ideology of village and forest that is later exploited in the stages of life system: retirees and renunciates who depart from society are particularly associated with the extrasocial world of the forest. It is also this forest world that gives its name to the forest books (Aranyakas). The theology of debt was the Vedic conception that people were born imperfect and in an imperfect world. This state of debt could be settled only through the practice of ritual sacrifice. This theology also effected the formation of the notions of karma and moksha as a system of debt and liberation. Debt theology, in some ways, was a principle that led to religious shifts in the Axis Age.

Malamoud's essays offer a useful supplement to the material in Molloy's text. Although some of the essays are more technical than others, the ones mentioned above can be assimilated both as lecture supplements and for student research. Additionally, many of the issues dealt with in the work continue as important concepts within later Hinduism. Ritual action has always remained of fundamental importance in India. Even though practice has shifted from Vedic fire rituals to the more widespread temple traditions of modern India, many Vedic conceptions and some practices still inform modern Indian religious life. Many modern Hindus maintain that the Vedas and their accompanying rituals are especially important in terms of their authority as fundamental texts. Even for those modern Hindus who do not understand the contents of the Vedas (as compared with the well-known Bhagavad Gita), these texts still remain a powerful symbol of tradition and religious authority that stretches back into antiquity.

Employing these essays in the suggested fashion allows the professor to demonstrate that while there was an axial shift around 500 B.C.E., it arose out of a set of speculations based on earlier materials. Additionally, these essays provide many insights into the ideology that supported a sacrifice-based religious system.

C. (Key words: Hinduism, religion in practice, India, Krishna, saints, Devi, guru, music and art)

The India volume of the *Princeton Readings in Religion* series, *Religions of India in Practice* (Princeton, NJ: Princeton University Press, 1995) edited by Donald S. Lopez, Jr., is a work by selected scholars that demonstrates the shift away from the study of philosophy and the religious expressions of elite groups. Although this approach is cumbersome for an instructor who is attempting a basic introduction, several of the twenty-six selections on Hinduism will prove useful. (There are additional entries on Buddhist, Jain, Muslim, and Sikh traditions.) The introduction, "A Brief History of Religions in India," by Richard H. Davis, provides an overview of Indian religious history that supplements Molloy's chapters on all of the above-named traditions. By providing a historical chronology, this chapter both supplements Molloy's presentation of Hinduism and provides a context for the diverse articles within the book. Although all of the included articles are helpful additions to any discussion of Hinduism, a few are of particular importance. Additionally, authors include suggested reading for more detailed research on each topic.

Under the heading of Devotional Hinduism, Molloy's text presents the many important gods of Hindu devotional worship. Neal Delmonico, in "How to Partake in the Love of Krishna" in *Religions of India in Practice,* offers a specific case study and accompanying text for the Caitanya Vaishnava tradition. In this tradition, worship of Vishnu is focused on his avatar, Krishna, and Krishna's lover, Radha. Worshipers are exhorted to follow rules of good conduct, to read and hear sacred scriptures, and to recite the many names of Krishna. After several years of religious development, followers undergo initiation and are taught by their spiritual teacher (guru) a set of esoteric incantations (mantras). By meditating on these mantras, followers are able to overcome ignorance and forgetfulness and therefore remember the divine and enduring enjoyment that can only come from Krishna and Radha. The collection also includes essays and texts devoted to the worship of Shiva, Vishnu (in other forms than Krishna), and the various goddess traditions.

Several articles in *Religions of India in Practice* are devoted both to the Divine Feminine (Devi) and the practices of Hindu women (see also section below). Tony K. Stewart, in "The Goddess Shashti Protects Children," illustrates an example of the widespread practice of women taking vows (vrata) in order to attain certain rewards from the goddess. Rewards include wealth, protection and maintenance of family health, and general prosperity. Specific deities who honor women's vows include such manifestations of the goddess as Lakshmi (provider of wealth) and Shashti (protector of children). Carrying out the vows include several elements: ritual items, verbal explanation of the goal of the vow, the demarcation of sacred space by the drawing of sacred designs with rice flour, and then the performance of the specific ritual. Another important article on women's religion in Hinduism is Lindsey Harlan's "Women's Songs for Auspicious Occasions." These songs are devoted to ancestors and goddesses and are held in conjunction with birthdays, weddings, and other important events. Women spend entire nights singing praises. Neglect of these songs can cause deities and ancestors to retaliate by sending sickness, poverty, or other mischief.

Because of the wide variety of traditional texts and accompanying essays, this work is a valuable resource. Its specificity for studying local texts and for practice over classical texts is not a detriment. It will be most helpful to the student or instructor who is interested in devotional Hinduism and modern India. Combined with Molloy's text and the volume's introduction, lecturers and students can easily adopt the articles in *Religions of India in Practice* for particular research projects or lecture subjects. This book was developed as a replacement for older anthologies, such as Hopkin's *The Hindu Religious Tradition* (1971), or Columbia's *Sources of Indian Tradition* (1958). For introductory students, it is probably better employed not as a replacement but as a resource to be used in tandem with more classical works of this type. Since Molloy's Hinduism chapter provides a well-rounded introduction, this work should be a useful supplement.

D. (Key words: devotional bhakti Hinduism, puja, Devi, Hindu goddesses, women's status, patriarchy, feminism, politics)

India's Hindu and Buddhist goddesses may give students a bridge into religious studies by analysis of the contemporary rediscovery of the goddess, while raising issues of patriarchy in religious society. Students may be introduced to gender topics and the experiences of women by examining the role of female deities—their images, devotional practices, and history—in the social standing, class status, and religious life of women. Do they empower women, or serve the interests of patriarchal culture? "Is the Goddess a feminist?" is one of the interesting questions that can develop small group discussions, by introducing the imagery of goddesses, such as Lakshmi, a goddess of wisdom and prosperity often embraced by women at all social levels in India. The book titled *Is the Goddess a Feminist? The Politics of South Asian Goddesses* by Alf Hiltebeitel and Kathleen M. Erndl, eds. (New York: New York University Press, 2001) considers the goddesses of South Asia by raising questions about images of deities as symbols that impact the actual daily lives of Hindu women. Contributors discuss contemporary Indian women who have embraced goddesses as spiritually and socially liberating, as well as the seeming contradictions between the power of Indian goddesses and the lives of Indian women. The book also critiques issues of sexual desire in the embodiment of female deities, and the question of goddess representation and contested interpretations. Western feminist use of Hindu and Buddhist goddesses as paradigms for feminist theology are analyzed in this collection. Kathleen M. Erndl is author of *Victory to the Mother: The Hindu Goddess of Northwest India in Myth, Ritual, and Symbol* (New York: Oxford University Press, 1993) in which she explores the vitality of Devi goddess worship in contemporary northwest India. Erndl interviews women and makes participant observations based on her scholarship to consider the nature of the goddess in the experience of her devotees. Beginning with an analysis of oral and written sources, Erndl's work includes written and oral traditions, pilgrimage, rituals, drama, and possession as case studies of women representatives "possessed" by the goddess who are then worshipped as her embodiment. Santoshi Ma is a more recent goddess that demonstrates the way popular culture absorbs and transforms ancient influences into contemporary culture. Another goddess, the fierce daughter of Durga named Kali Ma, is the subject of Lex Hixon's book *Mother of the Universe: Visions of the Goddess and Tantric Hymns of Enlightenment* (Wheaton, IL: Quest, 1994). David Kinsley's *Hindu Goddesses: Visions of the Divine Feminine in the Hindu Religious Tradition* (Berkeley: University of California Press, 1989) is a good introduction to this subject for students. It is interesting that the feminine faces of the divine from India's patriarchal and caste system traditions of religion are beginning to be reclaimed both at the popular level as well as by the feminist scholars of the Western academy.

E. (Key words: Shiva, Sanskrit, Tamil, bhakti)

Karen Pechilis Prentiss, in her article "A Tamil Lineage for Shiva Siddhanta Philosophy" (*History of Religions* 35, no. 3 [1996]: 231–257), discusses differences between the two philosophical traditions devoted to the worship of Shiva. One sect composed its texts in Sanskrit and the other composed its canonical texts in Tamil. The Tamil school differentiated themselves from the Sanskrit school by eliminating their connections with the traditional temple ritual and through their establishment of a Tamil lineage of bhakti poets. There was a distinct historical transformation of the sect from a pan-Indian Sanskrit school to a regional Tamil-based tradition. Sanskrit Shaiva siddhanta continued a tradition of philosophy, textual transmission, and commentatorial discourse. The Tamil school shifted its tradition to regional guru–disciple relationships, commentarylike texts, with some commentatorial discourse. The Tamil school moved beyond philosophical literatures into the realm of bhakti hymns. This created a canon of bhakti literature, philosophical interpretation of bhakti, and a Tamil language heritage.

This article offers some specifics relative to one of the many Shaivite schools. As the god of Shaivites, Shiva is conceived as the sole god beyond his more generally understood role in the Trimurti. What is particularly demonstrated in this research is the importance of the diversity across the Indian subcontinent. Although study of India often emphasizes the general nature of Vedic and Sanskritic culture, the Tamil culture of the south produced considerable social variety and history. It is also relevant that the division between philosophical schools and the devotional (bhakti) schools is often blurred by the vicissitudes of history.

Instructors will find this research helpful in offering a specific case example for several issues presented in the general text. Shiva worship, philosophy, bhakti, and cultural diversity are all considered in this article. Discussion might include consideration of the importance of historical change and sectarian development as important strands in the intricate tapestry of Indian religious life. Likewise, students can examine the mixture of different Indian religious trends within particular traditions.

F. (Key words: yoga, tantra, kundalini)

In "Mountains of Wisdom: On the Interface between Siddha and Vidyadhara Cults and the Siddha Orders in Medieval India" (*International Journal of Hindu Studies* 1, no. 1 [April, 1997]: 73–95), David G. White considers the complex and multilayered history of hatha yoga, alchemy, and tantra in medieval India. White traces the development of these important traditions from the cults of sacred mountains to the mythologies of demigod wizards (Vidyadharas) and perfecti (Siddhas), to historical human alchemists and *siddhas,* to alchemical apparatus (for sublimating mercury and achieving immortality), to hatha yoga practices. This is an example not just of historical development but also of simultaneous identifications: conceptualization of the "universe of the Siddhas is so constructed as to permit its practitioners to at once identify cosmic mountains with their own subtle bodies and alchemical apparatus, and to enter into those mountains to realize the final end of their practice, their transformation into the semidivine denizens of those peaks" (p. 91).

This article covers considerable history across Shaiva, Siddha, Tantric, and Jain sources. It demonstrates that while many Indian traditions focused on moksha, or liberation from the world, others sought a more this-worldly or "heroic" power. The study also provides details concerning the development of the subtle physiology of kundalini yoga from a combination of tantric, alchemical, and hatha yoga sources. The larger historical and geographic context is also considered. Although the specific details of the article are concerned with Hindu religious developments, Chinese, Syrian, and Persian parallels are also mentioned. Alchemical knowledge and legend traveled the Silk Road, connecting the Mediterranean with east and south Asia.

Accounts of and popularizations of kundalini yoga, hatha yoga, and tantra are continually increasing in circulation within the modern world. From this article, the instructor can demonstrate a portion of the complexity and history embodied in these traditions. Although these traditions are alive but waning in the context of modern India, they provided much of the content of medieval Indian religion. Hindu, Jam, and Buddhist streams of these medieval traditions are still found throughout Asia. As presented in the textbook, instructors may further demonstrate that there are many forms of yoga in Indian culture and history. Discussion could be focused on the polyvalence of the very term *yoga.* In this article, yoga is specifically understood in the context of hatha yoga and tantra, yet as presented in the text, there are also the very different traditions of karma yoga and bhakti yoga. How might all of these widely divergent activities and schools of thought be designated by the same term?

Notes on *For Fuller Understanding*

1. *Investigate to see whether examples of Hindu practice exist in or near your home or school. Visit a Hindu temple or center and attend a service if possible; then write a short description to share with others.*

   In urban areas, Hindu temples and meditation centers can often be found through a telephone directory. You may look under "church" in the yellow pages, and look for "Hinduism," "Vedanta Society," and "ISKCON" (International Society for Krishna Consciousness). In some areas, it may be helpful to make contact with an Indian national or immigrant; since U.S. higher education is internationally popular, Indian nationals are often to be found on college campuses as both professors and graduate students. Even though the individual Indian may belong to a different religion, he or she may know where persons who practice Hinduism are to be found and may even provide an introduction.

   Be sure your students are quite familiar with the contents of this chapter before they visit: familiarity will make the experience richer and allow for interesting conversations after the service.

   You can readily provide students with a template for the written report:

   Place and its description

   Occasion being celebrated

   Basic outline of service and time line

   [Drawing of place]

   Costume/decoration

   Notable actions

   Two or three readily identifiable features

   Two or three aspects you couldn't understand or identify

   How your experience helped you understand Hinduism

   What you might next investigate about Hinduism as a result of your experience

2. *Read one of the several excellent works by contemporary Indian novelists—works that involve life in today's India or in the communities of Indians who have emigrated to the West. Make notes on the elements of Hinduism you find in the novel.*

3. *Read from Walt Whitman's powerful group of poems* Leaves of Grass. *Copy three short selections that seem to have similarities with Hindu teachings. Read these aloud to friends and then discuss possible parallels with Hindu teachings.*

   This experience can be enriched in the classroom if students read some of the poems aloud. Videos of Whitman's life and thought might be used to accompany a classroom presentation.

4. *Investigate the life of Martin Luther King, Jr. How and when did he learn about the techniques of nonviolent resistance? Describe specifically how he made use of these techniques. What parallels do you see with the traditions of Hinduism and with the work of Gandhi?*

   This project can be enriched in the classroom with videos of the life and work of Martin Luther King, Jr. It might also be possible to invite to speak in the classroom someone who was involved in working for integration at the time of King.

5. *As part of a longer project, read some of the books that influenced Gandhi as he was working toward his philosophy of nonviolent resistance. What are the key ideas that you take from your reading? How might these ideas be applied to the problems and issues facing today's world?*

   Books that were influential were the New Testament (Matthew 5–7), Tolstoy's *The Kingdom of God Is within You,* Thoreau's *On Civil Disobedience,* and the Bhagavad Gita.

Video Resources

Hindu Ascetics

This program looks at the practices of some of India's holy men—sadhus (penitents), fakirs, and yogi—and at the powers with which the superstitious endow them; it also connects the rituals of these ascetic eremites to ancient Hindu and Buddhist rituals. This subject matter can be disturbing; preview this program before showing to younger audiences. (44 minutes) [Religion]

Hinduism: An Ancient Path in the Modern World

Hinduism is believed to be the world's most ancient living religion. This video provides an overview of its principles and beliefs, focusing specifically on the concept of transmigration of the soul and on the role of the guru. It illuminates the practice of Hinduism in the modern world, from the time of Mahatma Gandhi to today. It also looks at Sikhism—an outgrowth of Hinduism and Islam—and considers how Hinduism has survived despite the Muslim invasion, the British occupation, and pressures for social change from within India. (20 minutes) [Insight]

Hinduism and the Song of God: A Modern Interpretation of the Bhagavad Gita

Presenting images that are quintessential expressions of the spirit of India, this film explores Karma, the Four Stages of Life, and the Four Yogas. (30 minutes) [Hartley and Insight]

India and the Infinite

Dr. Huston Smith produced this picture of an India of paradoxes and extremes. Images gathered from Kashmir to Benares, from Bombay to Bangalore, combine with the poetry of Dr. Smith's words to produce a visual essay of lingering beauty. (30 minutes) [Hartley]

Sacred Trances in Bali & Java

Extraordinary examples of altered states of consciousness in animistic, Hindu, and Muslim rites. The film captures supernormal acts such as walking on fire, piercing cheeks with pins, and rolling on broken glass. (30 minutes) [Hartley]

Internet Resources

The Bhagvat Gita
http://iconsoftec.com/gita/

Gita: The Bhagavad Gita: a Hindu Pantheism
http://members.aol.com/Heraklit1/gita.htm

Hindu Home Page
http://www.hindutva.org/

Hinduism Page
http://www.d.umn.edu/~thats/hindu.html

Hinduism Online
http://HinduismToday.kauai.hi.us/

Hinduism Today Online
http://www.hinduismtoday.com

The Hindu Tantrik Home Page
http://www.hubcom.com/tantric/

Hindu Temples Reference Center
http://www.mandirnet.org

International Society of Divine Love (Radha Krishn, Hinduism, Supreme God)
http://www.isdl.org/index2.html

Spirituality/Yoga/Hinduism Home Page
http://www.geocities.com/RodeoDrive/1415/index.html

Tattvavaada
http://www.rit.edu/~mrreee/dvaita.html

Vedanta Page
http://www.sarada.com/

Multiple-Choice Questions

1. The word that means "liberation" is
   *a. moksha.
   b. karma.
   c. ahimsa.
   d. maya.

2. The word *Vedas* is related to the English word
   a. visit.
   *b. vision.
   c. vex.
   d. vertical.

3. Vedic worship was primarily
   *a. offerings to nature gods at fire altars.
   b. solemn circular dances.
   c. fasting for a month, beginning at the new moon.
   d. silent meditation.

4. A characteristic symbolic object associated with Krishna, indicative of the attractive power of the divine, is a
   a. shell.
   b. flame.
   *c. flute.
   d. flower.

5. A mantra is a
   a. sacred painting.
   b. form of meditation.
   c. breath exercise.
   *d. short chant.

6. What animal is treated with special devotion and care by Hindus?
   a. snake
   b. monkey
   c. elephant
   *d. cow

7. The term for the divine nature of each person is
   *a. atman.
   b. jnana.
   c. moksha.
   d. maya.

8. The Vedic god of fire was
   a. Soma.
   b. Indra.
   *c. Agni.
   d. Varuna.

9. The hallucinatory drink used in Vedic worship was called
   *a. soma.
   b. mantra.
   c. moksha.
   d. maya.

10. The oldest and most important of the Vedas is
    a. Sama Veda.
    b. Yajur Veda.
    c. Atharva Veda.
    *d. Rig Veda.

11. The Upanishads are
    *a. about 100 written works that discuss the nature of spiritual reality.
    b. sacred diagrams used in meditation.
    c. the seven centers of spiritual energy in the body.
    d. poems by Rabindranath Tagore.

12. When was the Bhagavad Gita written?
    a. 2000–1500 B.C.E.
    b. 1000–800 B.C.E.
    *c. 200 B.C.E.–200 C.E.
    d. 700–900 C.E.

13. The Bhagavad Gita is part of a long Indian epic poem called
    a. Iliad.
    b. Purana.
    c. Gita Govinda.
    *d. Mahabharata.

14. The prince who is counseled by Krishna in the Bhagavad Gita is
    *a. Arjuna.
    b. Ganesha.
    c. Lakshmi.
    d. Hanuman.

15. The term *maya* may be translated as
    a. liberation.
    b. nonharm.
    c. bliss.
    *d. illusion.

16. *Bhakti* means
    a. freedom from suffering.
    b. studying the sacred texts.
    *c. devotion to a god.
    d. working for the good of others.

17. The god Rama is frequently paired with
    a. Devi.
    *b. Sita.
    c. Lakshmi.
    d. Ganesha.

18. The Vedic god of storm and war was
    a. Soma.
    b. Surya.
    *c. Indra.
    d. Agni.

19. What god—ordinarily shown with the face of a monkey—helped return Sita after her abduction to Sri Lanka?
    *a. Hanuman
    b. Ganesha
    c. Ganga
    d. Lakshmi

20. The ideal of causing no harm to anything that can suffer is
    a. karma.
    b. moksha.
    c. jnana.
    *d. ahimsa.

21. The modern Indian who used nonviolent means to help lead India to independence in 1947 was
    *a. Mohandas Gandhi.
    b. Ram Mohan Roy.
    c. Rabindranath Tagore.
    d. Ramakrishna.

22. The religious practice of ordinary Hindus is primarily
    *a. devotion to deities.
    b. the practice of meditation.
    c. breathing exercises.
    d. study of ancient religious texts.

23. The law of moral cause-and-effect is called the law of
    a. moksha.
    b. jnana.
    *c. karma.
    d. ahimsa.

24. A Hindu social class, sanctioned by religion, is called a
    a. mantra.
    *b. caste.
    c. ahimsa.
    d. stratum.

25. Raja yoga is the yoga of
    a. knowledge.
    b. physical exercise.
    *c. meditation.
    d. devotion.

26. A brahmin is a
    *a. priest.
    b. warrior-noble.
    c. peasant.
    d. merchant.

27. This god is associated with destruction and rebirth.
    a. Vishnu
    *b. Shiva
    c. Rama
    d. Krishna

28. A major city of the pre-Vedic culture of the Indus River Valley was
    *a. Harappa.
    b. Benares.
    c. Madras.
    d. Pataliputra.

29. Om is a well-known example of a
    a. jiva.
    b. mandala.
    *c. mantra.
    d. yoga.

30. What deity is often shown with dark blue skin?
    a. Lakshmi
    b. Hanuman
    c. Shiva
    *d. Krishna

31. A guru is a
    *a. religious teacher.
    b. tree spirit.
    c. drink used in Vedic ritual.
    d. trance state.

32. An important symbol of Shiva is the
    a. stupa.
    *b. lingam.
    c. banyan tree.
    d. candle.

33. In Hinduism, *dharma* refers to
    a. postures used in meditation.
    *b. one's social duty.
    c. a style of drumming.
    d. faith in a teacher.

34. The absolute or divine reality is known as
    *a. Brahman.
    b. Brahma.
    c. brahmin.
    d. Bhagavad Gita.

35. A sannyasin is a
    a. craftsman or merchant.
    b. nature spirit.
    c. warrior-noble.
    *d. wandering holy man.

Essay Topics

1. Describe three geographical features of India that relate to Hindu devotional practice, and explain the connection.

2. What are the four Vedas about? Please describe them.

3. Describe the roles of the River Ganges in Hindu practice.

4. Define the concept of *Atman*. Describe how it is similar to yet different from the typical Western concept of self?

5. Define the concept of maya, and describe the impact of this concept on the Hindu understanding of death.

6. Describe the categories of the caste system and explain how they function within Hindu thought and practice.

7. What are the four stages of life and what are the obligations associated with each?

8. Describe three of the yogas and explain how they function within Hindu practice.

9. Name the three gods of the Trimurti. Describe the basic identities and roles of each of the gods.

10. Identify two Hindu deities usually portrayed in feminine forms. Describe a key characteristic of each.

11. Explain the concept of the guru. Offer two or three reasons why the concept has attained popularity in the capitalist Western world.

12. Explain the Hindu veneration of the cow in a way that would allow a Westerner to understand the basic Hindu belief behind the practice.

13. Describe two well-known examples of Hindu sculpture.

14. Describe how Hinduism of the past and present shapes the roles of women.

15. List three ways in which Gandhi has contributed to contemporary social issues. Describe how one of those contributions has resulted in political action beyond the traditional Hindu realm of influence.

16. Describe three areas of Hindu influence outside of India.

17. Assume that you have been asked to arrange a tour of the three most significant Hindu sites. What would they be? Why would you choose those sites?

18. Have you ever encountered someone in your culture who could be considered a sannyasin? Describe the characteristics that would allow you to make such an identification.

Chapter 4   Buddhism

Learning Objectives

After reading this chapter, the student should be able to

- describe the life story of the Buddha according to tradition.
- describe aspects of Hinduism that Buddha rejected.
- explain the content of the Four Noble Truths.
- discuss concepts of change and no self in Buddhism.
- discuss the spread of Buddhism from India.
- distinguish among the three major branches of Buddhism.
- discuss Zen and its unique expressions in art.

Chapter Outline

First Encounter
The Beginnings of Buddhism: The Life of the Buddha
The Basic Teachings of Buddhism
    The Three Marks of Reality
    The Four Noble Truths and the Noble Eightfold Path
The Influence of Indian Thought on Early Buddhist Teachings
    Ahimsa: "Do No Harm"
    The Soul and Karma
    Nirvana
The Early Development of Buddhism
Theravada Buddhism: The Way of the Elders
    Theravada Teachings and Literature
    Theravada Art and Architecture
Mahayana Buddhism: The "Big Vehicle"
    New Ideals: Compassion and the Bodhisattva
    Mahayana Thought and Worldview
        The Three-Body Doctrine
        Heavenly Bodhisattvas
        Shunyata
        Thathata
    Mahayana Literature
    Mahayana in China
    Mahayana in Korea
    Mahayana in Japan
    Some Major Schools of Mahayana
Zen Buddhism: Enlightenment through Experience
    Zen Techniques for Enlightenment
    Buddhism and the Arts of Japan
Vajrayana Buddhism: The "Diamond Vehicle"
    Origins, Practice, and Literature of Tibetan Buddhism
    Ritual and the Arts
Personal Experience: Visiting the Dalai Lama
Buddhism, the West, and Modern Challenges
Religion beyond the Classroom
For Fuller Understanding
Related Readings
Key Terms

Lecture Supplements

Molloy's introduction to Buddhism offers students a foundation in the life and teachings of Siddhartha Gautama, an overview of the main historical traditions and key concepts, and an introduction to diverse cultural forms of Buddhism. The "cultural expressions" approach is experiencing a surge in scholarship, notably represented in the *Life of Buddhism* (Berkeley: University of California Press, 2000), edited by Frank Reynolds, Jason Carbine, and Mark Juergensmeyer. This collection provides essay overviews by outstanding scholars, introducing aspects of Buddhist life in cultural contexts through sacred material culture and practices such as iconography, architecture, devotional practices, pilgrimages, gender roles, and other significant social characteristics. It includes current material on the lived experience of Buddhists in the West, both ethnic communities and new converts.

Another excellent collection of materials representing the cultural contexts approach is *Buddhism in Practice* (Princeton, NJ: Princeton University Press, 1995), edited by Donald S. Lopez, Jr. This book employs the framework of the Three Jewels (the Buddha, the Dharma, and the Sangha) to present diverse materials and articles on Buddhism. The organization forces the reader to read across geopolitical divisions, historical periods, and other traditional divisions. In order to establish the continuities across Buddhist traditions, the Three Jewels division mixes the articles that are devoted to topics situated in India, China, Japan, Tibet, and other areas. Like the other volumes in this series, articles include both scholarly introduction and commentary and traditional texts translated into English. Following Molloy's survey of geographical regions and the more substantial sections on Zen and Vajrayana branches of Buddhism, the concluding section of the text on Buddhism in the West gives students a chance to apply their learning to familiar issues. Several recent books are excellent for expanding on recent developments (e.g., see below Prebish, Fields, Coleman, and others), especially examining the ethnic and "elite" traditions Molloy discusses, and how Buddhism is transforming and hybridizing in Western cultures.

Buddhism is a term used for a wide variety of religious traditions represented by a long history, wide geographic and political distribution, and millions of adherents. There are as many approaches to understanding these traditions as there are discrete sects and schools. As demonstrated in the Molloy text, there are three major ways of dividing the myriad traditions of Buddhism. First, the various traditions can be divided according to the basic Buddhist self-division of its different dimensions, as in the Three Jewels: the Buddha, the Dharma, and the Sangha. Second, one could adopt the broad divisions among conservative schools represented today by Theravada, more inclusive traditions such as Mahayana, and the esoteric sects of Vajrayana. The third division can be mapped by geopolitical units and language differences: Indian, Chinese, or Japanese forms of Buddhism, or as Pali texts compared with Chinese or Tibetan texts. Different approaches to Buddhism generally rely on one of these divisional frameworks. Contemporary research tends to favor the third approach exemplified in the texts mentioned here, although the other methods are also employed.

A. (Key words: Mahayana, Vajrayana, mantra, meditation)

One article from the Princeton series volume on India, discussed above, is "The Power of Mantra: A Story of the Five Protectors," by Todd T. Lewis. As represented in Molloy's discussions of Pure Land, Nichiren, and Tibetan Buddhism, short phrases (mantras) have been widely employed by various Buddhists as prayers and tools of meditation. As demonstrated in these traditions, mantras are often employed for gaining rebirth in the Pure Land or for other powerful effects. Lewis explains how these short formulas "were regarded as concentrated expressions of truth that commanded power over the unseen forces; if spoken correctly and by appropriate individuals, their recitation could affect the world—and the mind of the reciter—in highly beneficial ways" (p. 227). Lewis further discusses the use of mantras as introduction to his translation of the "Five Protectors" text. He also discusses the use of this text by many different Mahayana groups in several languages.

The translation depicts the Buddha dwelling in a monastery on top of Mount Sumeru. The Buddha tells a story of how a monk benefited from knowing the correct mantra by being saved from punishment and subsequently redeemed. Some of the benefits of reciting the mantra include freedom from harm from demons, ghosts, madness, and sickness. In addition to recitation, the phrase can be written on paper and placed in an amulet worn around the neck. This will also free someone from harm and suffering.

Prayers and mantras have wide use throughout Asia. The example of mantras used for protection might be considered more mundane compared with mantras used for meditation and the achievement of enlightenment. Yet it is exactly this variety of practice that characterizes the diversity of the many Mahayana sects and traditions. Instructors will find this article and its accompanying text easily accessible to introductory students. It is short (seven pages) and offers a straightforward account of the beliefs associated with formulaic expressions (inantra).

B. (Key words: Theravada, preaching, rhetoric)

Preaching and teaching styles helped to spread Buddhism across Asia. Yet Buddhist preaching is often neglected in modern scholarship in favor of text, meditation, rituals, and so on. Mahinda Deegalle, in "Buddhist Preaching and Sinhala Religious Rhetoric: Medieval Buddhist Methods to Popularize Theravada" (*Numen* 44, no. 2 [May, 1997]: 1, 80ff), intends to overcome the scholarly tendency to ignore preaching rituals in Buddhism, with particular reference to Theravada Buddhism in Sri Lanka. The paper focuses on the term *bana*, which means "preaching." In Sri Lanka, preaching has served as a primary mode of religious rhetoric in the spread and popularization of Buddhism since the thirteenth century. Deegalle examines inscriptions to establish the importance of bana as a religious and historical category important to Sinhala (Sri Lankan) Buddhism. The author discusses, in particular, the Pujavaliya, a thirteenth-century text. Negotiations and communication between the religious establishment and its laity have often functioned successfully because of Buddhist preaching and educational styles. The text in question and the traditions that arose from it transformed Theravada intellectual framework by using popular terms such as *kama* (desire). Such terminology shifts helped to translate religious concepts into easily accessible language. Preaching, through employing popular rhetoric, influenced educational styles that have had profound influence on the attitudes and practices of Buddhists in Sri Lanka.

Although this article addresses few of the larger issues discussed in Molloy, it provides a crucial clue concerning the expanse of Buddhist influence. This case study is specific to Theravada schools in Sri Lanka, but it provides a useful corrective that is applicable to Buddhism everywhere. By generalizing from this example, it is easy to demonstrate that one factor that effected Buddhism's spread throughout the world was the importance of preaching and general missionary activities. Buddhism has maintained strong influence in the modern world, precisely in the locations where it has been integrated into popular culture. This factor is additionally represented by the recognition of scholars that Buddhism has many variations. Although there are core teachings such as the Four Noble Truths and the importance of meditation, Buddhism is much more than the sum of the historical Buddha's teachings.

Instructors will find this to be useful in its illustration of missionary, preaching, and educational activity. Many of the other traditions examined in Molloy do not find worldwide distribution. Popularization through preaching and active missions is one of the key factors in explaining why Buddhism, Christianity, and Islam are the world's numerically largest traditions. Students will find this article useful for research projects related to trends in Theravada traditions or as a piece that could be compared and contrasted with trends in Christian preaching.

C. (Key words: Tibetan Buddhism, Theravada/monastic Buddhism, Mahayana/messianic Buddhism, Vajrayana/ esoteric or magical Buddhism, Three Jewels, bodhisattvas, yoga, lama, Three-Body Doctrine)

Robert A. F. Thurman's *Essential Tibetan Buddhism* (New York: HarperCollins, 1995) is an excellent short course on the complexities and varieties of Buddhist history and tradition in Tibet. Thurman offers nine chapters, each devoted to the translation of a particularly important Tibetan Buddhist text. The selections provide examples from all the major schools of the tradition. Thurman's introduction (forty-five pages) is a useful supplement to Molloy's text. He emphasizes the importance of particular teachers as living representatives of enlightened Buddhas. He describes and discusses the major bodhisattvas of the tradition, such as Tara and Manjushri. He provides a brief history of Buddhism and its development in Tibet. Each of the translations is accompanied by detailed yet simple notes. Many terms are concisely explained, including mantra, Bodhisattva, Tantra, Dharma, and yoga. One section explains the institution of recognizing previous lamas in new incarnations. After important teachers die, children are sought out who embody the teachers' reincarnated selves. There are specific tests that demonstrate the validity of these identifications. This institution has provided considerable stability to the different schools. It also allowed for lineages that could not be passed on through heredity, since most schools of monks require celibacy.

Although no single volume could cover the diversity of the Tibetan traditions, this book delivers what it promises: the essentials. Thurman's experience as a monk and a scholar also makes this a particularly sensitive portrayal of an important Buddhist tradition. It can be helpful to students and lecturers alike because the introduction and notes are simple and the included texts provide primary sources for the tradition. Instructors might want especially to note Thurman's choice of English words for translating Buddhist concepts. His choices are consistent with contemporary American English and offer special insights not always available to introductory students. As with other scriptural traditions, many nineteenth- and early twentieth-century terms have become entrenched, yet these terms do not carry much meaning for the average student.

D. (Key words: Sangha, Buddhism in the West, Orientalism, Buddhist Americans, ethnic Asian immigrant communities, elite Buddhism, interreligious dialogue)

The emergence of Buddhism in the West makes an excellent topic for introducing issues in contemporary religious movements. The arrival of Buddha's teachings in Europe through travelers and intellectuals drawn to all things exotically "Oriental" demonstrates the initial tendency to distort or romanticize Asian religions. The transmission of Asian thought across the Atlantic to New England influenced such thinkers as Thoreau, Emerson, and William James and the development of abstract interpretations of Buddhism (sometimes called "Protestant Buddhism"). Thomas Tweed in *The American Encounter with Buddhism, 1844–1912: Victorian Culture and the Limits of Dissent* (Religion in North America) (Bloomington: Indiana University Press, 1992) gives a history of the early European influence. At the same time, ethnic Asian Buddhist immigrants who came across the Pacific Ocean to the West labored constructing railroads, mining, and building towns. Their communities established the earliest *sanghas* along the Pacific coast. For an excellent overview of the varieties of ethnic Asian Buddhist communities and their traditions in America, see Prebish and Tanaka's *The Faces of Buddhism in America* (Berkeley: University of California Press, 1998), which also examines some of the problematic questions regarding convergence with postmodern societies and misunderstandings by non-Asian scholars. Another significant influence on Buddhism in America emerged in the fifties with the "Beats" (e.g., Allen Ginsberg, Gary Snyder, Jack Kerouac). The American Trappist monk Thomas Merton also stimulated interest in Buddhism through his books and journals. Soon many Americans and Europeans encountered Asian teachings either through traveling in Asia, or from the newly arriving Asian Buddhists beginning to teach mainly young intellectuals and countercultural spiritual seekers. Some examples are Zen scholar Daisetz T. Suzuki and (not related) Shunryu Suzuki (author of the excellent *Zen Mind, Beginner's Mind,* founder of Tassajara Creek Monastery, San Francisco Zen Center, and Green Gulch Farm), and Tibetan Chogyam Trungpa Rinpoche (founder of Naropa University in Boulder). An excellent overview history of this phase of Buddhism in America is *How the Swans Came to the Lake* by Rick Fields (Boston: Shambhala, 1992), describing in narrative many of the key characters and events melting Buddhism into the diverse contexts of America. Another superb volume is *Luminous Passage: The Practice and Study of Buddhism in America,* by Charles Prebish (Berkeley: University of California Press, 1999), offering a scholarly appraisal of significant movements and issues, including the most current information on new developments and statistics and the emerging academic disciplines and scholars. Significant questions are also discussed in James Coleman's *The New Buddhism: The Western Transformation of an Ancient Tradition* (New York: Oxford University Press, 2001), providing students with ample in-depth material for exploring this contemporary historical development of Buddhism. For a scholarly treatment of the emerging discipline of American Buddhist studies, see *American Buddhism: Methods and Findings in Recent Scholarship* (Curzon Critical Studies in Buddhism) by Duncan Ryuken Williams and Christopher Queen, eds. (London: Curzon Press, 1999).

E. (Key words: ecology, environmentalism, engaged Buddhism, Dalai Lama, Tibetan Buddhist art, Kalachakra mandala).

Another thread following Molloy's approach to religions is the connection between Buddhism and ecology, exemplified especially in two anthologies. *Dharma Rain: Sources of Buddhist Environmentalism* by Stephanie Kaza and Kenneth Kraft, eds. (Boston: Shambhala, 2000) is a superb and scholarly collection of essays for exploring this significant element of Buddhist perspectives, demonstrating that ecological issues are a serious area of religious studies for the topic running through Molloy's text. Another similar but earlier collection is *Dharma Gai: A Harvest of Essays in Buddhism and Ecology* by Allan Hunt Badiner, ed. (Berkeley: Parallax, 1990), including excellent essays by the Dalai Lama and Gary Snyder, as well as other good materials. Harvard University Press has a series on Religion and Ecology, and their volume *Buddhism and Ecology: The Interconnection of Dharma and Deeds* (Religions of the World and Ecology series) by Mary Evelyn Tucker and Duncan Ryuken Williams, eds. (Cambridge, MA: Harvard University Press, 1998) emerges from a conference at the Harvard University Center for the Study of World Religions. This volume analyzes issues in Buddhism as an environmental resource for both theory and practice from Asian and American sources, and applies some of the practical aspects of ethics and engaged Buddhism (socially active Buddhist ethics) to current issues.

Molloy's visit with the Dalai Lama described in the text provides an opportunity to connect Tibetan Buddhism in America with popular issues for students. Because of increasing notoriety and such popular films as *Little Buddha, Seven Years in Tibet, Kundun,* and *The Cup,* and the Tibetan Freedom Concerts and student organizations, students can consider the questions raised by the encounter between Tibetan Buddhist traditions and modernity in the West. In keeping with the discussion of sacred arts in the textbook, Tibetan traditions of art may captivate and teach students the importance of material culture and symbolism, alongside those of Zen discussed in the text. One of the most sophisticated traditions of religious arts in the world, Tibetan Buddhism can raise questions about the "iconology" of symbol systems and "visual scriptures" in Buddhism. Two fascinating videos on Kalachakra ritual ceremony with spectacular mandalas include *Heart of Tibet: An Intimate Portrait of the Dalai Lama* (Mystic Fire, 1991) and the Irish film *Kalachakra, the Wheel of Time* (Mystic Fire, 1991). The first one presents a longer treatment of the Dalai Lama's visit to Los Angeles to give an elaborate ceremonial ritual, and the second one focuses specifically on the particle mandala construction in Dublin, Ireland. Both raise questions about Buddhism in the West. One of the many excellent treatments on Buddhism and the arts is *Wisdom and Compassion: The Sacred Art of Tibet* by Marilyn Rhie and Robert Thurman (New York: Harry Abrams, 1991). This book, based on an exhibition at the Asian Art Museum of San Francisco and Tibet House, New York, is lavishly illustrated and documented with essays explaining the role of art in Tibet. H. H. Tenzin Gyatso, the Fourteenth Dalai Lama of Tibet, has numerous books from which a teacher might select short readings for students. *The Four Noble Truths: Fundamentals of the Buddhist Teachings of His Holiness the XIV Dalai Lama,* translated and edited by Thupten Jinpa and Dominique Side (London: Thorson's, 1998) would make an excellent choice.

Notes on *For Fuller Understanding*

1. *Many immigrants from traditionally Buddhist countries continue to celebrate their cultural festivals and are usually quite welcoming toward visitors. If your area has such festivals, participate in one and make notes (or photos or a video) on what you see as Buddhist influences on the festivities.*

   Theravada Buddhists (Thai, Laotian, Cambodian) keep Vesak in May with religious services and community celebrations. Tibetans celebrate their New Year with religious celebrations of several days. Japanese frequently go to a temple on New Year's Eve and remember their deceased with O-Bon dances in summer. Chinese often keep Chinese New Year in late winter with Buddhist services. You can find out about Buddhist religious services by looking in the yellow pages under "church" (or something similar). Many immigrant groups have a yearly community gathering with dance, food, and religious elements. Information about cultural events can be found at university departments (religion, anthropology, Asian languages) and through Asian cultural organizations. Newspaper announcements about upcoming religious and cultural events can also be a source of information.

2. *Go on a virtual journey through Buddhist sites on the Internet, which range from semiprivate devotional Web pages through museum-based libraries of Buddhist art. Prepare an annotated bibliography of the Web sites that you found most valuable, and describe some of the insights and questions you came to as you explored.*

3. *Read a biography of the Dalai Lama and other books about Tibetan Buddhism. Prepare a written report on how the Dalai Lama's beliefs and actions earned him the Nobel Prize for Peace.*

4. *Find out if there is a Buddhist meditation center in your area. Visit it, gather information, even take a course, and then make a report to your class.*

   Theravada Vipassana, Tibetan, and Zen meditation instruction and practice are found in many cities. Look in the yellow pages under "church," or call a local university department of religion for information about the centers.

5. *Do some library research on American architect Frank Lloyd Wright and his connections with Japan. Is there any evidence to suggest that Wright could have been influenced by Buddhist ideas or forms?*

   In addition to books about Wright, students can read his autobiography. Books should be consulted that show photos of the major houses of his career, particularly "Fallingwater," the "Robie House," "Taliesin," and "Taliesin West."

6. *Around New Year's (or around Chinese New Year), phone Chinese restaurants in your area to see if any of them mark the occasion by serving* jai—*vegetarian "monk's food." If you find one, go—perhaps with a group of your classmates—for the feast, ask questions about its origins, and report (perhaps after additional research in a library) on what you learned.*

   For addresses and phone numbers, consult newspapers and other restaurant guides.

Video Resources

Buddhism and Black Belts
This video investigates how Buddhist practices influence daily life in modern Japan, looking at meditation, the tea ceremony, *ikebana* (flower arranging), calligraphy, martial arts, and archery. It also shows how Buddhism has been incorporated into Japanese education and how Zen thinking is used to discipline sports teams and to train police officers. (29 minutes) [Insight]

Buddhism, Man and Nature
This video captures the underlying philosophy of Buddhism rather than its historical manifestations, stressing its central tenets: that humans are part of nature, that emptiness has value, and that life is characterized by change that should not be resisted. (14 minutes) [Insight]

Buddhism: The Middle Way of Compassion
Filmed in India, Nepal, Thailand, and Japan, this video explores the development of Buddhism since the birth of Siddhartha Gautama. It explains the concept of karma, discusses the Noble Eightfold Way, and differentiates between Theravada Buddhism and Mahayana Buddhism. It also shows Buddhist rituals in different countries. (25 minutes) [Insight]

Buddhism: The Path to Enlightenment
This video traces the life of the Buddha from his birth as a prince through his search for a solution to life's sorrows and his years of preaching. Taking viewers to visit monasteries in southeast Asia, it examines how he influenced the lives of his followers. (35 minutes) [Insight Hartley]

Choice for a Chinese Woman: Enlightenment in a Buddhist Convent
Here is an extraordinary portrait of a Chinese teenager from a poor rural family who ran away to a Buddhist convent. This program looks at life inside the convent, at the religious conventions and convictions of a people trained since the Maoist revolution to disdain religion, and at the transformation of a young girl who has found peace in the search for enlightenment. (35 minutes) [Religion]

The Dalai Lama: A Portrait in the First Person
By the force of his words, the Dalai Lama has turned the disaster of the Chinese depredations in Tibet and the tragedy of his own exile from his roots and his spiritual home into a worldwide message of peace and strength. In this program, the Dalai Lama speaks of anxiety, anger, enlightenment, tolerance, and compassion. Your enemy, he says, is your best teacher; true compassion is what you feel toward your enemy. (24 minutes) [Religion]

Requiem for a Faith
This classic film tells the story of Tibetan Buddhism, alive today in a remote Indian refugee camp. Dr. Huston Smith's poetic narration guides us through a world of ancient rituals, continuous meditation, deep compassion, and a profound faith in humanity. (30 minutes) [Hartley]

Zen: The Best of Alan Watts
Featuring rare footage of the teacher who is considered the West's foremost interpreter of Eastern thought, Alan Watts comments on the basic teachings of Zen, Zen and nature, and how meditation helps one experience true calm. (60 minutes) [Hartley]

Internet Resources

Buddhist Art and Architecture
http://www.buddhanet.net/gallery.htm

Buddhist Resource File
http://pears2.lib.ohio-state.edu/BRF

Buddhist Studies—Art
http://kaladarshan.arts.ohio-state.edu/anu/buddhart.html

Dharmapala Centre School of Thangka Painting
http://www.bremen.de/info/nepal/Inhalt-e.htm

Kyoto National Museum
http://www.kyohaku.go.jp/meihin/menue.htm

Multimedia Buddhist Art Gallery
http://www.cmn.net/~hafer/artgallery.html

Sakyadhita—Bibliography on Women and Buddhism
http://www2.hawaii.edu/~tsomo/biblio.htm

Virtual Voyager at the MFA
http://www.chron.com/mandala/

Welcome to Kyoto
http://web.kyoto-inet.or.jp/org/saikosha/English/w1.html

Women in Buddhism, Past, Present, and Future
http://www.crosswinds.net/~campross/women.html

Zen Buddhist Info Web
http://www.dharmanet.org/infowebz.html

Multiple-Choice Questions

1. Siddhartha Gautama is the name of
   *a. the person who became known as the Buddha.
   b. one of the earliest disciples of the Buddha.
   c. a missionary who spread Buddhist teachings.
   d. an Indian translator of essential Buddhist texts who worked in China.

2. Tradition holds that which relative of the Buddha died soon after the birth of the Buddha?
   a. father
   *b. mother
   c. aunt
   d. grandfather

3. Regarding his social class, the Buddha was
   a. a priest.
   *b. an aristocrat.
   c. a merchant.
   d. a peasant.

4. The Buddha lived about this time.
   a. 958–878 B.C.E.
   *b. 563–483 B.C.E.
   c. 286–206 B.C.E.
   d. 79–159 C.E.

5. The Buddha was particularly troubled by the problem of
   a. whether there is an afterlife.
   b. the existence of the divine.
   *c. suffering and death.
   d. the exploitation of the poor.

6. The Buddha was shocked into going on a religious search by
   a. the death of his father.
   *b. the Four Passing Sights.
   c. his failure to have more than one child.
   d. his father's loss of wealth and property.

7. The Buddha left home to begin his life of wandering at what age?
   - a. 16
   - *b. 29
   - c. 45
   - d. 71

8. The Buddha was enlightened at what age?
   - a. 21
   - *b. 35
   - c. 51
   - d. 66

9. The Buddha died at what age?
   - a. 35
   - b. 49
   - c. 65
   - *d. 80

10. The basic outlook on life, formulated by Buddhism, is contained in
   - a. the four major yogas.
   - *b. the Four Noble Truths.
   - c. the four castes.
   - d. the Four Passing Sights.

11. One of the essential Buddhist teachings is
   - a. turn the other cheek.
   - *b. everything is changing.
   - c. live for yourself only.
   - d. you have only one life to live.

12. In regard to the common belief in a permanent soul, the Buddha seems to have taught that
   - *a. there is none.
   - b. each person has one, but it dies with the body.
   - c. the soul is more important than the body.
   - d. souls are constantly being reborn.

13. Buddhism began in
   - a. Sri Lanka.
   - b. China.
   - c. Thailand.
   - *d. India.

14. *Nirvana* seems to come from a word that means
   - a. expand.
   - *b. blow out.
   - c. fulfillment.
   - d. reach out.

15. A major goal of Buddhism is
   - a. union with God.
   - b. physical health.
   - c. reaching heaven.
   - *d. inner peace.

16. Buddhism developed into several branches. The branch that spread into Sri Lanka and southeast Asia is
   - a. Mahayana.
   - b. Vajrayana.
   - *c. Theravada.
   - d. Vipassana.

17. Literally, *Mahayana* means
    a. mind only.
    *b. big vehicle.
    c. great insight.
    d. compassionate heart.

18. A person of great compassion, willing to be reborn constantly to help others, is called
    *a. bodhisattva.
    b. arhat.
    c. karuna.
    d. sangha.

19. The essential collection of sacred books of Buddhism is called
    *a. Tripitaka (Tipitaka).
    b. Dhammapada.
    c. Vedas.
    d. Four Noble Truths.

20. *Zen* comes from a word that means
    a. joy.
    b. peace.
    c. insight.
    *d. meditation.

21. The ideal of the Theravada branch is the
    a. bodhisattva.
    b. scholar.
    *c. arhat (arahat).
    d. artist.

22. Tibetan Buddhism includes elements of
    *a. shamanism.
    b. Confucianism.
    c. Christianity.
    d. Islam.

23. The general name for that category of books that is said to give the words of the Buddha is
    a. abhidharma.
    *b. sutra.
    c. vinaya.
    d. dharma.

24. The unconditioned state of reality that is the highest goal of Buddhism is called
    a. moksha.
    *b. nirvana.
    c. dharma.
    d. trikaya.

25. The dissatisfaction and sorrow that life brings is called
    a. karma.
    b. bodhisattva.
    c. dharma.
    *d. dukkha.

26. Tibetan Buddhism
    *a. makes great use of ritual.
    b. uses animal sacrifice.
    c. does not value the role of the spiritual teacher.
    d. has spread to Malaysia and Indonesia.

27. Buddhism came to Tibet from
    a. China.
    b. Afghanistan.
  *c. India.
    d. Japan.

28. In Tibetan Buddhism, a vajra is frequently used together with
    a. a flower.
    b. a trumpet.
  *c. a bell.
    d. incense.

29. The Chan/Zen virtues are especially
    a. modesty and refinement.
  *b. intuition and naturalness.
    c. family harmony and family devotion.
    d. faith in a Buddhist deity.

30. The school of Chinese and Japanese Buddhism, which sees the Buddha as a divine savior, whose name the believer must constantly repeat with devotion, is
    a. Chan/Zen.
  *b. Pure Land.
    c. Gelugpa.
    d. Tiantai/Tendai.

31. Concerning words, Zen stresses that words are
    a. necessary.
  *b. not adequate.
    c. important.
    d. valuable when used in mantras.

32. What is most important in Zen is
    a. a master's tea bowl.
    b. a robe indicating authority.
    c. certain sacred books, including the Mumonkan.
  *d. enlightened awareness.

33. A koan is
    a. a poem.
  *b. a problem.
    c. a song.
    d. a dance.

34. The type of beauty that Zen particularly values emphasizes
    a. gorgeousness and wealth.
    b. what is rare and unusual.
  *c. simplicity.
    d. great size.

35. The Buddha of the Western Paradise is
    a. Maitreya.
  *b. Amitabha.
    c. Guanyin (Kuan-yin).
    d. Manjushri.

Essay Topics

1. Summarize the pivotal experiences that led the young Siddhartha to abandon his courtly life.

2. Describe the similarities between Siddhartha's experience of enlightenment and later Buddhist notions of enlightenment.

3. What, according to the conventional description of the life of the Buddha, was his final teaching before his death? What does it mean?

4. The Buddha is the first of Buddhism's Three Jewels. What are the other two, and what role do they play in Buddhism?

5. Give two examples from everyday life that show the Buddhist notion of impermanence. Please explain.

6. Contrast the Buddhist notion of *no permanent identity* with the Hindu notion of *Atman.*

7. List the Four Noble Truths. Explain how they illustrate the practical nature of Buddhist teaching.

8. Explain the Buddhist ideal of *ahimsa.*

9. In what key way is the Buddhist notion of *karma* different from the Hindu understanding of *karma?*

10. Explain the Buddhist notion of *nirvana.*

11. Describe three or four characteristic monastic practices in Theravada that illustrate Theravada's close adherence to the teachings of the Buddha.

12. List three symbols of the Buddha found in Buddhist art and explain their meaning.

13. Explain the Mahayana concept of *karuna.* Give two or three examples that show how karuna is fundamental to Mahayana teaching and practice.

14. Describe the three manifestations of the Buddha nature that are part of Mahayana teaching.

15. Explain the two types of bodhisattvas in Mahayana and explain their roles.

16. Explain and illustrate the Mahayana notion of *tathata.*

17. Explain the Buddhist notion of *skillful means.*

18. Select two of the major schools of Mahayana and describe several identifying characteristics of each.

19. Describe two typical practices associated with Zen and explain how they relate to the goal of achieving enlightenment.

20. Select two of the arts of Japan or China and explain how each illustrates a key teaching of Buddhism.

21. Explain the basic approach of Tantric Buddhism, describing how it differs from teachings in other more traditional forms of Buddhism.

22. Describe two ritual practices of Tibetan Buddhism and explain their meaning.

23. Describe two contemporary challenges to traditional Buddhism and explain how Buddhism is attempting to meet them.

24. Assume you are to arrange a tour for classmates to three of the most significant Buddhist sites. What sites would you choose? How would you defend each as "among the most significant"?

Chapter 5   Jainism and Sikhism

Learning Objectives

After reading this chapter, the student should be able to

- discuss the origins of Jainism.
- describe the key beliefs and ethical practices of Jainism.
- discuss similarities and differences among Jainism, Buddhism, and Hinduism.
- describe the emergence of Sikhism in India.
- explain the key beliefs and values of the Sikhs.
- discuss similarities and differences among Sikhism, Hinduism, and Islam.

Chapter Outline

First Encounter
Shared Origins
JAINISM
Background
Mahavira and the Origins of Jainism
Worldview
Jain Ethics
The Development of Jainism and Its Branches
    Digambaras
    Shvetambaras
    Sthanakavasis
    Terapanthis
Jain Practices
Jain Scriptures
Jain Art and Architecture
SIKHISM
Background
Nanak and the Origins of Sikhism
The Worldview and Teachings of Nanak
The Development of Sikhism
Sikh Scriptures
Sikhism and the Modern World
Personal Experience: A Visit to the Golden Temple
Religion beyond the Classroom
For Fuller Understanding
Related Readings
Key Terms

Lecture Supplements

Jains and Sikhs are two of the important religious minorities of India. Contemporary scholarship on both of these groups is often of a highly specialized nature. Even so, there are some recent articles and book chapters that are useful to the introductory student. Some current scholarship focuses on comparative frameworks for understanding these traditions.

Studying the Sikhs: Issues for North America (SUNY Series in Religious Studies) by John Stratton (Jack) Hawley and Gurinder Singh Mann, eds. (Albany: SUNY Press, 1993) is the best introduction to the key problems of scholarship regarding history, cultural and artistic studies, and diverse cultural and ethnic issues in Sikhism. This is a practical and useful book for scholars and teachers, including a syllabus and Sikh pedagogical models by two eminent scholars in the field. *The Sikhs* by Patwant Singh (New York: Knopf, 2000) is a comprehensive history by a Sikh scholar and pairs an insider's sympathetic perspective with a scholarly balanced approach to some of the problematic issues, including nationalistic conflicts and religious rivalry with Hindus. Patwant Singh's book on the Golden Temple of Amritsar, *Golden Temple* (Columbia, MO: South Asia Books, 1999), is an excellent source for examining the most sacred site of Sikhism, the shrine of the Adi Granth text. In *The Sikhs,* Patwant Singh discusses the development of the paradox among Sikh pacifist values, opposition to caste stratification, nonproselytizing, and the contrasting image and symbolism of warrior saints. He also discusses the Sikh paragon of discipline and loyalty in a religion of nearly 20 million worldwide, renowned for their education, their business practices, and their organizational success. This text delves deeply into the various historical figures and specific cultural contexts and material culture sites, such as Amritsar, with authenticity and substance.

John Cort's scholarship on Jains is authoritative, and the best text on the subject is undoubtedly *Jains in the World: Religious Values and Ideology in India* (New York: Oxford University Press, 2001). Cort's work is discussed below, but a good beginning for Jain studies is his essay in the *Journal of the American Academy of Religion,* "Art, Religion and Material Culture: Some Reflections on Method" (*JAAR* 64, no. 3 [Fall, 1996]), in which he discusses Jain temples and art and especially works on exhibition at a major show in Los Angeles. Cort uses the methodology of iconology of material culture, understanding the visual textuality of sacred art as revelatory of core values and devotion: the problem of "how to express trans-human perfection while remaining rooted in the physical reality of human form" (p. 622). A pantheon of Jain "Jinas" may simultaneously and paradoxically express a form of monotheism represented by the plurality of the divine. Further analyses of Jain sacred texts and other forms of art demonstrate that beyond texts, the transtextual or nonlogocentric sacred arts reveal far more than the reductive approach of limiting articulation of the sacred to books alone. "To the extent that human life is by its very nature embodied, physical and material, the study of religion therefore must involve itself with the study of material expressions of religion" (p. 631), Cort concludes.

David G. White's article "Mountains of Wisdom: On the Interface between Siddha and Vidyadhara Cults and the Siddha Orders in Medieval India" (*International Journal of Hindu Studies* 1, no. 1 [April, 1997]: 73–95) examines some elements of Jain practice and Jain texts. Mount Abu, mentioned in Molloy, is one of the mountains favored by the heroes of both Hinduism and Jainism discussed in the article. Mount Ahu also remains an important site of Jain temples. Elison Banks Findly, in "Jaina Ideology and Early Mughal Trade with Europeans" (*International Journal of Hindu Studies* 1, no. 2 [August, 1997]: 288–313), presents an interesting discussion of the interactions among Hindus, Muslims, Jains, and European traders in the 1500s and later. The article's most relevant point is that Jain ethics (particularly the notion of ahimsa, but also ethical constraints on Jain occupation choices) positively facilitated good trade relations between Indians and Europeans. Additionally, Sikhs have recently been discussed in comparative terms. David Scott, in "Buddhism: Sikh Encounters and Convergence" (*Studies in Religion* 26, no. 1 [1997]: 75ff), discusses the relative lack of Buddhist–Sikh comparative study. His article examines materials that suggest Buddhist influence on the formation of the Sikh tradition. Scott discusses similarities in doctrine, ethics, and meditation practices. Sikh tradition formation is often discussed in terms of Hindu and Islamic influences, but this article provides the lecturer with another angle on the issues. Even though these articles are specialized in ways that might not be as helpful for an introduction to Jains and Sikhs, they do provide the lecturer with information on academic trends, and they each maintain a comparative perspective that is useful in a world religions class. Some Sikh scholars maintain that the Muslim and British political climates in the early modern period actually created Sikh traditions by their policies. Others agree with the Sikh community and demonstrate that the Sikhs have had a separate self-identity from the time of Guru Nanak's life. The following summaries all come from *Religions of India in Practice,* the Princeton volume discussed previously under Hinduism. The volume includes four entries on Jains and three on Sikhs. All of the articles are short and easily assimilated by introductory students. Each author provides a brief introduction and a translation of a short text.

A. (Key words: Jain, Digambaras, Shvetambaras, Sthanakavasis, Jain image veneration)

Image veneration among Jain Shvetambaras is discussed by John E. Cort in "The Rite of Veneration of Jain Images." The Rite of Veneration is performed daily by both laity and mendicants. The author translates a description of the rite from a recent ritual manual. The rite has developed over centuries, and the translation represents several different languages. Jains sing hymns to Jain images in temples and on holy days. By venerating these images, Jains hope to absorb some of the superior qualities of the beings embodied in the image, which helps in the removal of karmic attachments. These practices are considered to both remove previous karma and prevent the accrual of future karma. The text includes both ritual instructions and several short songs. This text provides an explicit presentation of the important and personal nature of image veneration. It also exemplifies the particular kinds of behaviors that led to the formation of the Sthanakavasis.

The article demonstrates the distinctions between different Jain groups that are presented in Molloy's text. Instructors can use this short piece as focus for class discussion on the apparent discontinuities between Jain subsects. This article also provides a useful example of the overlap among Jain, Buddhist, and Hindu traditions. One might discuss how image-venerating Jains are more like Bhakti Hindus or Pure Land Buddhists and how the ascetic orders are more like Hindu renunciates or Theravada Buddhists. This is yet one more example of the simultaneous similarities and differences within the traditions that were developed in India.

B. (Key words: Sikh, the Divine Name, Adi Granth, Guru Arjan, Khalsa initiation, "Five K's")

The leading scholar of Sikhism, Hew McLeod, presents two important articles: "Sikh Hymns to the Divine Name" and "The Order for Khalsa Initiation." In the first article, McLeod discusses the importance of the Divine Name for the Sikh tradition. McLeod provides general overview notes similar to Molloy's text. He then supplies a translation of the Sukhmani hymn, which means both "Pearl of Peace" and "Peace of Mind." The hymn, written by Guru Arjan, celebrates the grandeur of the Divine Name and announces its importance in the quest for liberation. This hymn has wide popularity among both Sikhs and Hindus. Many Sikhs include it as part of the daily rites. The Sukhmani has several themes, including the importance of remembering the Divine Name, the liberating power of the Name over ancient scriptures, God's greatness, path of God, and the importance of the guru.

In his article about Khalsa initiation, McLeod discusses the importance of the Khalsa and the "Five K's" of the Sikhs. He outlines the differences between Sikhs who choose to enter the Khalsa and those who do not. Although there were many different codes of belief and behavior developed over the years, it was not until 1950 that the initiation and its code were standardized. The Sikh Code of Conduct manual that was published in 1950 has now won widespread acceptance. McLeod includes a translation of the initiation rite that is found in this code. The text discusses the five Khalsa symbols and provides the details of the ritual and the recitations involved.

These two articles provide easily accessible examples of Sikh texts and introductory material that mirrors the Molloy text. With these specific examples of Sikh literature, students can get a distinct sense of the mood of the tradition. The selections are short enough that they could be used as extra reading or could easily be assimilated in essays and other writing assignments. Mark Juergensmeyer's chapter on Sikh tradition in *Teaching the Introductory Course in Religion* (pp. 49–56) provides further basic information and various pedagogical approaches. It mentions scholars and textbooks relevant to introductory material. The bibliography at the end is a useful resource.

Notes on *For Fuller Understanding*

1. *Study present-day India and mark on a map the places where Jains are to be found.*

   Students should distinguish between the areas of the Digambaras and the Shvetambaras and mark Jain centers of pilgrimage, sacred mountains, and important Jain temples. Ask students to find photos of as many of these places as they can.

2. *Construct arguments for and against the Jain acceptance of religiously inspired self-starvation.*

   Students can research modern arguments for and against suicide, especially in the case of terminal illness, and investigate organizations that support suicide, such as the Hemlock Society.

3. *Investigate Sikhism to find out where Sikh communities exist in North America. If there is a Sikh community in your area, find out more about it, visit its temple, and give a report.*

   Sikh centers exist in many large cities in the United States and Canada.

Video Resources

Trip to Awareness: A Jain Pilgrimage to India
Visiting the Jain temples of Palitana, Mount Abu, Shrevana Belgola, and Ellora, this program explains the tenets of contemporary Jainism. It examines Jainism's roots, its recipe for self-realization, and the concept of ahimsa. (30 minutes) [Insight]

Internet Resources

The Golden Temple—Homage to Amritsar—The Harimandir Sahib
http://www.goldentemple.com/

Jain Center of Northern California
http://www.jcnc.org/

Jainism: Principles, Sources, Images, History
http://www.cs.colostate.edu/~malaiya/jainhlinks.html

Jain Meditation International
http://www.jainmeditation.org/

Jainworld
http://www.jainworld.com

Jiv Daya Committee, JAINA
http://www.jivdaya.org/

Online Sikh Museum
http://www.sikhmuseum.org/

The Sikhism Home Page
http://www.sikhs.org/

Welcome to Jainworld
http://www.jainworld.com/

Multiple-Choice Questions

JAINISM

1. Jainism places great emphasis on
   *a.   ahimsa.
   b.   sacrificial rituals.
   c.   self-defense.
   d.   ritual dance.

2. The Jain worldview holds that a Creator
   a.   made the world.
   b.   created only good things.
   *c.   does not exist.
   d.   created evil as well as good.

3. Hylozoism, the background philosophy of Jainism,
   *a.   sees life in everything, even what is inanimate.
   b.   holds that religion and culture are the same.
   c.   recommends celibacy and the monastic life.
   d.   sees women as equal to men in possibility of spiritual development.

4. Jains allow and even recommend
   a.   long periods of sleeplessness to attain unusual states of consciousness.
   *b.   gentle suicide after a long life of virtue.
   c.   use of bodily passions to gain spiritual insight.
   d.   living by farming and fishing as ways of staying close to nature.

5. The Jains consider Mahavira to be
   *a.   the twenty-fourth "crossing-maker."
   b.   the first person to have reached the top of the universe.
   c.   the third god in their trinity.
   d.   one of the twenty major disciples of Ramakrishna.

6. Jain monks differ from Buddhist monks in allowing
   a.   the eating of food after noon.
   b.   refusing to beg for food.
   *c.   nakedness.
   d.   the drinking of liquor.

7. In the story of their lives, Mahavira and the Buddha show similarities, such as
   a. the fact that they both came from the south of India.
   b. their both being of the brahmin caste but rejecting its rituals.
   c. the fact that they both were orphaned as children.
   *d. their both practicing extreme asceticism.

8. Jainism sees reality as made up of
   *a. life (jiva) and nonlife (ajiva).
   b. three principles: energy, inertia, and stasis.
   c. five elements: earth, water, air, fire, and consciousness.
   d. only physical matter, taking many different shapes.

9. *Tirthankara* is the Jain name that is translated
   *a. crossing-maker.
   b. released from bondage.
   c. gone away.
   d. one who has overcome.

10. The name *Mahavira* literally means
    a. ford-finder or path-maker.
    b. big vehicle or big boat.
    *c. hero or great man.
    d. great virtue or great insight.

11. Jainism seems to be most strongly concerned about
    a. correct ritual at the statues of the tirthankaras.
    b. circumambulation and pilgrimage.
    c. living the longest life possible.
    *d. breaking the power of bondage to the physical world.

12. Jains believe that perfected souls
    *a. disappear from the world and live at the top of the universe.
    b. are reborn in new bodies in order to help others.
    c. live in a paradise in the western sky.
    d. are absorbed into the divine and lose all individuality.

13. Jainism, as taught by Mahavira, emerged in India about the time of what other great teacher?
    a. Mohandas Gandhi
    *b. Siddhartha Gautama, the Buddha
    c. Guru Gobind Singh
    d. Sri Aurobindo

14. Jain monasticism has split into how many branches?
    a. 2
    b. 3
    *c. 4
    d. 5

15. The name of the Digambara branch literally means
    a. white lotus.
    b. upper-sight.
    *c. sky-clothed.
    d. painfree.

SIKHISM

16. The religion of Sikhism first developed in
    a. Kashmir in northern India.
    b. Northeast India, near Calcutta and Benares.
    *c. the Punjab region of India and Pakistan.
    d. Southeast India, near Madras.

17. The center of the Sikh religion is at
    a. Benares.
    b. Lahore.
    c. Colombo.
    *d. Amritsar.

18. The turning point in Nanak's life was a
    *a. prophetic call near a river.
    b. near-death experience from sickness.
    c. request by his spiritual teacher to preach.
    d. dream of a child who told Nanak to leave home.

19. A Sikh temple is called a
    a. guru.
    *b. gurdwara.
    c. kesa.
    d. kara.

20. Which religions accept the eating of animals?
    a. Jainism and Sikhism
    b. Jainism and Hinduism
    *c. Sikhism and Islam
    d. Sikhism and Hinduism

21. Nanak, after leaving home to teach, wore
    a. a white robe and a rosary of amethyst beads.
    *b. clothing that blended Muslim and Hindu styles.
    c. nothing, as a sign of total submission to God.
    d. a Sufi robe of brown wool with a Buddhist begging bowl.

22. The Khalsa was created to be
    *a. a protective social organization.
    b. a group of copyists who created a permanent library of Sikh literature.
    c. a group of devotees who would read aloud continuously in the Golden Temple for the sake of the faithful.
    d. the organization that cleaned the Golden Temple.

23. One of the requirements of the Khalsa was
    a. no use of weapons.
    *b. no alcohol.
    c. daily begging for food.
    d. no eating food after noon.

24. The name *Adi Granth* means
    a. final history.
    b. first beauty.
    *c. original collection.
    d. multiple meaning.

25. The Adi Granth is the
    a. Sikh name for the Golden Temple.
    *b. most important Sikh scripture.
    c. name of the vow that members take to enter the Khalsa.
    d. sword with which baptismal water is stirred.

26. Some Sikhs want a
    *a. Sikh nation, separate from India.
    b. wider use of Sikh principles in the government of Pakistan.
    c. return to the early principles of ahimsa.
    d. union of Sikhism with Islam.

27. How many Sikh gurus were there before the human line of gurus ended?
    a. 3
    b. 5
    *c. 10
    d. 33

28. Nanak's name for God was
    a. The Inconceivable.
    b. Radiance.
    c. The Void.
    *d. True Name.

29. Nanak, like the Hindus, believed in
    a. worship of many gods.
    *b. reincarnation and karma.
    c. daily puja at home altars.
    d. vegetarianism and devotion to cows.

30. Guru Granth is
    *a. an honorary title for the sacred book of Sikhism.
    b. the last of the Sikh gurus, who was assassinated.
    c. another name of Nanak, in his capacity as Sikh teacher.
    d. a Sikh community association, created to help widows and orphans.

Essay Topics
JAINISM

1. Explain the Jain belief in *ahimsa*. By what other religion is this belief espoused?

2. Summarize the story of the life of Mahavira. Include at least three details.

3. Explain why Jainism rejects the notion of a Creator God.

4. Explain the Jain concepts *jiva* and *ajiva*. How do they help explain the human situation?

5. Explain briefly three of the basic Jain ethical principles.

6. What is the fundamental Jain goal? How does it relate to the idealization of self-starvation?

7. Contrast the Jain notion of liberation with the Buddhist notion.

8. Name two of the four main branches of Jainism, and list key identifying characteristics of each.

9. Describe two typical Jain devotional acts and explain how each relates to Jain belief.

SIKHISM

10. What is the literal meaning of the word *sikh*? Why is it appropriate? Please explain your answer.

11. When did Nanak live and what was the key moment in his life story?

12. Describe the basic Sikh understanding of God.

13. What are the two key functions of the *sangat*?

14. Describe three elements of Khalsa dress. How do these elements relate to Sikh belief?

15. Describe two practices that involve the Adi Granth.

Chapter 6   Taoism and Confucianism

Learning Objectives

After reading this chapter, the student should be able to

- describe the basic elements of traditional Chinese belief that appear in later developments of Chinese religions.
- relate basic details of the lives of the key founders of Taoism and Confucianism.
- define the meaning of Tao.
- discuss Taoist values and ideals, and the images used to convey them.
- discuss the focus and goals of Confucianism, especially in terms of the Five Great Relationships, the Confucian Virtues, and the notion of the "noble person."
- describe how Taoism and Confucianism shaped Chinese arts.

Chapter Outline

First Encounter
Basic Elements of Traditional Chinese Beliefs
    TAOISM
The Origins of Philosophical Taoism
    Laozi (Lao Tzu)
    The Tao Te Ching
    Zhuangzi (Chuang Tzu)
The Basic Teachings of Philosophical Taoism
Taoism and the Quest for Longevity
Religious Taoism
Taoism and the Arts
Taoism and the Modern World
    CONFUCIANISM
The Tao in Confucianism
The Life of Confucius
Living According to Confucian Values
    The Five Great Relationships
    The Confucian Virtues
Confucian Literature
The Development of Confucianism
    Schools of Philosophy
    Development of Confucianism as a Religious System
Confucianism and the Arts
Personal Experience: At a Confucian Temple
Confucianism and the Modern World
Religion beyond the Classroom
For Fuller Understanding
Related Readings
Key Terms

Lecture Supplements

As a result of the modern state of Western relations with China, trends in scholarship are uneven in nature and scope. Much of the philosophical literature of Taoism, although once the primary focus of scholarship, is currently being ignored in favor of in-depth study of religious Taoism. On the other hand, although suppressed in its land of origin, Confucian and neo-Confucian philosophy are widely discussed in academic journals devoted to issues of philosophy. Because of this, the religious dimensions of Confucianism are not receiving widespread attention. Although Confucianism still suffers in modern China, some public rites are being performed again, and Confucian veneration of ancestors (with its accompanying rituals) is being practiced in rural areas. The Molloy text covers the basics of the traditions quite thoroughly, yet there are some additional sources that are helpful for both scholars and introductory students.

Three volumes cover many of the important issues. The Princeton series, discussed in reference to India and Buddhism, has also published *Religions of China in Practice* (for general discussion of this series, see the section on Hinduism). Because of the organization of the chapters, Confucianism is not dealt with in an explicit fashion but is synthesized into other divisions. Taoism and Buddhism receive several entries, most of which can be easily synthesized for lecture supplementation or student research. Each provides a translation of a specific text and the author's introduction, commentary, and suggestions for further reading. The introduction also serves to supplement and reflect the general issues presented in Molloy.

Additionally, Molloy suggests Kristofer Schipper's *The Taoist Body* (Berkeley: University of California Press, 1994) in his Related Readings section. This work is one of the best volumes available on Taoism. A translation from French, it is readable and can be surveyed by both students and professors for further research. The Lyden book discussed under Chapter 1 also has useful short sections on both Confucianism and Taoism (see above for the details of each selection and suggested use). These entries are presented from the philosophical and doctrinal perspective and thus supplement the suggested readings, which are mostly of religious or ritual sort. For those interested particularly in Taoism, an older volume, N. J. Girardot's *Myth and Meaning in Early Taoism* (Berkeley: University of California Press, 1983), is an excellent work.

A. (Key words: popular religion, spirits, bureaucracy, ceremonial practices, syncretism, society, folk religion, elite religion)

For *Religions of China in Practice,* edited by Lopez (Princeton, NJ: Princeton University Press, 1996), Stephen Teiser wrote the introduction chapter titled "The Spirits of Chinese Religions." This offers a succinct and useful way to prepare for the contemporary problems of scholarship presented by Chinese religions. Teiser discusses the "syncretism" of Taoism, Confucianism, and Buddhism within the popular religions of China, including diverse regional issues of local practices. The subsection, "The Problem of Popular Religion," discusses the way that religion is shared by people of China in general, including popular festivals and holidays, particularly the New Year's festivals and other celestial calendar days. Teiser also discusses the role of spirits and spirit mediums functioning as shamans in the performance of religious practices in the lived experience of common folk. This is a helpful clarification of how the popular religion reflects the class distinctions between the elite or literate traditions of Confucianism and Taoism based on the classic writings and philosophies, and those of the actual experiences of people in regional settings with spirits and practices that reflect a cultural approach. The folk traditions have become a very serious area of religious studies in these traditions. Another subsection, "Kinship and Bureaucracy," describes the function of spirits in Chinese society regarding ancestor worship and hierarchy of spirits. It is quite useful in sorting out the issues of filial piety (xiao) and hagiography of gods. In the "Spirits of Chinese Religions" subsection, Teiser discusses the Chinese cosmologies and the basic substance of the cosmos known as *qi* (*chi*), which he helpfully explores as "psychophysical stuff" or vital energy. He also helpfully sorts out some of the various interpretations of the Yin and Yang modalities, exploring how Taoists and Confucians have interpreted this important symbolism (which students will all recognize) in various ways over history. It is this key concept of change and harmony that will anchor students in their appreciation of the Taoist and Confucian approaches and distinctions. His treatment of shen (spirit, spirits, and spiritual) is a helpful discussion. Teiser also gives brief but clear overviews of the concepts of Taoism and Laozi (Lao Tzu), Confucianism and Kong Qiu (Confucius), and Buddhism (*Fojiao*) in China with its various formulations (this section would also be helpful in the discussion of Buddhism). The *Chinese Religions in Practice* collection of materials provides a patchwork of diverse Chinese sources demonstrating the varieties of religious experience, correlating with Molloy's methods.

B. (Key words: Taoism, Taoist ritual, Confucianism, Buddhism, gods, Jiao rite of cosmic renewal)

A current work on Chinese religion that is particularly lauded by scholars is *Taoist Ritual and Popular Cults of Southeast China* (Princeton, NJ: Princeton University Press, 1993) by Kenneth Dean. Even though the book is particularly devoted to Taoism, it is important because it deals with all three major traditions of China: Confucian, Taoist, and Buddhist. As a result of the softening of governmental pressures, traditional religious practices are having a revival throughout China, especially in small villages and rural areas. Festivals for the birthdays of local gods are being held again, and local temples are receiving needed repairs and reordination. Temple affiliations bring communities together, revealing overall regional religious structures. Birthday festivals of the gods structure local life. Different types of ritual specialists perform the local rituals: ritual masters, spirit mediums, and Taoist or Buddhist priests. Ritual masters and spirit mediums work in the courtyards outside the temples. Vegetable or animal offerings are brought by the communities. The atmosphere is one of crowds, smoke, firecrackers, and incense fumes. The mediums chant, dance, and drum to produce trances. In trance, the mediums cut and pierce themselves with swords and skewers. Inside the temples, Taoist or Buddhist priests perform elaborate classical rituals. Dean discusses the Jiao rite of cosmic renewal and how it is being practiced in many communities for the first time in decades. The process of the development of local cult spirits into members of the heavenly pantheon is central to the work. City and village gods are seen as local spirits who receive ordination and assignment from the Taoist Celestial Master.

Case studies of three particular cults are provided. Each case study focuses on the spread of the cult temple network, the processions of the gods, and the elaboration of specifically marked rituals for different social groups in a community. The gods of these cults represent all three major religions: a Taoist doctor, a Buddhist monk, and a paragon of Confucian filial piety. Taoist ritual plays an important role by providing a framework for the universalization of the local cults. This process of interaction between Taoism and popular cults is reflected in the composition of invocationary songs, hagiographies, Taoist scriptures for the local god, and continual integration of observances into the Taoist ritual framework. Each chapter also discusses tension between state and local communities, especially concerning the pace of restoration. Dean concludes that religion is embedded in community and that doctrine is generally not of primary importance. He articulates the general assumption that orthopraxy (right action) is of greater relevance than orthodoxy (right belief) in Asia. He stresses an approach to religion in China that focuses on the role of ritual and liturgy within family, lineage, and communal groups.

Dean's book addresses and offers considerable details for almost every aspect of religious Taoism mentioned in Molloy. It also is an important supplement for Molloy's section on Taoism and the modern world. Instructors could draw specific examples from this work for lecture, discussion, and further reading. It is particularly useful for its presentation of the state of affairs in modern China. Accompanied by the introduction, any of the chapter case studies could be used as the basis of research projects for students. Discussion can easily reflect on the mixed nature of religious life in China. This work demonstrates that the borders among folk, Taoist, Confucian, and Buddhist traditions are permeable.

B. (Key words: cosmology, cultivation, Confucianism as a religion, classics, nature)

Two recent articles discuss the importance of realizing the religious dimensions of Confucianism. Both articles are devoted to Confucianism in Japan, but they are applicable to the larger issues of the tradition. These articles are found in a special edition devoted to religious dimensions of Confucianism (*Philosophy East & West* 48, no. 1 [January, 1998]: 5ff, 46ff). Mary Evelyn Tucker discusses several important issues in "Religious Dimensions of Confucianism: Cosmology and Cultivation." Tucker considers the religious nature of Confucianism through her discussion of the terms *cosmology* and *cultivation*. She also discusses how political dimensions often obscure religious ones. She criticizes Western categories such as transcendence and immanence because they further obscure the subject. The religious dimension is particularly expressed in the dialectical relationship between the self and the universe that is concerned with both inner and outer harmony. Cultivating the self is illustrated as the proper moral response to society, politics, and nature. Tucker discusses two Japanese neo-Confucians as exemplars of religious Confucians.

John Berthrong addresses the issues of religion in "Confucian Piety and the Religious Dimension of Japanese Confucianism" in the same issue of *Philosophy East & West*. He takes a different position from that of Tucker. He relies more on some of the theoretical categories that Tucker avoids. He discusses the religious dimension as represented in the canon of classics in terms of a transcendent referent, which he describes in terms of ultimate concern. He argues that for the Confucian the secular is the sacred, and he discusses the distinctive characteristics of this tradition's development in Japan. Both of these articles are interesting in the references to some of the issues presented in Molloy's first chapter. The first rejects Western terminology and theory, while the second affirms classical approaches to religion (with references to the theories of Tillich and Eliade).

These articles are somewhat specialized yet are relatively straightforward and specifically address issues of religion. Instructors will find them helpful as supplements to lecture notes. They could be used in class discussion as a point of return to the central issues of study presented in Chapter 1. Many of the journal articles currently available are of this type. If the instructor is more interested in the philosophical dimensions of Confucianism, these will help to balance the focus on ritual found in the Dean and Princeton texts.

Notes on *For Fuller Understanding*

1. *Try to describe the personality of Confucius. Do you know of any person in recent times who has a similar character and values? Compare the two.*

   The person may be a figure from politics, film, television, or general culture. He or she could also be a friend or relative.

2. *Describe how Taoism and Confucianism are complementary.*

3. *List the differences that you see between the Confucian "noble person" (junzi) and the Theravada Buddhist monk.*

4. *Do you see any contradiction between the Taoist ideal of gracefully accepting death, suggested by the Tao Te Ching, and the Taoist search for long life and immortality? Can the two goals be reconciled? Please explain.*

   Perhaps examples can be given either from the world of film and television or from family members and friends.

5. *Do some research on contemporary life in Korea and Japan. Look particularly for evidence of Confucian virtues that seem to play roles there and that contribute to their international successes.*

   Some cities have cable television stations that broadcast Japanese and Korean films and television series. Recent immigrants might also be valuable sources of information. Novels in translation and newspaper items about these countries could also be consulted. Topics could include attitudes toward education, marriage, divorce, the roles of husband and wife, and the loyalty of employees to a company.

6. *Consider your own "home culture." If Confucianism became an influence, how would its principles or rules be expressed in everyday language and activity?*

   Imagine an American city transformed by Confucianism. What would the schools be like? How would life on a big-city street or in a subway be different? How might family life be different?

7. *Investigate whether your area has a Chinese garden, and visit it if you can. Find books in the library with photographs of Chinese gardens. What themes and images common in Taoism do you find there?*

Video Resources

Taoism
Set against the backdrop of contemporary China, this video illuminates the central tenets of Taoism and examines its call for a return to primitive social forms and an abandonment of conventional values. John Blofeld, a respected authority on Taoism, explains how Taoism has influenced other Eastern religions and practices. (25 minutes) [Hartley and Insight]

Taoism: A Question of Balance
In Taiwan, multiple gods are worshiped in thousands of Buddhist and Taoist temples. Documenting the rituals of Taoism, this program shows how religious life weaves together a Confucian respect for ancestors, the cosmic pattern of the Tao and its oracles, a belief in local gods who dispense justice and favors, and the hungry ghosts of the dead. (52 minutes) [Insight]

Internet Resources

The Abode of the Eternal Tao
http://www.abodetao.com/

China WWW VL—Internet Guide for China Studies (ANU Heidelberg Univ.)
http://sun.sino.uni-heidelberg.de/igcs

Chinese Philosophy
http://www.hku.hk/philodep/ch/

Chinese Philosophy Page
http://main.chinesephilosophy.net/index.html

Daoism Depot
http://www.edepot.com/taoism.html

Taoism Information Page
http://www.clas.ufl.edu/users/gthursby/taoism/

Taoism: The Temple of the Immortal Spirit—The Western TAOIST
http://www.thetemple.com/

Multiple-Choice Questions

TAOISM

1. The notion of *wu wei* is
    a. social responsibility.
    b. filial piety.
    *c. no unnecessary action.
    d. education and discipline.

2. Literally, *Tao Te Ching* means
    a. book of light and shadow.
    b. mountain-silence-scripture.
    c. dark-path-poetry.
    *d. way-power-classic.

3. From a Taoist perspective, the proper job a person should have would be determined by
    a. whatever his or her family decides.
    b. the caste she or he belongs to.
    c. what the government decides is needed.
    *d. what the individual is most capable of doing.

4. The man who dreamed he was a butterfly was
    a. Laozi (Lao Tzu).
    *b. Zhuangzi (Chuang Tzu).
    c. Zhu Xi.
    d. Mengzi (Mencius).

5. Applying the notion of yin and yang, we could say that Taoism shows a special love for
    *a. allowing things to develop naturally.
    b. creating a large corporation.
    c. getting as many academic degrees as possible.
    d. having many children and educating them carefully.

6. The most important image to be found in the Tao Te Ching, the image that best expresses its ideals, is
    a. fire.
    b. music.
    *c. water.
    d. light.

7. At the end of his life, Laozi (Lao Tzu) is said to have
    a. disappeared in a large cave in southern China.
    b. sailed with friends off the eastern coast of China to find the Isles of the Blessed.
    c. died when a tall, heavy bookcase fell over on him.
    *d. left China riding on an ox.

8. Taoists aim at enjoying a long life but also accept death because
    a. the soul will be reborn, possibly in a better life.
    b. the soul can go to heaven.
    *c. death is a part of the natural order of things.
    d. accepting death shows strength of character.

9. The aspect of reality that expresses itself in silence, receptivity, and darkness is called
    a. wu wei.
    *b. yin.
    c. tao.
    d. yang.

10. The Tao Te Ching is written in approximately how many Chinese characters?
    a. 100
    b. 1,000
    *c. 5,000
    d. 25,000

11. The Tao Te Ching is known for its
    *a. deliberate obscurity.
    b. careful prose.
    c. logical organization of themes.
    d. mention of important sites in China.

12. Tao is the origin of
    a. mathematical certainty.
    *b. the rhythms of nature.
    c. the human intuition of beauty.
    d. our ability to distinguish between right and wrong.

CONFUCIANISM

13. Confucianism has been especially concerned about relationship
    a. with God.
    *b. between human beings.
    c. with nature.
    d. between human beings and animals.

14. Confucius lived during what years?
    a. 1221–1156 B.C.E
    b. 860–780 B.C.E
    *c. 551–479 B.C.E
    d. 437–502 C.E

15. Confucius worked almost all his life as
    *a. a teacher.
    b. a priest.
    c. an artist.
    d. a librarian.

16. The Analects are
    a. the principal source of Legalist philosophy.
    *b. the sayings of Confucius.
    c. a reaction against Mohist thought.
    d. a compilation of ancient poetry, saved by Confucians.

17. The Doctrine of the Mean
    a. is a long work on the history of the state of Lu.
    b. is the basis for the Legalist emphasis on strict punishment.
    c. reflects the Taoist love of contemplation.
    *d. is a short book on moderation and harmony.

18. The Mencius
    a. advocates the ideal of the bodhisattva.
    b. offers advice about magical ritual that was thought to raise agricultural productivity.
    *c. presents the teachings of a Confucian thinker.
    d. was a stone memorial to Confucius placed in his home town of Qufu.

19. Confucius's ideal society would live according to the ideals of the
    *a. Five Relationships.
    b. Four Noble Truths.
    c. Seven Sacraments.
    d. Five K's.

20. Confucius hoped to
    a. introduce new ideas about architecture.
    b. stop the destruction of books by the emperor.
    *c. restore the social harmony of the past.
    d. reestablish appreciation for simple living.

21. The Yi Jing (I Ching)
    a. was a central library, where many ancient texts were kept.
    b. recounts tales of the mythic life of the Yellow Emperor.
    c. is a book of prophecy and poetry.
    *d. is a book, valued by Confucius, that is used for divination.

22. In their view of human nature, the Confucianists
    a. seem to be the most optimistic of the philosophical schools.
    b. emphasize that people are rapacious and predatory, needing the strictest controls.
    *c. see human beings as needing the shaping of their characters by education.
    d. see education as a pursuit that primarily develops human intellect.

23. The personal ideal or hero of Confucianism is the
    a. teacher.
    b. businessman.
    *c. gentleman.
    d. simple peasant.

24. The social period in which Confucius lived was
    *a. disorderly.
    b. peaceful.
    c. a time when China was ruled by a single emperor.
    d. a time of a classless society.

25. Mencius (Mengzi, Meng Tzu) was a
    a. Legalist with a pessimistic view of human nature.
    *b. Confucian with a positive view of human nature.
    c. Mohist with a stern view of human nature.
    d. Taoist with a very optimistic view of human nature.

26. In regard to Confucianism, the Communists after the Communist Revolution
    a. encouraged it in order to build up a sound economy.
    b. spread it because of its support of government.
    *c. rejected it as being undemocratic.
    d. rejected it because of its emphasis on individual freedom.

27. The most fundamental relationship for Confucius seems to have been that between
    a. friends.
    *b. father and son.
    c. elder brother and younger brother.
    d. husband and wife.

28. The virtue of filial piety means
    a. doing what is appropriate to a situation.
    b. love of education.
    *c. devotion to one's family.
    d. doing only what is spontaneous.

29. The ideal of benevolence or humanheartedness in Chinese is a written character made up of which pictographs?
    a. two hearts, one beside the other
    b. a person under a roof
    c. a mother and a child
    *d. a person and the number two

30. The most significant Confucian art form has been
    a. garden design.
    *b. calligraphy.
    c. stone carving.
    d. music.

Essay Topics

1. List five of the common Chinese beliefs and practices that have been a part of Mahayana Buddhism as well as of Taoism and Confucianism. Describe each briefly.

2. Explain *yang* and *yin,* using examples as necessary to illustrate your explanation.

3. Recount the life story of Laozi.

4. What is the Tao Te Ching, and what roles has it played in the Taoist religion?

5. Define the Tao—or explain why we cannot define the Tao, yet can experience it.

6. What does the collection called the Zhuangzi add to basic understanding of the Tao?

7. Explain the ideal of *wu wei.*

8. Summarize four of the basic teachings of philosophical Taoism.

9. Describe three or four elements or practices that came to be associated with religious Taoism.

10. Describe with some detail four classical Chinese arts and show how they exhibit some of the concerns of Taoism.

11. What particular aspects of the Tao are of primary interest to the Confucian?

12. What two ideals were sought by Confucius?

13. Explain, from a Confucian perspective, what it would take to be an "excellent" human being.

14. List the five great relationships and summarize the responsibilities of the related persons in each of the five.

15. What is *Ren*? How does one show it?

16. Explain *Wen* and describe how it shows itself in practice.

17. Explain the Confucian notion of sincerity and contrast it with the common Western notion.

18. Identify two of the Four Books of Confucianism and describe a key characteristic of each.

19. Describe what Mencius brought to Confucianism by contrasting his thought with that of Confucius.

20. Pretend that you have been asked to begin a Confucian school. What would be studied? What practices would be evident in everyday life?

21. Summarize Zhu Xi's contributions to Confucian thought.

22. What is the greatest of Confucian arts? Why?

23. Summarize three key arguments against Confucianism that became prominent during the twentieth century.

24. In what ways are Confucian virtues at odds with typical Western virtues?

Chapter 7   Shinto

Learning Objectives

After reading this chapter, the student should be able to

- retell portions of the Shinto creation story.
- explore the tensions and accommodations among Shinto, Buddhism, and Confucianism.
- describe the focus and practice of Shinto.
- discuss the contributions of Shinto to Japanese culture and history.
- describe characteristics of the New Religions that are Shinto offshoots.
- discuss the features of Shinto that make it relevant to the modern world.

Chapter Outline

First Encounter
The Origins of Shinto
The Historical Development of Shinto
    Accommodation with Buddhism and Confucianism
    Shinto and Japanese National Identity
Essentials of Shinto Belief
Shinto Religious Practice
    Worship at Shrines
    Celebration of the New Year
    Observances of the Seasons and Nature
    Other Practices
Personal Experience: A Temple High above Kyoto
Shinto and the Arts
    Architecture
    Music and Dance
Shinto Offshoots: The New Religions
Shinto and the Modern World
Religion beyond the Classroom
For Fuller Understanding
Related Readings
Key Terms

Lecture Supplements

Shinto is a remarkable tradition composed of both ancient and modern elements. Scholarship on the tradition appears particularly in East Asian studies journals and in other materials specific to Japan. Shinto's characteristic of being both modern and ancient and its social and economic dimensions are two primary areas of interest. Several recent books are devoted to the topic. *The Religions of Japan in Practice*, edited by George Tanabe from the Princeton series (Princeton, NJ: Princeton University Press, 1999), is an essential volume for background and recent scholarship. It provides an introduction, short articles, and translations accessible and easily assimilated by both lecturers and introductory students. Tanabe adequately introduces various typologies of Japanese religions and the problematics with different historical periods. Especially helpful for students is the background material in the chapter "Shinto in the History of Japanese Religion: An Essay by Kuroda Toshio" that explains *kenmitsu* Buddhism, or the blending of Shinto and Buddhism. Toshio explains the distinction that "Shinto" is a modern invention in retrospect to describe the indigenous religions of the *kami,* which were later systematized for the purpose of unifying the disparate peoples following the impact of the more organized structures of Buddhism. He demonstrates the various stages of development of a Shinto religion to distinguish the Japanese synthesis of Taoism and Buddhism with the various *kami* represented in the *Kojiki* and *Nihon shoki* creation texts and ritual descriptions. Various interpretation theories are offered. The Shinto deities of the ancient period were transformed over time into what could later become a national unification religion reflecting Japanese identity. Its formulation into a secular nationalist ideology leading up to the Emperor's role in religious leadership is a significant example of religious impact on society and ideology. That this formulation also became known as the "indigenous religion" of Japan gives an ironic example of the way that religion may be applied as a later concept over the folk traditions of smaller regional and tribal identities with little conceptual religion. The shrines and spirits that inhabit them, and the folk traditions of localities, are sometimes lost in the need for societies to unify through ideologies. Buddhism's bodhisattvas and the *kami* were syncretized and/or hybridized into a symbolic system functioning in diverse regions that later evolved into a national religion as the result of political policy, Toshio argues. It is therefore significant that Buddhism played a role in providing a framework for systematizing religious practices that were later appropriated by political elites for secular power. An excellent case study for Shinto is the essay in *Religions of Japan in Practice*, "Motoori Norinaga on the Two Shrines at Ise" by Mark Teeuwen, exploring the significance and functioning of the remarkable shrine to the kami Amaterasu, the sun goddess. This shrine and the role of Amaterasu would make a stimulating illustration for students of the complexities of religion in Japan. Many Shinto shrines may also be represented on Web sites that would give students an opportunity to make a short research study of a specific shrine and the kami associated with it, along with practices of a local religious tradition.

Two other volumes of note are John K. Nelson's *A Year in the Life of a Shinto Shrine* (Seattle: University of Washington Press, 1996) and Irit's *The Gods Come Dancing: A Study of the Japanese Ritual Dance of Yamabushi Kagura* (Ithaca, NY: East Asia Program, Cornell University, 1995). Both works present detailed materials on Shinto and will be helpful for student research projects. Ian Reader's *Religion in Contemporary Japan* (Honolulu: University of Hawaii Press, 1991) and Winston Davis's *Japanese Religion and Society: Paradigms of Structure and Change* (Albany: SUNY Press, 1992) contain many insights on Shinto. Although these works deal with a larger set of issues, they each have sections or chapters devoted to Shinto in the context of society and religion, in general.

Lecturers will discover a wide range of sources on the World Wide Web; for example, International Shinto Foundation (Shinto.org), as well as many others on history, shrines, gardens, and related topics. Students who do not have local representations of Japanese culture will find these sites useful for their many visual representations of the nature and art associated with the tradition. The tradition of Shinto has remained strong in modern Japan in spite of its perceived connections with Japanese failure in World War II and its essentially primal, or oral, religious core. Pilgrimage is popular among Japanese of all classes and religions; thus, even someone not deeply interested in Shinto is likely to visit shrines and travel to holy mountains and other locales central to Shinto.

A. (Key words: Shinto, primal religion, international)

Michael Pye, in "Shinto: Primal Religion and International Identity" (*Marburg Journal of Religion* 1, no. 1 [1996]: 5 virtual pages), discusses the nature of Shinto in modern Japan. Shinto continues to be important even in the age of globalization or internationalization. Pye discusses how Shinto is blended with other traditions in Japan: Buddhism and some new religious movements. During the early part of the century, Shinto was enmeshed in many racial, political, and authoritarian issues. Since the end of World War II, and especially in the past two decades, Shinto followers are forced to address issues of globalization and religious pluralism both at home and abroad. Pye discusses some of the options and possibilities for the tradition in the modern setting.

This article is a brief summary of particular issues of Shinto tradition's development, explicitly in the modern period. It is brief and therefore provides the student with an easily assimilated resource. By discussing Shinto as a primal religion, Pye raises several issues that could be adapted to class discussion. How is Shinto like oral religions? Although it shares many of their characteristics, it does not exist in the same kind of cultural setting. Students might want to explore this issue by debate. They could represent both sides of the debate: Shinto is a primal religion or Shinto is not.

B. (Key words: Shinto priests, Shinto in the modern world)

John K. Nelson, in "Warden + Virtuoso + Salaryman = Priest: Paradigms within Japanese Shinto for Religious Specialists and Institutions" (*Journal of Asian Studies* 56, no. 3 [August, 1997]: 678–707), presents a straightforward discussion of the priest role in modern Shinto. Although some Japanese might see Shinto priests as no more than quaint reminders of the past, Nelson argues that Shinto priests have adapted well to the changes arising in modernity. Since the 1980s, the financial boom in Japan has increased the patronage of Shinto rites and festivals. Priests also play a strong role in modern tourism. Nelson depicts the Shinto priests by what they are and are not. They are not celibate (although they may abstain in reference to particular festivals and rites). They do not often live at shrines but instead are normative citizens in the family and living arrangements. The priests' primary religious role is maintaining proper relations between humans and nonhuman powers through both ritual and social actions. Priests do operate in a structured organization. Pay and reputation are based on seniority and on performance. Priests must also pass exams in order to move up through the ranks: they are tested on history, rites, myths, and the like. Shinto's origin in and similarities to oral religion are somewhat discontinuous because Japan is not an oral culture in any sense. Active management strategies (of a business type) and trained specialists have allowed Shinto to remain in step with modern Japan while maintaining its characteristics of traditional, naturalistic religion.

Although this article does survey a broad range of sources and theoretical positions, its discussion of the priests is clear and concise. Students can use this material as a way to realize the connections between traditional and modern religious professions. Lecturers can directly summarize the roles of the priest from this article for discussion or comparison with other religious professions or life roles: monks, priests of other traditions, preachers, prophets.

C. (Key words: teachings, history, mythology, shrines)

A comprehensive work devoted to Shinto is Stuart D. B. Picken's *Essentials of Shinto: An Analytical Guide to Principal Teachings* (Westport, CT: Greenwood Press, 1994). Picken defines Shinto and discusses obstacles to understanding. He provides a detailed history and discusses Shinto mythology and texts and how they should be interpreted. The imperial connection with Shinto and its funeral rites and shrines are described in detail. Several issues concerning understanding of the kami are considered. Shrines receive special attention: architecture, primitive styles, roof design, and ornamentation. Picken considers several other issues (priests, rituals, new religions, etc.) and concludes with several comparative reflections. This work could support a whole course devoted to Shinto. Lecturers and students who want to do in-depth research will find this text useful. Professors might also employ the book as resource for lectures, especially if they want to focus on a particular issue, such as architecture. The work is too long and detailed for class reading but is an excellent resource.

Notes on *For Fuller Understanding*

1. *Design a "new" religion that builds upon some of the elements of Shinto while perhaps incorporating traditions from other religions and institutions.*

   Have students consider some of the essential traits of Shinto—respect for nature, emphasis on cleanliness and purification, love of beauty, and use of ritual. They can blend those traits with other elements that they value. One can even draw on nonreligious elements—for example, business and technology.

2. *Pick one Shinto "New Religion" as a focus for research. Look into its origins, its current status, and its spread. Use your research to predict its future course.*

   Tenrikyo has been the most active beyond Japan and might therefore be a good subject to study. If it has a place of worship in your area, students might attend a service and interview one of its leaders.

3. *Most of the Shinto "New Religions," such as Omoto and Tenrikyo, have offices dedicated to international outreach. At a library, find out the address of the Japanese headquarters of one of these religions, and then write, requesting information in English. Share the information with your class.*

   Omoto publishes a regular newsletter in English, *Aizen*. This can be requested and reviewed. Tenrikyo has many publications in English, and its offices will be happy to send some.

4. *Using a library, an architects' association, and/or the Internet, look at recent trends in Japanese architecture, both grand (public spaces) and small (private homes). Write a report that highlights connections between recent trends and traditional Shinto attitudes and arts.*

   One area that is also interesting to investigate is Japanese adaptation of Western architectural forms. For example, some American-style homes now being built in suburbs are designed with a *genkan* (entry area) where shoes are to be removed, in order to help keep the house clean.

Internet Resources

Early Shinto
http://www.wsu.edu/~dee/ANCJAPAN/SHINTO.HTM

Noh Dancing
http://linus.socs.uts.edu.au/~don/pubs/noh.html

Shinto
http://www.japan-guide.com/e/e2056.html

Shinto & Buddhism: Wellsprings of Japanese Spirituality
http://www.askasia.org/frclasrm/readings/r000009.htm

Shinto Divinity Hikogami, Japan
http://www.museon.nl/objextra.eng/shinto.html

Shinto Online Network Association
http://www.jinja.or.jp/english

Multiple-Choice Questions

1. Shinto often makes use of
   *a.   purification rituals.
   b.   sitting in meditation.
   c.   repetition of the name of Amida Buddha.
   d.   the cutting of the priest's hair as a form of initiation.

2. The sun goddess of Shinto is
   a.   Izanagi.
   *b.   Amaterasu.
   c.   Susanowo.
   d.   Inari.

3. The primeval female kami who was burned by the fire god is
   *a.   Izanami.
   b.   Susanowo.
   c.   Izanagi.
   d.   Tsukiyomi.

4. The color most often associated with Shinto is
   a.   black.
   b.   green.
   c.   purple.
   *d.   white.

5. The torii is
   *a.   often used as a gateway to a sacred location.
   b.   a wand used by a Shinto priest for purification.
   c.   the name of a basin where one washes before prayer.
   d.   worn around the neck as a good-luck charm.

6. The name for a god in Shinto is
   *a.   kami.
   b.   koan.
   c.   o-mikoshi.
   d.   gagaku.

7. The Shinto shrine that is dedicated to Amaterasu and is the shrine of the imperial family is located at
   a.   Tokyo.
   b.   Hiroshima.
   *c.   Ise.
   d.   Mount Fuji.

8. A major Shinto shrine in Tokyo is named after what emperor?
   a. Jimmu
   *b. Meiji
   c. Hirohito
   d. Akihito

9. An important element of ritual at a Shinto shrine is
   a. lighting a candle.
   b. offering incense.
   c. bodily prostration.
   *d. hand clapping.

10. The term *Shinto* comes from two Chinese words that mean
    a. the fulfillment of nature.
    *b. the way of the gods.
    c. bridge of light.
    d. perfect life.

11. The country that before modern times had the most influence on Japan was
    a. India.
    b. Mongolia.
    c. Vietnam.
    *d. China.

12. The primary focus of Shinto worship is directed toward
    a. a single, all-powerful male God.
    b. Mount Fuji and other sacred mountains.
    *c. the gods of nature.
    d. female deities.

13. Among Shinto values and practices, which task is quite important?
    *a. purification
    b. cleaning one's house before prayer
    c. confessing one's wrongdoings to a priest
    d. writing sacred texts by hand

14. Shinto puts great emphasis on
    a. strong beliefs.
    *b. careful ritual.
    c. following the commands of a spiritual teacher.
    d. regular meditation.

15. *Kamikaze* is a term used for referring to
    *a. suicide pilots.
    b. high winds, like typhoons.
    c. gods who live at the top of mountains.
    d. the special hats of Shinto priests.

16. State Shinto refers to
    a. the special role of the emperor in Shinto.
    b. a springtime rice-planting ceremony, done for the good of the nation.
    c. Shinto ceremonies carried out at the beginning of each day in schools.
    *d. a former system of national shrines.

17. The Nihongi is
    a. the painting of a pine tree, a frequent background for Noh plays.
    b. a special dance used in Noh plays.
    *c. a collection of stories of the gods and early history.
    d. the name of one important branch of Shinto.

18. The ideal of the warrior, promoted by Shinto during World War II, is called
    a. kamikaze.
    *b. bushido.
    c. harai.
    d. mikoshi.

19. The emperor renounced his title to divinity when
    a. Buddhism first entered Japan.
    b. Christianity first entered Japan.
    c. Japan first began to modernize.
    *d. World War II ended.

20. Tenrikyo, which grew out of Shinto, has its headquarters near
    a. Tokyo.
    b. Kobe.
    c. Osaka.
    *d. Nara.

21. The founder of Tenrikyo was
    a. Kamo Mabuchi.
    b. Motoori Norinaga.
    c. Deguchi Nao.
    *d. Nakayama Miki.

22. Omoto is a new religion that emphasizes the value of
    *a. art.
    b. business.
    c. study.
    d. technology.

23. Omoto, in order to encourage international understanding, gives a special place to the study and use of
    a. Latin.
    b. Chinese.
    c. Spanish.
    *d. Esperanto.

24. Shinto and Buddhism
    a. have developed separately in Japan.
    b. began to blend in the nineteenth century.
    *c. began to blend soon after the introduction of Buddhism.
    d. were forced to separate from each other before 1200 C.E.

25. The Japanese people
    a. have always enthusiastically adopted foreign cultures.
    b. adopted the culture of Vietnam for about 500 years.
    *c. seem to be a blend of several peoples.
    d. rejected the culture of China.

26. It has been a traditional teaching that the imperial family is descended from what kami?
    a. Susanowo
    b. Tenri-no-o-mikoto
    c. Inari
    *d. Amaterasu

27. It is possible that the creation myth that tells of numerous kami
    *a. unites the beliefs of several clans or tribes.
    b. originated in Okinawa.
    c. is a Japanese retelling of an ancient myth from India.
    d. has some historical truth.

28. Shinto and Confucianism particularly had what feature in common?
    a. love of art and imagery
    *b. veneration of ancestors
    c. idealization of the simple life of the farmer
    d. appreciation for ritual dance

29. The emperor of Japan came to be considered a father figure for the whole country. This
    a. arose from Shinto love of ritual.
    b. was a necessity after the attempted Mongol invasion of Japan.
    *c. seems to show the influence of Confucianism.
    d. came from the Buddhist ideal of the loving bodhisattva.

30. Shinto
    *a. has helped the Japanese maintain a sense of their unique identity.
    b. has been quite warlike throughout its long history.
    c. is a religion with organization and strong structure.
    d. developed a statement of belief and a set of commandments after 1400 C.E.

Essay Topics

1. Explain the derivation of the term *Shinto*. What does the name tell us about the relationship with China and with Buddhism? Please explain.

2. How did Amaterasu come into being? What role, according to legend, did she play in Japanese history?

3. Describe how areas of influence are typically divided between Shinto and Buddhism in Japan. How might this be evident at a Japanese temple complex?

4. Explain the emergence of State Shinto within the context of the Meiji Restoration. What was the Meiji Restoration and why did it establish State Shinto?

5. Explain the basic Shinto notion of *kami*. Describe and name the most important kami.

6. How are ancestors understood according to basic Shinto belief?

7. Describe the basic rituals associated with visiting a Shinto shrine, and relate the rituals to Shinto belief.

8. List at least three ceremonies that are typically performed by Shinto priests.

9. Summarize New Year rituals associated with Shinto.

10. What roles does the emperor of Japan play in Shinto ritual?

11. Describe a torii. What is its function? Where may it be found?

12. Describe the key beliefs of Tenrikyo.

13. Describe the key beliefs of Omotokyo.

14. Describe at least four ways in which Shinto beliefs and practices are relevant to the problems of the modern world.

Chapter 8   Judaism

Learning Objectives

After reading this chapter, the student should be able to

- discuss developments in the four general periods of Jewish history.
- describe the three parts of the Hebrew Bible.
- retell some of the major stories in the Hebrew scriptures.
- describe Jewish religious practices.
- explain the characteristics of the major divisions within Judaism.
- discuss the history of persecution that culminated in the Holocaust.
- discuss challenges Judaism faces in the modern world.

Chapter Outline

First Encounter
An Overview of Jewish History
The Hebrew Bible
Biblical History
    In the Beginning: Stories of Origins
    The World of the Patriarchs and Matriarchs
    Moses and the Law
    The Judges and Kings
    Exile and Captivity
    Return to Jerusalem and the Second Temple
Cultural Conflict during the Second-Temple Era
    The Seleucid Period
    Responses to Outside Influences
The Development of Rabbinical Judaism
    The Canon of Scripture and the Talmud
    Islam and Medieval Judaism
    The Kabbalah
    Christianity and Medieval Judaism
Questioning and Reform
Judaism and the Modern World
    Hitler and the Holocaust
    Creation of the State of Israel
Personal Experience: A Visit to Anne Frank's House
Jewish Belief
Religious Practice
    The Jewish Sabbath
    Holy Days
    Jewish Dietary Practices
    Other Religious Practices
Divisions within Contemporary Judaism
    Culturally Based Divisions
    Observance-Based Divisions
The Contributions of Judaism
Jewish Identity and the Future of Judaism
Religion beyond the Classroom
For Fuller Understanding
Related Readings
Key Terms

Lecture Supplements

Judaism has long been understood as a tradition that is both a religion and an ethnic identity. Its millennia of history is usefully divided by Molloy as biblical Judaism and rabbinical Judaism. This division maps important shifts in self-identity, historical context, and religious practice. Because of the tradition's importance for both Jews and Christians (and in a derivative sense for Muslims), the earlier period, biblical Judaism, has been studied by scholars and historians of varying backgrounds. Rabbinical Judaism, also researched in detail, has been primarily studied by Jewish scholars, although some modern secularist scholarship exists as well. There is a wide range of scholarship on these topics. The subject Judaism boasts more journals and topic-specific studies than any of the world's traditions except Christianity. Often these sources emphasize either one or the other side of the historical division between biblical and rabbinical. Of the many sources available, there have been some recent studies that are accessible to introductory students. From these sources, students can gain general overviews and some detail-specific materials. Lecturers should refer back to the Lyden summary provided for Chapter 1. Lyden presents several key entries on Jewish response to the nature of God, the meaning of death, and so forth.

A. (Key words: ancient Israel; biblical Judaism; social context; social institutions: politics, economics, diplomacy, law, and education).

Victor H. Matthews and Don C. Benjamin present a reconstruction of the social context of the Hebrew Bible in *Social World of Ancient Israel, 1250–587 B.C.E.* (Peabody, MA: Hendrickson, 1993 [Revised 1995]). The book is a selective study that focuses on early Israel and the period of the monarchy. Although the book provides numerous details, the authors admit that they selected only representative social institutions for those two worlds: institutions that provide insight into the world of the Hebrew Bible. The study is meant to suggest overall patterns via specific institutions, not to provide an exhaustive study. The book assumes that gaining an understanding of the social context of the Hebrew Bible is imperative for anyone reconstructing either the "story" of the text or the "history and culture" behind the text.

The text focuses on social institutions selected from daily life: politics, economics, diplomacy, law, and education. The characteristics of these institutions demonstrate the communal character of the biblical world. The work seeks to explain this communal world to the modern audience, which understands and appreciates individuals more than institutions. Oftentimes, modern readers have reconstructed and interpreted the Hebrew Bible as if written by and about typical individuals in the world of the Bible. For example, the authors discuss institutions as social forces first in villages and later in the state. The text states: "Politics is the power of a father, mother, monarch, or virgin to protect and provide for a village or state. Economics is the power of a farmer, herder, midwife, priest, or slave to work the land and bear children. Diplomacy is the power of a host, chief, legal guardian, or prophet to make war or to trade with strangers. Law is the power of the elder, widow, or lawgiver to solve problems between neighbors. Education is the power of the wise, the fool, and the storyteller to hand on culture to the next generation." The authors explore the ways in which knowing how "players" function in these institutions, such as "father/mother," "prophet/wise one," "host/stranger," better shapes our understanding of earliest Israel.

The first part focuses on ancient Israel as villages. Several different roles are explored. One is the father, whose duty was to protect and provide for his land and children. He could adopt or excommunicate sons and daughters, recruit workers and warriors, negotiate marriages and covenants, host strangers, designate heirs. Another role examined is that of the mother. She was to protect and provide for children, to bear children and arrange for other wives to bear children, to manage the household by supervising domestic production and rationing, and preparing food. She was also in charge of processing and storing beer. She taught children the clan traditions, mediated domestic conflicts, and often designated heirs. The book next turns to various topics, such as farms and farmers, herders, and the care of animals. The importance of midwives is expressed. One of the most interesting topics (Chapter 6) deals with the host and the stranger and the importance of hospitality codes. Other roles discussed are the chief, the legal guardian, the elders, and the widows. Wisdom and foolishness are dealt with in the context of communal behavior and application of social pressures relative to the term *shame*.

Ancient Israel as a state is discussed in the second part of the book. The text states: "When the land and children of a village culture are continuously threatened, a state forms to centralize power in a monarch." This power is discussed in terms of the monarch, the virgin, the priest, the slave, the prophet, the lawgiver, and the storyteller. For example, the prophet is described as a social actor who "analyzes the short-term consequences for the state of the decisions of its monarch to impose taxes, negotiate covenants, and wage war." The prophet represents the state before the divine assembly at its annual meetings to evaluate the fulfillment of Israel's and Judah's covenants with the Hebrew God. The prophet promulgates the decisions of the divine assembly regarding the state with words and pantomimes while in a state of prophetic ecstasy. Each role and category is defined and presented by the use of either biblical illustrations or Near Eastern comparative materials.

The book gently exposes the inefficiency of past anthropological models for interpreting the relationships, attitudes, and social conventions of early Israel. Its corrective insights will enable scholar and student alike to plot new approaches for studying the Hebrew Bible and the ancient people of Israel. Other works often present resources that are specialized and beyond the abilities of the introductory student. This book offers a straightforward framework for understanding the broader picture of ancient Israel. The work demonstrates the use of cultural anthropology and biblical analysis and thus, while straightforward, is contemporary in its methods and explanatory framework. The expert, the lecturer, and the student should all find this book useful for research, presentation, and discussion.

Professors who are interested in further research relative to "social-world" approaches might also refer to Thomas W. Overholt's *Cultural Anthropology and the Old Testament* (Guides to Biblical Scholarship) (Minneapolis: Fortress, 1996) and to *The Savage in Judaism: An Anthropology of Israelite Religion and Ancient Judaism* (Bloomington: Indiana University Press, 1990) by H. Eilberg-Schwartz. Neither work is as user-friendly as the Matthews and Benjamin text, but both offer considerable help in reconstructing the historical and cultural context for the writing of the Hebrew Bible.

B. (Key words: Psalms, pilgrimage, calendars, Middle Eastern shared heritage)

Thomas McElwain suggests that the Psalms show textual evidence for a pilgrimage tradition that was practiced between the tenth and twelfth month of the Israelite civil calendar. In "A Structural Approach to the Biblical Psalms: The Songs of Degrees as a Year-End Pilgrimage Motif" (*Temenos* 30 [1994]: 113–123), McElwain argues that the Psalm in question supports the thesis that there was a shared pattern of pilgrimage practice that corresponds to modern Islamic pilgrimage practices. This pattern, which is demonstrated in the ancient Jewish text, was part of a shared set of cultural practices, not a later invention specific to the practice of Islam. McElwain suggests that the structure and content of the Psalms provide a basis for judging the Islamic pilgrimage events as reflecting an ancient Near Eastern tradition that was practiced in Israel and the surrounding areas.

Another article devoted to the particulars of the Psalms is William P. Brown's "A Royal Performance: Critical Notes on Psalm 1 l0:3ag–b" (*SBL Journal of Biblical Literature* 117, no. 1 [Spring, 1998]: 93–96). This article provides a brief discussion suggesting the Psalm's use as part of royal ritual. This article is of a specialized nature, discussing the particulars of translation of one verse. Its bibliography and introductory materials are helpful for illustrating the various uses of the songs drawn together in the book of Psalms.

Scholars have often approached the Psalms as a storehouse of information on general characteristics of Israelite and Canaanite culture, since many of them predate the formalization of the Hebrew scriptures. Because they are songs, they tend to be recorded and thus, in some ways, are safe from the editors' hands. Lecturers can adopt these types of articles into their notes in reference to the religious practices of ancient Israel. Since choral and individual music were practiced throughout the early history of Judaism, these types of specific articles help to reconstruct some of the accompanying practices. Additionally, the first article that is devoted to pilgrimage offers a good resource for comparative discussion concerning the widespread practice of pilgrimage throughout the world's religions.

C. (Key words: rabbinical Judaism, Talmud, formation of tradition)

For most of the twentieth century, there has been a relatively straightforward view of the formation of rabbinical Judaism. Jacob Neusner challenged the tradition with his "Why There Never Was a 'Talmud of Caesarea'. Saul Lieberman's Blunders" (*Temenos* 30 [1994]: 175–195). Neusner states that the origin of the two Talmuds is the fundamental issue for understanding the formation of rabbinical Judaism. The two Talmuds defined the Judaic system: one originated in Babylonia (ca. 600 C.E.), the other was codified in the land of Israel (ca. 400 C.E.). Neusner suggests that the generally accepted theory—that the Israel Talmud began with three tractates devoted to civil law— is flawed. He evaluates the editing and dating of the rabbinical document "Talmud of Caesarea" to demonstrate his conclusions.

This article deals with a specific text that was important to rabbinical tradition formation. Although it is specialized in nature, it addresses many of the important issues of dating and editing that are crucial to the understanding of texts. Lecturers will find it helpful if they are interested in fleshing out the emergence of the rabbinic traditions. Since these traditions shaped Judaism from late antiquity to the present, the origin and formation of the textual basis is important. This article is also useful to the lecturer who wants to better understand how theories about history and texts tend to become ingrained and often need reevaluation. Students are likely to find this article helpful if they are researching the historical shift from biblical to rabbinical Judaism.

D. (Key words: Orthodox Judaism, modernity)

Aryei Fishman, in "Modern Orthodox Judaism: A Study in Ambivalence" (*Social Compass* 42 [1995]: 1, 89–95), discusses the struggles of the tradition of Orthodox Judaism in the context of the modern world. Authority is an important category for this tradition, and there is considerable tension between the power of tradition and the necessity of change in the contemporary world. Orthodox identity is in a state of constant formation that arises from the traditions of the past but is also transformed by the conditions of the present. Modern manifestations of Judaism do not seem to offer the same meaning and authority for some Jews. Orthodox Jews feel that the traditions of the past provide a deeper and more authentic model for religious life than the patterns of behavior that are present in other religious trends. Orthodoxy is well established throughout the Western world and in Israel, but issues of relevance and legitimacy are working to widen the division between the modern and traditional characteristics of Orthodox identity.

This article recognizes the difficulties that exist for many traditional life paths (both inside and outside of Judaism). Although Orthodox Jews do not represent a pristine group unaffected by historical context and development, there are many tensions within the Orthodox groups. This raises questions concerning how to be traditionally religious when the traditional world no longer exists. Self-identity has always been important for Jews, especially since the destruction of the Second Temple. This struggle continues to work within the tradition and is sometimes aggravated by the existence of other Jewish observance-based divisions.

Instructors will find this article useful for those interested in the Judaisms of the modern world. The formation of the state of Israel and the inclusion of many different divisions within Judaism present not one unified people but peoples of differing views and identities. Students will find the article helpful because it presents issues relative to one of the groups that on first look might seem more exotic or anachronistic. This article goes far to demonstrate how identity construction is always an ongoing practice, not a product of frozen history.

E. (Key words: Jewish identity, modernity, Judaism and the arts, Judaism in films, cultural impact)

Contemporary Judaism in America and the modern world is especially observed through various forms of art and the media. Although there are many branches of Judaism, and especially in the United States a diversity of Jewish ways of expressing identity and practice of faith, the arts are a primary expression of Jewishness and Jewish sensibility. Judaism's relationship with the arts is shaped in part by the "aniconic" tradition that directs "thou shalt make no images" of the divine (similar to the aniconic tradition of Islam). However, the religious impulse toward material expression has produced a long history and variety of uniquely Jewish forms of art, including the struggle between the artist and faith. Jewish novelists abound, and Jewish literature and writers and critics have significantly influenced contemporary intellectual life. A novel that expresses the difficulties of being traditional and yet feeling the deep creative urge to paint, *My Name Is Asher Lev* by Chaim Potok, illustrates the dilemma of a modern Jew and the sacred creativity of an artist. Marc Chagall's paintings illustrate Molloy's chapter on Judaism, and among the great contributions to modern culture that Molloy discusses, modern film is high on the list. The Jewish Film Archive (http://members.aol.com/jewfilm/index.html) lists hundreds of significant films by Jews and about Jewish themes. A film based on Chaim Potok's novel *The Chosen* is an especially accessible film for discussion of Jewish identity in class. Recently the Holocaust has been a significant theme in films, perhaps most notably *Schindler's List* by Jewish filmmaker Steven Spielberg, or *Europa, Europa* and *Life Is Beautiful,* to name a few. Yet whether Jewish artists express their faith through traditional religious imagery or depict the struggle with modern identity issues in more veiled and anguished themes, the subject of Judaism and the creative genius of Jewish artists impact modern American popular culture. Television shows like *Seinfeld* and *The Simpsons* (mentioned by Molloy) make Jewish humor and experience an element of American self-criticism. Woody Allen's films have created their own intellectual niche by exploring the contemporary dilemmas of Jewish identity. One of his most sobering films is *Crimes and Misdemeanors,* on the ethical and moral dilemmas of modernity. The novels of Elie Wiesel are another example of ways Jewish identity is explored in the arts. The Internet offers numerous resources for this topic, and a beginning place is About.com's *Judaism Arts and Literature* (http://judaism.about.com/religion/judaism/cs/art/index.htm), edited by Lisa Katz. This is a topic with too many examples to mention, yet with a wealth of ways for students to explore Jewish religious experience.

Notes on *For Fuller Understanding*

1. *If your area includes a synagogue or a museum that chronicles Jewish history, visit it and make an oral report on the highlights to your class.*

Many synagogues have a collection of artifacts and photos recalling the local practice of Judaism in the region. Have students ask to see the collection (it may be in a basement or an adjoining hall). Synagogues frequently run a bookstore with limited hours, carrying books of local interest, as well as of general interest. One of the largest collections of Judaica is in the Jewish Museum in New York City. Other cities (such as Chicago) also have museums dedicated to Judaism.

2. *With a few classmates, undertake a comparative study of women's roles in several religions, including Judaism. Give particular attention to changes that took place during the twentieth century and changes that you might predict for the twenty-first century.*

Perhaps the most obvious changes have gone on in Reform Judaism and Protestant Christianity, which have begun to ordain women as rabbis and ministers. Mahayana Buddhism has also seen wider roles for women.

3. *Using library and computer lab resources, examine models and diagrams of the Second Temple. Prepare an illustrated report in which you explain the various Temple courts and the services held there.*

4. *Choose an artist, composer, or writer whose work suggests the influence of Jewish thought and practice. Study several of that person's works, making note of the ways in which Judaism left its mark.*

Composers worthy of study are Leonard Bernstein and Ernest Bloch. Marc Chagall is an obvious choice for a painter. Isaac Bashevis Singer, Bernard Malamud, and Chaim Potok are writers whose works are quite approachable.

Video Resources

The Dead Sea Scrolls
For decades, a small group of researchers monopolized the study of the Dead Sea Scrolls. Attention to the scrolls focused on the scientific scandal surrounding them. Now, the focus has changed to the messages that these valuable records of our biblical past convey. In this program, two Scroll experts share their views on the conclusions that can be drawn from the ancient documents. Controversy surrounding the research is examined by Robert Eisenman, who has been ostracized by fellow researchers for his views. (28 minutes) [Religion]

The Life of Anne Frank
The life of Anne Frank told through quotations from her diary, pictures of her hiding place, photos from the Frank family album, and historical documentary footage. This documentary provides the historical background for *The Diary of Anne Frank* as it follows the flight of the Frank family to Holland, persecution of the Jews in Holland, and the family's clandestine existence until it was betrayed and Anne was deported to Bergen-Belsen. (25 minutes) [Religion]

Internet Resources

Dead Sea—Intro
http://www.ibiblio.org/expo/deadsea.scrolls.exhibit/intro.html

FIU Libraries Judaism Internet Resources
http://www.fiu.edu/~library/internet/subjects/religion/reljud.html

A Great Assemblage
http://www.library.yale.edu/exhibition/judaica/

Jewish/Israel Index Communities & Synagogues
http://www.maven.co.il//subjects.asp?S=171

The Jewish Museum London
http://www.jewmusm.ort.org

The Jewish Quarterly
http://www.jq.ort.org

Jewish Studies: Internet Resources
http://www2.lib.udel.edu/subj/jew/internet.htm

Judaism 101
http://www.jewfaq.org

Judaism Alive
http://www.judaismalive.org/

Judaism Reading List: Introduction and General
http://www.faqs.org/faqs/judaism/reading-lists/general

Maven—More than 5,600 Jewish/Israel Links!
http://www.maven.co.il/

Reform Judaism
http://rj.org

A Teacher's Guide to the Holocaust
http://fcit.coedu.usf.edu/holocaust/

Welcome to Israel Museum Web Server
http://www.imj.org.il/main.html

United States Holocaust Memorial Museum
http://www.ushmm.org/

Multiple-Choice Questions

1. Judaism traces itself back to what legendary patriarch who is written about in the book of Genesis?
   a. Moses
   b. David
   *c. Abraham
   d. Nehemiah

2. The biblical book that describes the origins of the human race is
   a. Proverbs.
   *b. Genesis.
   c. Isaiah.
   d. Psalms.

3. Zionism is
   a. the practice of seeking archeological evidence to discover the truth of biblical stories.
   *b. a movement that urges Jews to live in Israel.
   c. the practice kept by males of not cutting the beard or the hair in front of the ears.
   d. the Jewish culture that grew up in Eastern Europe after 1000 C.E.

4. The Hebrew Bible sees history as
   a. a purposeless circular movement of events.
   b. something over which human beings have no control.
   c. unreal and illusory.
   *d. signs of divine activity.

5. The moral conscience of the Hebrew people was the
   *a. prophets.
   b. patriarchs.
   c. kings.
   d. psalmists.

6. According to the Book of Exodus, what disaster was the last to strike the Egyptians?
   a. plague of frogs
   b. hail
   c. darkness
   *d. death of firstborn male children

7. The Jewish view of God is best expressed as
   a. God is an impersonal force.
   *b. God makes moral demands.
   c. God is the pattern of nature.
   d. God created the world but does not interfere in it.

8. The Torah is
   a. a name for the books of Psalms and Proverbs.
   *b. the first five books of the Bible (Pentateuch).
   c. another name for the Writings (Ketuvim).
   d. the historical books of the Bible.

9. The destruction of the Second Temple changed the nature of the Hebrew religion in that afterward
   *a. the Jewish religion began to focus on the written word.
   b. animal sacrifice became more important as a part of worship.
   c. Judaism spread to Egypt.
   d. the Jews began to adopt Persian culture.

10. The Talmud is
   a. the earliest part of the Kabbalah.
   b. the Hebrew name of the prayer shawl.
   c. the writings of medieval thinkers.
   *d. a long work of commentary based on biblical principles.

11. The Jewish Day of Atonement, the most sacred day of the Jewish year, is
   a. Rosh Hashanah.
   b. Hanukkah.
   c. Passover.
   *d. Yom Kippur.

12. Contemporary Judaism has split into four parts. The most liberal is called
   a. Reform Judaism.
   *b. Reconstructionist Judaism.
   c. Orthodox Judaism.
   d. Conservative Judaism.

13. The general Jewish attitude toward physical matter and bodily pleasure has generally been that
   *a. both matter and the body are innately good.
   b. the whole goal of life is pleasure.
   b. matter and the body are dangerous and we should avoid all physical attachments.
   d. the aim of life is to develop the soul by disciplining the body.

14. When the Jewish boy turns thirteen, he is considered an adult in the religious community. This ceremony takes its name from his new status.
   a. Mazal Tov
   *b. Bar Mitzvah
   c. Seder
   d. Tefillin

15. Which division of modern Judaism stresses strict beliefs and careful keeping of dietary laws?
   a. Conservative
   b. Reform
   *c. Orthodox
   d. Reconstructionist

16. Which Jewish festival recalls the event related in the Book of Exodus about liberation of the Hebrews from oppression in Egypt?
    a. Yom Kippur
    b. Hanukkah
    c. Rosh Hashanah
    *d. Passover (Pesach)

17. Which book is part of the Torah or Pentateuch?
    *a. Leviticus
    b. Isaiah
    c. Song of Songs
    d. Jonah

18. The Reform movement that began to spread in the nineteenth century attempted to
    *a. modernize Judaism.
    b. reject Zionism.
    c. return to traditional practices that were in danger of being lost.
    d. popularize Yiddish culture.

19. The three categories of the Hebrew Bible are
    a. Torah, Prophets, and Proverbs.
    b. Psalms, Chronicles, and Proverbs.
    c. History, Prophets, and Psalms.
    *d. Torah, Prophets, and Writings.

20. The Sadducees were
    a. a Jewish semimonastic community.
    *b. an aristocratic, priestly party centered in Jerusalem.
    c. very patriotic Jews who were violently anti-Roman.
    d. a movement in Judaism interested in studying and commenting on Jewish law.

21. The Jewish Sabbath is kept from
    *a. sunset Friday to sunset Saturday.
    b. sunrise Saturday to sunrise Sunday.
    c. sunrise Saturday to sundown Sunday.
    d. sunrise Sunday to sunrise Monday.

22. The biblical book of song lyrics sung in worship at the Second Temple in Jerusalem is
    a. Ecclesiastes.
    *b. Psalms.
    c. Song of Songs.
    d. Book of the Twelve.

23. Jewish dietary laws forbid eating
    *a. pork.
    b. lamb.
    c. beef.
    d. fish.

24. The Jewish New Year occurs at what time of year?
    *a. autumn
    b. winter
    c. spring
    d. summer

25. The Passover occurs at what time of year?
    a. autumn
    b. winter
    *c. spring
    d. summer

26. On what feast are Jewish children given presents for eight days?
    *a. Hanukkah
    b. Rosh Hashanah
    c. Pesach
    d. Purim

27. The Bible says that God spoke to Moses
    *a. on Mount Sinai.
    b. in Egypt near the Nile River.
    c. near the Dead Sea.
    d. in Iraq.

28. The day of Rejoicing in the Torah comes at the end of what festival?
    a. Pesach
    *b. Sukkot
    c. Purim
    d. Hanukkah

29. The Southern Kingdom was destroyed in 586 B.C.E. by
    a. Assyria.
    b. Persia.
    *c. Babylonia.
    d. Egypt.

30. Sephardic Jews have lived primarily in
    a. Yemen.
    b. Russia.
    c. Ethiopia.
    *d. the Mediterranean region.

31. The language of Sephardic Jews has been
    *a. Ladino.
    b. Yiddish.
    c. Farsi.
    d. Basque.

32. The Yiddish language, though written in Hebrew characters, is a type of
    a. Greek.
    *b. German.
    c. Ethiopian.
    d. Spanish.

33. The first two kings of the Israelite Kingdom were
    a. Solomon and Hezekiah.
    b. Nathan and Solomon.
    *c. Saul and David.
    d. Ezra and Nehemiah.

34. A dietary law kept by traditionalist Jews is that what items may not be eaten at the same meal?
    *a. meat and dairy products
    b. fruit and nuts
    c. fish and wine
    d. bread and olive oil

35. Traditionalists sometimes interpret the command not to work on the Sabbath as including no
    a. walking outside the house.
    *b. use of the telephone.
    c. reading of books.
    d. talking with friends.

Essay Topics

1. Explain why Judaism may be said to have either 2000 or as many as 4000 years of history.

2. List three reasons that the Hebrew Bible is important to Judaism, independent of its contributions to the historical record.

3. Describe four identifying characteristics of God as described in the story of Eden.

4. Describe the role of Eve in the story of the Garden of Eden. In what ways might a Westerner view her role both positively and negatively? What kind of influence has this story had on Western culture?

5. Briefly describe three theophanies recounted in Genesis and Exodus.

6. Summarize key points in the debate over whether Judaism was from the beginning monotheistic.

7. List three of the contributions of the legendary King David to Hebrew history, according to the biblical account of him.

8. Define *prophet* in the Hebrew tradition. Recount briefly the tale of one of the prophets.

9. Describe one contribution of the Babylonians and another of Zoroastrianism to Hebrew thought.

10. List the four factions that emerged in response to foreign influences on Hebrew ways at the time of the Second Temple. Describe in detail the thinking of one of the factions.

 11. Describe the end of the Second Temple. What did the event mean in the history of Judaism?

12. How did the Hebrew scriptures achieve their final form? What is the role of the Talmud in conjunction with the scriptures?

13. In what ways did the rise of Islam influence Jewish life?

14. Identify and then summarize the importance of the Kabbalah. Why do you think it took on special importance during the Middle Ages in Europe?

15. In broad terms, what impacts did the dominant Christians have on European Jews?

16. Describe the two directions in which Judaism moved in reaction to ideas that came to dominate during the Renaissance.

17. What was the Nazi rationale for the extermination effort that came to be known as the Holocaust? What was its ultimate cost in human lives?

18. Summarize the three steps by which the state of Israel came into being.

19. Summarize four of the central beliefs of Judaism.

20. Summarize the main practices and obligations of Jews relating to the Sabbath.

21. What is Yom Kippur, and how is it observed? (Other feast days may be substituted.)

22. What is the Seder, and how is it significant? List three practices associated with the Seder and explain their meaning.

23. What are the biblical roots of kosher practice? List three practices that must be observed in a home that keeps the kosher dietary laws.

24. Describe three or four characteristics that distinguish Sephardic from Ashkenazic Judaism.

25. List five practices or beliefs that distinguish Orthodox Judaism.

26. Briefly summarize the development and practice of Reform Judaism.

27. Explain why Jewish contributions to the visual arts (painting, sculpture) are quite limited.

28. Describe two or three ways in which Jewish thought may have influenced philosophy, literature, or music.

29. Assume that you have been asked to create a tour to the three most significant sites in Hebrew/Jewish history. What sites would you choose? Why?

* Describe the five schools of Judaism

Reflections

①

Chapter 9   Christianity

Learning Objectives

After reading this chapter, the student should be able to

- summarize the life and teachings of Jesus, especially in the context of his times.
- describe the structure and content of the New Testament.
- explain Christian doctrines and practices.
- discuss the growth of Christianity.
- describe medieval and modern developments.
- explain the origins of the major branches of Christianity.
- assess the impact Christianity has had on the arts.

Chapter Outline

First Encounter
The Life and Teachings of Jesus
    Jesus in the New Testament Gospels
    The Two Great Commandments
Early Christian Beliefs and History
    Paul and Pauline Christianity
    The New Testament: Its Structure and Artistry
        The Gospels
        The Acts of the Apostles
        The Epistles
        Revelation
The Essential Christian Worldview
The Early Spread of Christianity
Influences on Christianity at the End of the Roman Empire
    Augustine
    Benedict and the Monastic Ideal
The Eastern Orthodox Church
    Early Development
    Monasticism in the Eastern Church
    Eastern Orthodox Beliefs
Personal Experience: Inside the Monasteries on Mount Athos
Christianity in the Middle Ages
    Christian Mysticism
    The Crusades, the Inquisition, and the Founding of Religious Orders
    The Late Middle Ages
The Protestant Reformation
    Martin Luther
    Forms of Protestantism
        Lutheranism
        Calvinism
        The Church of England (Anglican Church)
        Sectarianism
The Development of Christianity Following the Protestant Reformation
    The Catholic Reformation (Counter Reformation)
    The International Spread of Christianity
    Nontraditional Christianity
        Church of Jesus Christ of Latter-day Saints
        Christian Science and the Unity Church

      Jehovah's Witnesses
      African Independent Churches
      Unification Church
Christian Practice
   Sacraments and Other Rituals
   The Christian Year
   Devotion to Mary
Christianity and the Arts
   Architecture
   Art
   Music
Christianity Faces the Twenty-First Century
   The Challenges of Science and Secularism
   Contemporary Influences and Developments
Religion beyond the Classroom
For Fuller Understanding
Related Readings and Musical Recordings
Key Terms

Lecture Supplements

In Molloy's approach to Christianity, the methods of cultural experience and sacred arts are employed in ways that may, by this point in the course, give students the opportunity to experience Christianity in a similar way. The diverse range of Christianities seen through the lens of different cultural contexts against the background of other traditions might look quite different from what is expected. This is a religion that many students anticipate with personal "cultural baggage" from their own aversions or attractions out of family histories and cultural impressions. Undoubtedly the media and the local experiences of Christianity in typical modern societies give a confusing and wide-ranging set of images and negative stereotypes, as well as the personal convictions or belief systems that students may bring to this subject. Because of the persistence of theological exclusivism and belief systems, and because of ideologies of supremacy and missionizing, the approach to Christianity is problematic. Here is an opportunity for students to gain an appreciation of the varieties of cultural expressions through sacred arts, of mystical traditions now subjugated by scientific and materialist assumptions of modernity, and of new ways that Christianity is adapting to the changing societies of the twenty-first century. New movements that stress fresh approaches to identity issues, inter-religious dialogue, environmental theologies, human rights and liberation theologies, and affirmation of other religions might stimulate discussion and breakthroughs in student intellectual grasping for meaning. Often students are afraid to have cherished beliefs subverted by new perspectives on familiar religious beliefs. But the sensitive way Molloy handles the subject, with a consistent pattern of methodologies and themes, gives the instructor the opportunity to really open up new breakthroughs in religious studies. The later chapter on alternative religions will be able to build on this carefully constructed platform.

Christianity is the world's largest tradition. As such, it includes hundreds of sects, denominations, divisions, and coalitions. Because of the tradition's breadth, there are varying sorts of research from general overviews to studies of the smallest minutiae. Many of the journals devoted to the topic of religion have a large portion of their articles devoted to the history, texts, and cultures of the Christian world. Instructors who have particular interests will find sources on everything from the first-century church to new religious movements arising out of Christian contexts. As Molloy points out, there are various ways in which the tradition can be approached.

A. (Key words: Christian origins, gospels, New Testament, historical Jesus, Christ, mythology)

The controversial questioning of the historical Jesus and the biblical texts has given rise to new insights and exciting opportunities to take fresh approaches to this subject. One scholar who might be especially useful with students is Marcus Borg, whose book *Meeting Jesus Again for the First Time* (San Francisco: Harper, 1994) introduced in historical context the critical studies of the historical Jesus and questions regarding the Gospels that many Christians find threatening and subversive. Borg is a rigorous scholar and professor of religion at a state university and member of the Jesus Seminar (some of the biblical scholars leading the new investigations of scriptural authenticity), yet his sensitivity as a practicing pastor puts him in a unique position to introduce students feeling fear about this approach into a fresh frame of mind. Borg's Web site, *A Portrait of Jesus* (http://www.united.edu/portrait/), is also an excellent resource for further class materials.

The scholar of Christian origins Burton L. Mack has written a comprehensive explanation of the writing and formation of the New Testament. In *Who Wrote the New Testament? The Making of the Christian Myth* (New York: HarperCollins, 1995), Mack discusses who wrote the New Testament and why it was written. He describes both the social and the cultural context of the New Testament. Mack does not view the gospels as complementary accounts of a single set of events. Instead, he demonstrates that the gospels represent a history of divergent Christian communities and anonymous writers who wrote different chronicles for distinct purposes and audiences. This process of gospel writing developed over a period of more than a hundred years. Mack delineates how Christians in later centuries assigned the names of apostles and disciples to the stories about Jesus and his teachings, adjusted the chronology, and erased cultural differences. All of these editorial and revisionist activities were done so that the tradition could present a coherent history of the faith and invest the new church with authority and authenticity.

The work is easy to understand and should be accessible to any audience. It challenges the readers to reconsider the New Testament as dynamic myth that has been reinterpreted many times throughout history. Mack rejects a reading of the text as a timeless and static statement of one single truth. Like other mythic works, such as *The Iliad,* the New Testament writers mythologized events and figures. This mythologizing activity worked to transform the historical Jesus, a human philosopher, into the Christ, messianic son of God. For Mack, the New Testament represents the codification of a religious mythology similar to the myths of the world's many religions.

In the first part Mack discusses Jesus' transformation into Christ. He begins with the clash of cultural values between Greek tradition and Semitic tradition. This clash was characterized by Greek emphasis on philosophy and individualism versus the Semitic concept of collective well-being. Mack states that Jesus' teaching of the kingdom of heaven was not otherworldly but was a search for a better way to live by bringing the two cultures together. In discussing teachings from the Jesus movements, Mack examines the Q source, Pronouncement Stories, Gospel of Thomas, Miracle Stories, and the Pillars of Jerusalem to show the characteristics of the first forty years of the Jesus movement. At first, Jesus was remembered as a teacher, and his concept of Kingdom was vague. To gain new social identity and legitimate themselves as a people, the Christians needed Jesus to become more than a teacher. Mack further describes the fragments from the Christ cult (Christ Myth, Ritual Meal, Christ Hymn). The differences between Christ cult and Jesus movements are considered. The Christ cult focused on the significance of Jesus' death and destiny and created a spiritual presence with hymns, prayers, acclamations, and doxologies—rituals and meals. The Jesus movement focused on philosophy and teachings.

In the second part Mack discusses "Christ and the Hinge of History." Mack discusses the specific epistles of Paul as important because they are the primary text for the modern theory that Christianity was born as an apocalyptic movement. Mack states that the Christ myth was not based on an apocalyptic message. He argues that Christianity was born out of a Jewish law-gospel conflict and that this conflict made it possible to be justified by faith instead of by works. Mack suggests that Paul's Letters to Greeks and Romans were aimed at justifying a mixed congregation of Jews and gentiles as the children of the God of Israel. Mack continues with detailed reading of several New Testament books and how they demonstrate Paul's mission of converting gentiles. Mack continues to employ the same method for discussion of all the books of the New Testament. He then discusses the shift from focus on Jesus and his authority to interest in his disciples as apostles and missionaries—what Mack calls the apostolic period. The role of the early Christian fathers in this process is also discussed. Mack's epilogue focuses on the historical fascination with the Bible: he argues that the formation of the Bible was necessary for the church to speak with authority.

This work is an attempt at an explanative approach to early Christianity. Although it will meet with various forms of criticism from within the communities of Christians, it is consistent with the approaches to religion demonstrated in the other chapters of Molloy. Instructors will find it a valuable research and lecture tool for introducing historical method into the student's understanding of the tradition. This work could be used by students for comparison with studies of specific New Testament books. Since Mack attempts to understand the broader view of the formation of the canon, specific New Testament sources could be compared and contrasted. Likewise, this topic presents ample opportunity for discussion. How can Christians view themselves and their tradition when Christianity is placed in historical context? Mack's is not the only available interpretation of events. What other approaches are historically accurate but different? This is also a fundamentally useful text for its cultural information, even for those who do not agree with Mack's analysis. Mack is often controversial in his presentations and conclusions, yet he offers a powerful and sophisticated study of the formation of canon in the Christian tradition.

For a different but supplementary view of early Christian history, see "Antiquity and Christianity" (*Journal of Biblical Literature* 117, no. 1 [Spring, 1998]: 3–22) by Hans Dieter Betz. This is a comprehensive treatment of several of the issues of formative Christianity; it is broad in scope and therefore useful as a short overview of the important issues. It provides a sweeping view from antiquity to the present. Additionally, Rodney Stark's *The Rise of Christianity: A Sociologist Reconsiders History* (Princeton, NJ: Princeton University Press, 1996) is a useful book for those who are interested in social scientific approaches to Christianity. This work demonstrates the use of better methods of social scientific research than are often employed in biblical scholarship. The work is primarily focused on the rate of growth and expansion of Christian traditions. Stark attempts to explain the growth of Christianity in social scientific terms, employing patterns and statistics in the same way that sociologists study the spread of modern religious movements.

B. (Key words: mysticism, desert, ocean)

Students who develop an interest in Christian mysticism should look at Bernard McGinn's "Ocean and Desert as Symbols of Mystical Absorption in the Christian Tradition" (*Journal of Religion* 74, no. 2 [1994]: 155–181). The author has devoted specific study to the use of desert and ocean metaphors and motifs in Christian mysticism. Because of the biblical setting, desert symbolism has been more dominant over the centuries, even as Christianity spread to other climates and locales. McGinn discusses the two motifs and the way that mystical union is described and understood. Specific study is devoted to the mystical idea of absorptive union with God.

Although this is a specific article tracking but one point on the vast field of Christian thought, it does provide a window into the world of mysticism. Lecturers who want to discuss mystical Christianity will find this article useful; students doing specific research should find it helpful, as well. This article might have wider appeal to introductory students because of its emphasis on symbols and motifs. Students majoring in English, literature, poetry, psychology, and some other fields might find this an interesting article with which to tie the subject of religion to their other interests. Discussions might be focused on questions raised in this article. What would mystical language sound like if Christianity had started in a tropical area? How does space and environment shape mystical and poetic language?

C. (Key words: heaven, Christian eschatology, New Testament, Dante Alighieri)

Jeffrey Burton Russell, in *A History of Heaven: The Singing Silence* (Princeton, NJ: Princeton University Press, 1997), presents a general introduction to Christian eschatology. Specialists and researchers might find this book too general, but it is an excellent overview for the beginning student. (Consider Caroline Bynum's *Resurrection of the Body in Western Christianity, 200–1336* [New York: Columbia University Press, 1995] for a more in-depth discussion.) Russell's theme is a consideration of the fulfillment of human longing for unity with the cosmos. He examines this theme in Christianity from the New Testament to the medieval period. Resurrection of the body, spirituality, representations of heaven, and the Last Judgment are all considered in the text. The work is full of Russell's own theological reflections, which enrich the work. The longing of the human for heaven is discussed in terms of theology, spirituality, and artistic expression.

This book is straightforward and easy for introductory students to read. Although it is not comprehensive, it accurately presents the basics of early and medieval Christian ideas of heaven and its place in Christian thought. Lecturers will find it a useful survey for fleshing out lecture notes and a good source for introductory research. Russell has also published several works on the history of the devil in Christian conceptualizations of evil. All of his works provide useful insights into particular images and beliefs concerning spiritual beings and places important in Christian spirituality.

D. (Key words: Pope, Vatican, bureaucracy)

A different type of discussion of Christianity is presented in Thomas J. Reese's *Inside the Vatican* (Cambridge, MA: Harvard University Press, 1996). This is not a work of theology or spirituality. This book is helpful for lecturers who are interested in the actual politics of the Vatican. The Roman Catholic Church is one of the largest religious organizations in the world. As such, it has developed a complex bureaucracy and maintains considerable financial resources. Reese provides the following breakdown of the Vatican bureaucracy: internationalization has increased in recent years; staff are usually overworked; officials tend toward conservatism by screening out critical voices; qualification for positions is not measured by exams or other means; staff positions are not evaluated; bishops often send their least capable priests to work at the Vatican, saving the best priests for home duty; a patronage system of protection and promotion still functions; and networking and connections are more important than ability. Reese also explores and reports on several issues related to finances. Reese suggests a limited reform agenda. He argues that the bureaucracy is too introverted and that too few cardinals actually elect new popes.

This book is helpful for lecturers and students who desire insight not into theological issues but into the mechanics of a religious institution. Numerous insights are presented on the day-to-day operations of the Vatican organization. This is a work of political science and journalism. It is a different way to view certain theological choices within the Roman Catholic hierarchy. Not every lecturer or student will be interested in this particular topic. Works such as this do demonstrate the broader range of available studies of Christian society and history. Other works of this type also exist for Protestant organizations, the Eastern Orthodox Church, and newer movements such as the Church of Jesus Christ of Latter-day Saints (Mormons). All of these types of works can inform introductory students that religion is not just belief and practice; it is also politics, institution, and finance. Students interested in social sciences and business will find this work (and ones like it) helpful for tying their areas of interest to the larger topic of religion.

E. (Key words: feminist theologies, women, syncretism, ecofeminism, ecotheology, liberation theology)

Christian theology has been revolutionized in recent decades by new approaches to theological issues. The feminist theologies that are currently excavating the roles of women throughout Christian history and who also are applying feminist methodologies of biblical hermeneutics have raised fresh issues that shape the experience of many contemporary Christians. Various female intellectuals throughout history were subjugated or marginalized (or persecuted) by institutional patriarchal and hierarchical leadership. Their stories are now being told by numerous theologians and reassessed in ways that demonstrate a more feminine side to Christian history. Women in non-Western traditions are especially contributing new perspectives and examining ways that institutional Christianity has oppressed women, often with little biblical foundation. Many of the biblical accounts of women have been examined in new light and reinterpreted or critiqued for their patriarchal cultural perspectives. The articles and books on this subject abound, but the following volumes are recommended starting points. *Searching the Scriptures: A Feminist Introduction* by Elisabeth Schussler-Fiorenza (New York: Crossroad, 1997) is one of the most authoritative texts used by scholars around the world. For a survey of key women figures in church history, *Friends of God and Prophets: A Feminist Theological Reading of the Communion of Saints,* the latest volume by Elizabeth A. Johnson (New York: Continuum, 1999), is a comprehensive treatment. Womanist theology is a significant and compelling perspective especially from African American perspectives. One of the best texts to begin with is *If It Wasn't for the Women . . .: Black Women's Experience and Womanist Culture in Church and Community* by Cheryl Townsend Gilkes (Mary Knoll, NY: Orbis, 2000). Traditional symbolism of Mary has also been a stimulating area of reinterpretation. Our Lady of Guadalupe, the most ubiquitous example in the Americas, is especially vital for class discussions. *Our Lady of Guadalupe: Faith and Empowerment among Mexican-American Women* by Jeanette Rodriguez, with foreword by Virgilio P. Elizondo (Austin: University of Texas Press, 1994) explores the symbol with feminist, liberation theological, and syncretist lenses. This symbol is especially useful in class for examining the way religious iconography is contested from different perspectives, such as official church positions versus the views of indigenous peoples who see her as a goddess and the feminine face of God. Ecofeminism and ecotheologians examine environmental topics with renewed theological perspectives, and both aspects may be explored in the excellent collection *Ecotheology: Voices from South and North* by David G. Hallman, ed. (Mary Knoll, NY: Orbis, 1994). For a more widely collected selection of readings on ecotheologies see *This Sacred Earth: Religion, Nature, Environment,* edited by Roger Gottlieb (New York: Routledge, 1996), which includes the significant critique of Christianity's role in the degradation of the environment by Lynn White, and other responses that address those issues (see also this subject in the section, Alternative Religions).

Notes on *For Fuller Understanding*

1. *Compare and contrast at least two Christian denominations by conducting interviews with the pastors of different denominational churches. Work up an inventory of questions (perhaps by rereading this chapter) that will guide your interviews. Write up a report that highlights both the common beliefs and the divergences.*

   This exercise will be more interesting if one church is fairly traditional Protestant or Catholic Christianity and the other is less traditional or less well known—such as Unity, Christian Science, Mormon, Jehovah's Witnesses, Seventh-Day Adventist, Eastern Orthodox, and so on.

2. *Inventory the important Christian art and architecture in your area. Prepare a brief guide that a visitor who is interested in art and architecture might use on a self-study tour.*

   A good way to start is to determine what is important. "Important" means artistically important, and this can be determined by consulting travel guides to one's region, art museums, and experts. It is also possible to define "important" as important for historical reasons, important to an ethnic group, or important to an individual.

3. *Assume you have been offered an all-expenses-paid one-month trip to Europe—if you are willing to guide a tour group to cities and sites that played major roles in the early spread of Christianity. Do research that guides you in choosing an itinerary. Then write a script of what you will visit and study at each of the sites you choose.*

Topics could include cities associated with the missionary activity of Paul in Greece, Malta, and Italy (Turkey might also be included); centers of the spread of monasticism, important basilicas and other churches in important early centers of Christianity (e.g., Istanbul, Rome, Milan, Lyons). This itinerary can be expanded to include later periods, too—for example, all major Christian sites in Europe, Gothic cathedrals, Baroque churches, important museums of Christian art, and so on.

4. *If you belong to a Christian congregation, arrange to interview both church elders and relative newcomers. What does being a member of the congregation mean to members of each group? What particular satisfactions do they find in membership? What do the elders miss from the "old days," and what sorts of things do younger members hope to change? Prepare a display that celebrates the members you interviewed.*

5. *See if there are any Christian nuns in your area. Arrange to visit their convent if possible, or seek to talk with several nuns. Try to uncover the stories of their choices, their joys, and their hopes. Write up your report as a collection of life stories or as part of a study on the status of women in various religions.*

Christian traditions that include nuns are Roman Catholic, Eastern Orthodox, and Anglican (Episcopal). The regional bishop's office at the cathedral of each of these denominations can provide information.

6. *Experience the choral Sunday service at an Episcopal cathedral (or major church) in your area. Make a report on the composers and types of music.*

Most newspapers have advertisements in Saturday editions for services on Sunday. Major choral services are at the late-morning service, beginning usually at 10:00 A.M. or 10:30 A.M. Some churches also have evensong or late afternoon services, beginning sometime between 3:00 P.M. and 5:30 P.M. Students may also telephone churches for information.

Video Resources

The Amish
This program helps discredit the stereotype of the Amish as quaint relics who refuse to evolve along with the rest of civilization. Instead, we see that they have declined to advance themselves through technological "improvement" and have instead chosen a more spiritual path. Their gentleness and respect for God, nature, and each other provoke us to reconsider our priorities and what kind of world we have made. Featured are vignettes of Amish farm life, school, worship, recreation, childhood, and courtship. (54 minutes) [Palisades]

Byzantium: From Splendor to Ruin
This program covers the founding of Constantinople as a second Rome; its flowering when the Roman Empire in the West was shattered; its gradual decline under the impact of Normans, Turks, Venetians, and the Crusades; and finally, its fall in 1453. It describes the history, art, and religious significance of Byzantium, its attempts to restore the Roman Empire, and its influence in the West. (43 minutes) [Religion]

Christ in Art
Art critic Oliver Hunkin takes us on a guided tour of the works of Leonardo da Vinci, Botticelli, Michaelangelo, Raphael, Rembrandt, Fra Angelico, and others, as they depicted subjects such as the birth of Christ, the madonna and child, and the faces of Christ. Hunkin provides historic background and points out significant details to enrich our appreciation. (45 minutes) [Palisades]

Christian Mysticism and the Monastic Life
This film imparts the peace and the passion of the monk while providing views of Europe's cathedrals and the great monasteries of both Europe and America. (20 minutes) [Hartley]

Contemplating Icons: An Introduction to Icons and Prayer
The video begins by telling us, "An icon is like a window opening on the invisible, spiritual world." The program includes five parts: (1) *Icons of Christ,* representations of the face of Christ reveal the heart of Orthodox tradition and beliefs. (2) *The Mother of God,* the variety of icons portraying Mary emphasizes her importance within the Eastern Church. (3) *Saints and Prophets,* "Those who are more Christ-like," as the Russian word *saint* signifies. (4) *The*

Iconostasis, the history and liturgical significance of "the place where icons stand." (5) *Liturgical Solemnities,* which explores some of the icons of the Twelve Feasts throughout the liturgical year. Narrated by Cormac Rigby. (50 minutes) [Palisades]

The Crusades

Looking closely at the major Crusades, this program examines the political and military divisions, economic incentives, and military pressures that gave rise to the Crusades. It traces the path of the Crusaders to the Holy Land and considers the effects of the holy wars and the influence of the returning Crusaders on the developing culture of Western Europe. (23 minutes) [Insight]

Gothic Cathedrals

Reaching heavenward, made of stone and glass, Gothic cathedrals stand as rich and complex designs. From their immense buttresses to the intricacies of stained glass, from the legendary Notre Dame and Chartres in France to Washington National Cathedral, the engineering behind these great testaments to faith has not changed dramatically in 900 years. (50 minutes) [Palisades]

The Greek Orthodox Church

The island of Patmos is the backdrop for this account of the Greek Orthodox Church, its history, and its living tradition. Interwoven with the spectacular Holy Week celebrations, the program records the sometimes contradictory attitudes of the church and of the islanders, some of whom regret, while others welcome, the passing of the old way of life. (30 minutes) [Religion]

Gregorian Chant: The Monks and Their Music

This video explores why chant soothes the soul and what accounts for its current popularity. Chant, with its meditative quality, can turn off the chaos of the modern world and return us to another time when life was simpler. Along with covering the history of chant, its roots in Jewish psalmody, and the cataloging of chants by feast and festival that Pope Gregory undertook in the year 600, the music is sung by the Monastic Choir of St. Peter's Abbey, Solesmes, France. (30 minutes) [Palisades]

The Life of Father Bede Griffiths: A Human Search

An intimate portrait of a great mystic and thinker. Born into the English middle class in 1906 and educated at Oxford, Father Bede was a Benedictine monk and scholar for more than twenty years. He lived his last thirty-seven years in southern India where he developed a spiritual and scientific understanding that transcends all dogma. Cardinal Hume, Archbishop of Westminster, said of Father Bede, "He is a man in search of that which is fundamental to all religions: the search for the absolute and that which transcends all human limitations. He is a mystic in touch with absolute love and beauty." (59 minutes) [Palisades]

Mother Teresa

This film is considered the definitive portrait of the 1979 Nobel Peace Prize winner, Mother Teresa. Shot during a period of five years in ten countries on four continents, this award-winning film follows Mother Teresa into the world's most troubled spots. From the war in Beirut to Guatemala under siege, from the devastated streets of Calcutta to the ghettos of the South Bronx, the film is a close-up experience of the way Mother Teresa transcended all political, religious, and social barriers. (82 minutes) [Palisades]

Radiant Life: Meditations and Visions of Hildegard of Bingen

She was a twelfth-century Rhineland mystic, composer, author, activist, and healer—a remarkable woman by the standards of any time. At age forty-two, Hildegard began having lucid visionary experiences about our sacred relationship to God and the natural world. She also composed brilliant liturgical chants for women singers. (40 minutes) [Hartley]

Religion in the South Seas

This program begins with the story of the young Samoan who became the first native cardinal in the South Pacific; as a result of Bishop Pio's many innovations, traditional dress and ceremonial dancing and singing have become part of his church. Missionaries in the eighteenth century sought to apply a narrower view of Christianity on Cook Islanders; the second segment of this program tells the story of two young native people who defied the Blue Laws. Finally, we look at the most famous and feared Kleva Man—one of those gifted people elsewhere known as seers, high priests, shamans, or wise men; here we observe Aviu, who used his powers to heal the sick, mend ailing marriages, and fix broken machines. (28 minutes) [Religion]

The Roman Catholic Church in Poland

This program captures the intensity behind Catholic worship in Poland, where the church has been one of the main factors in preserving a sense of Polish identity. Interviews with Solidarity activists recall the church's struggle in the 1980s. The program also looks at the role of the church in the political life of post-Communist Poland. (30 minutes) [Religion]

The Roman Catholic Church: The Vatican and Italy

With privileged access to the Vatican, this program offers a concise account of the relationship between the autonomous nations of the Vatican and Italy. In addition to showing the basilica, the electrifying spectacle of a papal audience, and the profoundly moving Maundy Thursday ceremony at Saint John Lateran's, the program also considers the reality of the pope's own diocese, Rome, and explores the dilemmas of practicing Catholics, laypeople, and clergy. (30 minutes) [Religion]

The Russian Orthodox Church

This program captures the other-worldly color of the revived Orthodox Church in Russia and traces its history from oppression under Stalin to its newfound freedom. Interviews with families of believers complement the visual splendor of church worship. The program also examines the new challenge to Orthodoxy presented by the rival Catholic church. (30 minutes) [Religion]

The Shakers

A beautifully photographed study of the Shakers that celebrates in pictures and words their tradition of simplicity in all things. Narrated by Ben Kingsley, the film opens with the beginning of the Shaker movement in the French Huguenot community and the founding of the American Shaker community by Ann Lee in the 1700s. While the Shakers' vow of celibacy has led to its near extinction, the spirit of the Shakers lives on in its artifacts. Exquisite still-life photography of their unadorned furniture and utensils and of their meetinghouses and barns (in particular, the round barn in Hancock, Massachusetts) creates moving and illustrative testimony to the timelessness of simplicity. (52 minutes) [Palisades]

The Swedish Lutheran Church

Sweden was one of the last European countries to adopt Christianity and now appears likely to be the first to abandon it. This program gives a concise account of Lutheranism and examines how—or even whether—organized religion can survive in an affluent and liberal society. (30 minutes) [Religion]

Taizé: That Little Springtime

The community of Taizé in France is an ecumenical "experiment" comprised of eighty Brothers—Catholic and Protestant—dedicated to bringing about peace and Christian unity. Founded in 1942 by Swiss philosophy student Roger Schutz, now Brother Roger, Taizé today attracts thousands of people, mostly young adults, from all over the world. They come to pray with the Brothers in the Church of Reconciliation, participate in the Bible classes and discussion groups, and communicate with people from other countries. (26 minutes) [Palisades]

The Vatican: Fortress of Christianity

This documentary traces the historical development of Catholicism in Europe and throughout the world as well as the establishment of the Vatican as the spiritual center of Christianity. The program looks at this geographically tiny nation within the confines of the city of Rome and at Saint Peter's Basilica and other majestic examples of Roman architecture. (29 minutes) [Religion]

Washington National Cathedral

During its almost one hundred years, the Cathedral Church of Saint Peter and Saint Paul, commonly known as Washington National Cathedral, has represented more than just a magnificent architectural achievement. Known for its soaring Gothic architecture, striking interior vista, and glorious stained glass windows, the Cathedral also stands as a testament to the people who built it and those who worship there. This program combines breathtaking cinematography, archival film footage, and sacred hymns with interviews with national leaders, theologians, architectural experts, and master craftsmen. (60 minutes) [Palisades]

Where Luther Walked

This video travels from Eisleben, Luther's birthplace, to Wittenberg, the center of his ministry, to Worms, where he was tried for heresy. It recounts major turning points in Luther's life. (30 minutes) [Insights]

Internet Resources

Catholic Files
http://listserv.american.edu/catholic/

Catholic Resources on the Net
http://www.cs.cmu.edu/People/spok/catholic.html

Christus Rex
http://www.christusrex.org/

Church of England
http://www.church-of-england.org/

Encyclopedia Coptica
http://www.coptic.net

The Episcopal Church, USA
http://www.dfms.org

Gregorian Chant Home Page
http://www.music.princeton.edu/chant_html/

A Guide to Christian Literature on the Internet
http://www.iclnet.org/pub/resources/christian-books.html

Guide to Medieval Christian Spirituality
http://www.chass.utoronto.ca/~degregor/spirituality.html

The Holy See
http://www.vatican.va/

The Lutheran Church—Missouri Synod
http://www.lcms.org

The Order of Saint Benedict
http://www.osb.org/

The Orthodox Christian Page in America
http://www.ocf.org/OrthodoxPage/

Outline of Objects and Topics in Scrolls from the Dead Sea
http://www.ibiblio.org/expo/deadsea.scrolls.exhibit/overview.html

The Religious Society of Friends
http://www.quaker.org/

United Methodist Church Home Page
http://www.umsource.net

World Council of Churches
http://www.wcc-coe.org/

Multiple-Choice Questions

1. The gospel that is oriented toward a Jewish audience and that portrays Jesus as the "new Moses" is
   *a. Matthew.
    b. Mark.
    c. Luke.
    d. John.

2. "I am the Light of the world" is a statement found in what nonsynoptic gospel?
    a. Matthew
    b. Mark
    c. Luke
   *d. John

3. Many fine portraits of women are found in what gospel, that emphasizes compassion and also contains the story of the Good Samaritan?
   a. Matthew
   b. Mark
   *c. Luke
   d. John

4. Jesus said that all important religious laws could be summed up in the
   a. Ten Commandments.
   *b. Two Great Commandments.
   c. Commandments in the Book of Leviticus.
   d. teachings of the Pharisees.

5. In Jesus' time, what power controlled Israel?
   a. Greece
   b. Egypt
   c. Persia
   *d. Rome

6. Which of these books is found in the New Testament?
   a. Genesis
   b. Samuel
   c. Psalms
   *d. Hebrews

7. The Jewish monastic community that may have strongly influenced John the Baptist and Jesus was the
   a. Jewish patriots.
   b. Pharisees.
   *c. Essenes.
   d. Sadducees.

8. An essential part of the teaching of Jesus was
   a. Be one with nature.
   b. Meditate in order to know your true self.
   c. Find and follow a spiritual teacher.
   *d. Love one another.

9. When the early Christian belief spread outside Israel, it was spread particularly by what missionary?
   a. Andrew
   *b. Paul
   c. Amos
   d. Augustine

10. In 1054, what happened between the Eastern (Greek-speaking) Church and the Western (Latin-speaking) Church?
    a. They published an edition of the Bible on which all Christians could agree.
    b. They agreed on the official date of Easter.
    *c. They split apart.
    d. They moved the capital of the Empire to Constantinople.

11. The Christian bishop of North Africa who wrote his *Confessions* and influenced much later Christianity was
    a. Benedict.
    b. Basil.
    c. Francis.
    *d. Augustine.

12. Perhaps the most important ritual of Christianity is a sign of entry into the church, or
    *a. baptism.
    b. anointing.
    c. ordination.
    d. infallibility.

13. The color that symbolizes sorrow for sin and repentance and is used during Lent is
    a. red.
    b. gray.
    c. green.
    *d. purple.

14. A letter to an early Christian community is called
    a. a gospel.
    *b. an epistle.
    c. an apostle.
    d. a psalm.

15. Regarding traditional Jewish practices, Jesus seems to have thought that
    *a. human happiness was an important goal.
    b. traditional practices should be kept strictly.
    c. dietary laws were important.
    d. rules about not working on the Sabbath were the most important and should be kept the most strictly.

16. The major Christian rituals, such as baptism and the Lord's Supper, are often called
    a. confessionals.
    b. rosaries.
    c. indulgences.
    *d. sacraments.

17. Christianity added its books to those of the Hebrew Bible; the distinctively Christian books are called
    *a. the New Testament.
    b. Revelations.
    c. Epistles.
    d. Pearl of Great Price.

18. What movement, growing after 500 C.E. in Europe, helped spread Christianity widely throughout Europe?
    a. the Holy Roman Empire
    b. the university system
    *c. monasticism
    d. the spread of the Cyrillic alphabet

19. The Gothic cathedrals were built primarily during the
    a. Dark Ages.
    *b. Middle Ages.
    c. Renaissance.
    d. Enlightenment.

20. Gothic architecture, although it arose in France, may be traced back to
    *a. Persia.
    b. Ethiopia.
    c. India.
    d. Russia.

21. The Protestant Reformation was started by
    a.   John Calvin.
    *b. Martin Luther.
    c.   John Wesley.
    d.   Meister Eckhart.

22. The founder of the Church of England was
    a.   John XXIII.
    b.   Clement IX.
    c.   Elizabeth II.
    *d. Henry VIII.

23. The branch of Christianity that is significant in Russia, Bulgaria, Greece, and Romania is called
    a.   Catholic.
    *b. Eastern Orthodox.
    c.   Lutheran.
    d.   Anglican.

24. The central sacrament (ritual act) of the Roman Catholic Church is called
    a.   penance.
    b.   ordination.
    *c. the Mass.
    d.   anointing.

25. The bishop who is the most important bishop in the Eastern Orthodox Church is the patriarch of
    a.   Antioch.
    *b. Constantinople.
    c.   Jerusalem.
    d.   Alexandria.

26. In 313 the emperor Constantine published an Edict of Toleration, which allowed
    a.   Jews to live outside ghettos.
    *b. Christians to worship publicly.
    c.   non-Romans to become Roman citizens.
    d.   Christians to live in Israel.

27. Christianity first spread in
    a.   Russia.
    b.   the South Pacific.
    c.   central Europe.
    *d. the Mediterranean region.

28. Lent is
    a.   a period of preparation for Christmas.
    *b. a period of preparation for Easter.
    c.   the time after Easter.
    d.   the forty days after Ascension.

29. The history of the early Christian Church is found in what biblical book?
    a.   Genesis
    b.   Daniel
    c.   Mark
    *d. Acts

30. What is the oldest branch of the Protestant Reformation?
    a. Calvinism
    b. Christian Science
    c. Church of England
    *d. Lutheranism

31. The branch of Protestantism that especially has stressed the religious value of work and discipline is
    a. Lutheranism.
    *b. Calvinism.
    c. Anglicanism.
    d. Russian Orthodox.

32. The dramatic style of church architecture that Catholics frequently used in order to oppose the Protestant Reformation is called
    a. Greek.
    b. Romanesque.
    *c. Baroque.
    d. Byzantine.

33. The person whose Rule for Monks helped organize and spread Western monasticism was
    *a. Benedict.
    b. Francis.
    c. Paul.
    d. Dominic.

34. The term *A.D.* means
    a. After Death.
    *b. Anno Domini (in the year of the Lord).
    c. Adest Divinitas (the divine is present).
    d. A Deo (from God).

35. The view that the end of the world is near is called
    a. messianism.
    *b. apocalypticism.
    c. adoptionism.
    d. monophysitism.

Essay Topics

1. Explain the belief in end times and in a Messiah as the context for Jesus' life.

2. Explain the case of Jesus at the time of his arrest. How was he viewed by the Romans, by Jewish patriots, and by his followers?

3. Explain how a historian would be likely to view the accounts contained in the four Gospels.

4. What was the core teaching of Jesus? Give at least two examples from the Gospels that show Jesus emphasizing this teaching.

5. Describe what we know of Jesus' personal life and teachings as they relate to marriage and family.

6. Summarize the early Christian message as preached by Peter.

7. What was Paul's mission? How did he become aware of it? How, typically, did he practice it?

8. Paul is said to have defined the relationship of Christians to Judaism. Summarize the significant teachings of Paul in this regard.

9. What is the meaning of "synoptic" gospels? What are they? Why is the Gospel of John viewed differently?

10. Describe several of the images and symbols used in the Gospel of John. What sense of Jesus emerges from this account?

11. Was Paul the author of the so-called Pauline epistles? Explain why your answer should or should not be a major concern for Christians.

12. Explain, with at least two illustrations, how Jews and Christians understand the Hebrew Bible differently.

13. Summarize the essential Christian view of God, Jesus, and the Holy Spirit.

14. Explain the essential Christian view of life after death. How does it differ from the Hindu notion of rebirth and moksha?

15. Explain the two approaches to reconciling differences used by Christians in the first thousand years of Christianity.

16. How did the Roman Empire influence the growth and shape of Christianity? Give at least three examples to show how its influence lived on even after the Roman Empire in the West no longer existed as a political entity.

17. Summarize at least two contributions made by Augustine to the Christian worldview, and show how they reflected the particular circumstances of his life.

18. Who were the Essenes? Summarize at least three ways in which Essene practice and belief may have influenced Christianity.

19. What are the essential characteristics of monasticism? Describe at least three ways in which Benedictine monasticism had a lasting influence on Christian practice.

20. What is the meaning of *orthodox,* and in what countries of the world is Orthodox Christianity dominant?

21. Describe three controversies that led to the distinctions between Orthodox and Western Christianity.

22. Describe two ways in which a visit to Mount Athos is likely to illustrate practices of Orthodox Christianity.

23. List three people associated with a mystical orientation in medieval Christianity. Describe briefly a contribution associated with each.

24. Describe the stated reason for the first Crusade. In what ways did the Crusades ultimately change Christianity?

25. What was the Inquisition? Where and how long did it operate? What were its goals?

26. Describe three practices associated with the dominant church that became focal in the movements known as the Protestant Reformation.

27. Describe Martin Luther as a traditionalist Catholic might have seen him and as a reformist might have viewed him.

28. Describe at least two characteristics or attitudes that distinguish Lutheranism, Calvinism, and Anglicanism.

29. Describe distinguishing characteristics of three Sectarian groups.

30. Describe three results of the Catholic Reformation.

31. Summarize three paths that extended Christianity beyond its European boundaries.

32. Select one of the nontraditional Christian sects. Summarize its history and key teachings. It what way is it broadening (or challenging) traditional Christianity?

33. Identify the two key Christian sacraments. Describe the beliefs and practices associated with each.

34. What are the two most important seasons of the Christian year? Describe the beliefs and rituals associated with each of the seasons.

35. Summarize the history of devotion to Mary. In what ways is it a source of contention?

36. Identify three styles associated with church architecture. Describe key characteristics of each.

37. Summarize three contributions of Orthodox Christianity to architecture and art.

38. Describe three traditional uses of music in Christian worship services.

39. How is science a challenge to contemporary Christianity?

40. Summarize key events and attitudes in the ecumenical movement.

Chapter 10   Islam

Learning Objectives

After reading this chapter, the student should be able to

- describe Muhammad's life and the major events that shaped Islam.
- describe the Muslim view of God.
- describe the Five Pillars of Islam.
- discuss the significance and content of the Qur'an for Muslims.
- explain the differences between the Sunni and Shiite branches of Islam.
- describe the belief and practices of Islam's mystics.
- discuss Islam's influence on the arts.

Chapter Outline

First Encounter
The Life and Teachings of Muhammad
Essentials of Islam
    The Five Pillars of Islam
    Additional Islamic Religious Practices
    Scripture: The Qur'an
The Historical Development of Islam
    Expansion and Consolidation
    The Shiite and Sunni Division within Islam
Sufism: Islamic Mysticism
    Sufi Beliefs
    Al-Ghazali and Sufi Brotherhoods
    Sufi Practice and Poetry
Personal Experience: Ramadan in Morocco
Islamic Law and Philosophy
    Islamic Law and Legal Institutions
    Islamic Philosophy and Theology
Islam and the Arts
    Architecture
    Fine Art
Islam and the Modern World
    Islam and Contemporary Life
    Islam in the West and Beyond
Religion beyond the Classroom
For Fuller Understanding
Related Readings
Key Terms

Lecture Supplements

Islam is widely discussed in books, religion and social science journals, and journals devoted solely to Islam. As in many other fields of religious studies, attention is shifting to examining Islam in diverse sociocultural contexts and the lived experience of Muslims. Religion journals have recently been focusing on numerous issues associated with the Sufi traditions, political dimensions of Islam, and fundamentalism in the modern world. Journals dedicated to Islam tend to focus on particular texts and philosophical issues. Much research is focused on Islam in the Middle East and North Africa (the Muslim states), but there is also work on Islam throughout Asia. For example, the *Religions of India in Practice* series discussed relative to Hinduism and Buddhism offers several accessible articles devoted to

Islam in India. The Muslim minority in China receives thoughtful treatment in *Islam in China: A Critical Bibliography* by Raphael Israeli (Westport, CT: Greenwood Press, 1994) and "Ethnic Survival: Islam and Other Middle Eastern Religions" by Julia Ching (*Chinese Religions* [1993]: 170–183). There are also recent works devoted to Indonesia, which despite having the largest Muslim population of any modern state has largely been ignored in Muslim studies.

The Oxford History of Islam (New York: Oxford University Press, 1999) offers instructors a comprehensive approach to the many and varied topics in Islamic studies and fills in many of the gaps in the former framework. Editor John Esposito has collected works from sixteen leading Muslim and non-Muslim scholars that establish a historical background for continuing to expand the horizon of Islamic studies. The topics discussed range from the early teachings and revelations of the prophet Muhammad to the development of Islamic culture and empire throughout Southeast Asia, China, and Africa. This source also gives much needed attention to Islam in the modern world by offering two chapters, "The Globalization of Islam," authored by Yvonne Yazbeck Haddad, and "Contemporary Islam," by John L. Esposito. These chapters focus on modernity and globalization of Islam through human migration patterns, the impact of nation-states on ethnic and religious composition, and interfaith relations. In addition *The Oxford History of Islam* contains in-depth articles on art, architecture, and science.

Introducing students to Islam is challenging in part because of what Edward Said describes as "Orientalism": the lens through which we see with Western eyes constructed by the colonial and imperial preconceptions of the exotic "other" or "Oriental" world. Said's brilliant work *Orientalism* (New York: Random House, 1979) discloses how intellectual traditions in the West are created and transmitted as concepts of that which is "other" than the Occident, and therefore inferior. The "other" may be romanticized, but it is seen in contrast to that which is familiar. Said, a Palestinian scholar at Columbia University, has shifted discourse about Islam toward a recognition that even contemporary intellectuals distort the "Middle East" (east of where?). Scholarship continues to project images of violence and irrationality in Islam as much as our politics and society do through the media (e.g., images of terrorism, radical fundamentalism, shrouded faces, etc.). Through viewing an excellent film, *Edward Said on Orientalism* ([30 minute video recording] Media Education Foundation; executive producer and director, Sut Jhally; producer and editor, Sanjay Talreja, 1998), students may have a visually stunning variety of film clips with interviews and explanations of Orientalism. This film can be very instructive for dissolving preconceptions and for looking differently not only at Islam, but also at our own biases, stereotypes, and preconceptions when approaching other cultures. At this stage of the course, students are very receptive to approaching Western religions with new perspectives and sophistication.

With the increasing importance of discussions of modernity, there have been several useful works on Islam. Seyyed Hossein Nasr, in *Sufi Essays* (Albany: SUNY Press, 1991), addresses the importance of Sufi teachings for contemporary problems. He discusses comparative religious study, ecology, and the problems of spiritual meaninglessness in the modern secular world. Bruce Lawrence presents a helpful, easily assimilated work on Jewish, Protestant, and Islamic fundamentalists in *Defenders of God: The Fundamentalist Revolt against the Modern Age* (San Francisco: Harper & Row, 1989). Another work that is useful for nonspecialists is Julian Johansen's *Sufism and Islamic Reform in Egypt: The Battle for Islamic Tradition* (New York: Oxford University Press, 1996). Although this study is specific and detailed, it provides a useful research tool for students who want to further understand the issues of modernity and Islamic traditions.

A. (Key words: Sufi spirituality, Qur'anic hymns and *suras,* food, poetry)

The spiritual values and practices of core Islamic communities are necessary to understanding the experiential nature of Islam. John Renard's text *Seven Doors to Islam* (Berkeley: University of California Press, 1996) discusses the religious faith and traditions of Muslims from Morocco to Indonesia to the Americas. Renard presents an accessible view into the marginalized role of mystics and seekers in Islam. The companion text *Windows on the House of Islam* (Berkeley: University of California Press, 1998) is an excellent source for instructors wishing to explore the themes of Islamic spirituality and religious life. This text utilizes visual and primary sources to expand the reader's understanding of ritual and personal worship of the divine. *Windows on the House of Islam* includes numerous accounts that represent the practice of Islam throughout history in a variety of cultural contexts. John Renard's collection is composed of a broad spectrum of Islamic society and religious experience, including translations from Arabic, Persian, Chinese, and Indonesian sources. Another approach to Islam and material culture may be found in Valerie J. Hoffman's "Attitudes toward Food in Sufi Traditions" (*Journal of the American Academy of Religion,* Fall, 1995) in which she addresses the development of Sufi traditional practice as a reaction to worldly influences, specifically how food consumption is not a neutral act but an opportunity to strengthen devotion and limit temptation to highlight the all-encompassing nature of Islamic practices. These new approaches to the experiences of Islamic spirituality transform students' preconceptions of Islam to appreciation of diverse cultural perspectives.

In keeping with Molloy's experiential methodology, *Approaching the Qur'an: The Early Revelations* by Michael Sells (Ashland, OR: White Cloud Press, 1999) introduces and translates the early revelations through sound and hymnic *suras,* including an enriched CD recording of various Qur'anic reciters. The CD contains a variety of thirty-three reciters from different cultures as well as several stunning recordings of the *Adhan* call to prayer. This is not only a rich cultural source text but also a scholarly approach through material culture beyond texts. Honoring the rhythm of hearing the Qur'an in the original Arabic, while following in poetic translations, students may gain a deeper appreciation of the sensory power of the faith of Muslims in the revelations of Muhammed. Instructors might also consider introducing Islamic poetry through such towering writers as Rumi (Coleman Barks, tr., *The Essential Rumi* [San Francisco: Harper, 1995] and *Hafiz* (Daniel Ladinsky, tr., *The Gift: Poems by Hafiz the Great Sufi Master* [New York: Arkana, 1999]). Few writers in history have written with such powerful and sensuous words about the divine experience.

B. (Key words: Sufi thought, visions, mysticism, dreams)

Two recent articles in *Religion* 27, no. 1 (1997) explore several interesting issues relative to the role of visionary experience in the Islamic tradition: Marcia K. Hermansen, "Visions as 'Good to Think': A Cognitive Approach to Visionary Experience in Islamic Sufi Thought" (pp. 25–43), and Valerie J. Hoffman, "The Role of Vision in Contemporary Egyptian Religious Life" (pp. 45–64). Hermansen's article examines an eighteenth-century text by an Indian Sufi. She wants to describe and consider the role of visionary experience in providing special knowledge for action in the world (these experiences are discussed as cognitive or gnostic visions). Visions have a long history of association with saints and mystics going all the way back to Muhammad. Hermansen describes visions as useful for gaining specific knowledge about mundane events and for the clarification of interpretation and theology. Her selected text presents the practice of intensive reflection on particular issues that employ symbolic interpretations. This process of religious reflection is said to initiate a mystical experience. These experiences are then interpreted through the traditional symbolic modes to solve problems or as divinatory practices. Arabic culture maintains a long history of divinatory and dream interpretation practices that have continued to be followed and elaborated up to the present.

Hoffman's article is broader in scope, dealing with both Egyptian Muslims and Coptic Christians. Recognizing that the general geographic environment is as important as religious divisions (such as Muslim or Christian), she discusses further the role of visions and dreams. There are several varieties of visions: dreams, appearances of light, or even apparitions. Hoffman points out that dreams must be included in a discussion of Islamic mysticism because they are one of the most widespread forms of visionary experience. She warns against the view of mystics as a rare, pathological, or exceptional group. Instead, in the Egyptian context, visions are not the property of a mystic elite. Visions of all types have large frequency and are not only tied to people of unusual behavior or talents but also occur in all levels of society, among both traditional and modern Egyptians. In these communities, visions have the same function as detailed by Hermansen.

These articles present a practical view of the role of visions and dreams in Muslim everyday life. As such, they provide a helpful view of the importance of personal relationship with Allah, as demonstrated through submitting and listening and looking for mystical guidance. Instructors and students interested in the broad range of Islamic mysticism will find these articles useful. They can be thoughtfully combined with the explanations and conclusions of other works such as Jonathan G. Katz's *Dreams, Sufism and Sainthood: The Visionary Career of Muhammad al-Zawai* (New York: E. J. Brill, 1996). This work discusses the failure of Muhammad al-Zawai to be recognized as a Sufi saint. Although it does not focus on a successful or recognized saint, the book explores the importance of visions and visionary experience for the tradition.

B. (Key words: women, Islamic modernism and fundamentalism, women's rights, democracy)

The *Journal for the Scientific Study of Religion* 37, no. 1 (March, 1998) presents two articles on the changing roles of women in the modern Islamic world. Mansoor Moaddel, in "Religion and Women: Islamic Modernism versus Fundamentalism" (pp. 108–130), discusses the different discourses on women in the Muslim world. First, Islamic fundamentalists view women in the traditional way: demanding that they cover their bodies, except for face and hands; stay outside of social affairs; and remain inferior in status to men. Modernist Muslims claim the reverse of these traditional views and demonstrate their positions via Qur'an exegesis. They champion equal rights and access to education as well as the rejection of traditional practices such as polygamy. Moaddel argues that a pluralistic environment (such as in Egypt and India) produced the modernist interpreters, whereas monolithic cultural contexts (such as in Iran) have developed along fundamentalist lines during the modern period. The article further discusses the stated issues as an avenue toward understanding the relationship between religion and women.

Katherine Meyer, Helen Rizzo, and Yousef Ali worked together on the second article, "Islam and the Extension of Citizenship Rights to Women in Kuwait" (pp. 131–144). This article provides a specific study that relates well to the more general discussion in the first article. Through random samples, the authors interviewed several Kuwaiti citizens. The article was provoked by consideration that Islamic beliefs were not compatible with democratization. The authors demonstrate that this is an oversimplification. Without specific studies and samples, such as this one, conclusions are speculative. Women's rights are considered one of the important indicators of democratic ideals, and this is why this category was explored. The article finds that regardless of sect or class, Islamic orthodoxy was compatible with providing greater rights to women, yet Islamic religiosity was not compatible. Sunni and Shia respondents did answer differently to the sample questions but the overall conclusions were similar. It is apparent that religious practice and traditional conceptions of social roles, not Islamic theology or orthodoxy, prevent the granting of greater rights to women.

These articles address one of the strongest issues of the contemporary Muslim world. Students interested in women's issues will find these articles a useful starting point. Additionally, the broader issues of modernity, fundamentalism, and democracy are also discussed. These issues can provide several avenues for class discussion of religion in general and current news events in politics and economics in particular. These articles help the students and lecturers address how social issues are also religious issues.

Notes on *For Fuller Understanding*

1. *List differences in attitudes toward women in Islam, Protestant Christianity, and Hinduism. Organize a panel to discuss this topic.*

   Many areas and quite a few colleges have a Muslim community that supports a Muslim center or mosque. Often members happily provide speakers who will go to classrooms and schools. Some of the most willing are converts to Islam, who provide thought-provoking arguments for their conversion. These speakers might be included in the discussion or panel.

2. *Do research on the differences that you see in the way that death is viewed and treated in Islam and Hinduism.*

3. *Islam is becoming an important presence in Europe and North America. Discuss what kind of contributions Islam might make there. Also discuss how those cultures might influence or change the practice of Islam (for example, could Islamic worship begin to adopt congregational music of some kind?).*

   In Europe, Islam is especially present in the immigrants who have come to England from Pakistan, to Spain from Morocco, to France from Algeria, and to Germany and Scandinavia from Turkey. Many of these immigrants are now raising families whose children no longer feel a connection with their parents' country but who remain Muslim. The blend of cultures should be considered. In the United States, Muslims are both immigrants and converts. How will American and European culture change the traditional values of Islamic families? Will Islam influence Western society as well? It would be helpful to invite a Muslim—either from among the students or from outside—to speak about these questions. This topic is frequently given journalistic treatment, which can be consulted.

Video Resources

Beyond the Veil: Are Iranian Women Rebelling?
In this program, a female reporter dons the *hijab*—"modest dress"—and goes undercover to find out how Iranian women feel about the government-enforced dress code and about their diminished role in Iranian society. Proponents of the *hijab*—Islamic scholars, a woman doctor, and a female student—discuss the practice within the context of Islamic religious tradition and the social benefits derived from it. Professional women and others discuss the broader issue of Islam's right to subjugate women by shaping who they are and how they think. (22 minutes) [Religion]

The Five Pillars of Islam
The essential principles on which Islam rests—its five pillars—are described, discussed, and put into historical context in this program. The program introduces the huge international mosaic of Muslim believers and the conflict between traditional teaching and the effects of industrialization. (30 minutes) [Middle East/Video]

I Am a Sufi, I Am a Muslim
This program introduces Sufism, a branch of Islam that is much less well known in the West than some of the more fundamentalist forms that are frequently in the news. The program travels to India, Pakistan, Turkey, and Macedonia

to explore exactly what Sufism is and observe how it is practiced in various parts of the world today. Among the many aspects of Sufism featured in the program are the whirling dervishes of Turkey, who find God through ecstasy; ecstatic fakirs in Macedonia, where there is a big revival in popular Sufism; and the vital role of music in Sufism in India and Pakistan. The program also features Nusrat Gateh Ali Khan, perhaps the most well-known performer of Qawali music (52 minutes) [Religion]

Islam: The Faith and the People
This video examines the beliefs of Islam and how they have influenced Western culture. Explaining how Muslims view Muhammad, it examines the five pillars of Islam and explains how they dictate aspects of daily life. The program considers the role of the mosque, looks at how the crusades affected Islam, discusses the artistic and scientific contributions of Islam, and details the effects of colonialism on Islamic countries. (22 minutes) [Insight]

Islam Today
Oil is, of course, the impetus that brought Islam into the later twentieth century. The conflicts between traditional values and modern lifestyles, between vast wealth and indigenous poverty, between the civilization once believed eternally monolithic and the thousands of voices each demanding satisfaction on a different level—these are the seismic fracture points of the Islamic world today. (30 minutes) [Middle East]

Islamic Art
Forbidden by Islamic law to represent the human form, Muslim art burst forth in the characteristic decorative style we know as arabesque. This program discusses the architecture and sculpture of mosques and Qur'anic schools, the illumination and calligraphy of sacred texts, music, the art of the garden, and the influence of the abstract arabesque on Western art. (32 minutes) [Middle East]

The Islamic City
In the middle of deserts or steppes, towns assume vast religious, cultural, economic, and political influence. Cairo, Damascus, and Sanaa exemplify the Islamic city, centered around the traditional medina, mosques, and souks, and beset by the modern problems of industrialization and overpopulation. (30 minutes) [Middle East]

Islamic Mysticism: The Sufi Way
A study of Islam and its mystical core, Sufism, this program examines Muslim rituals and the teachings of the Qur'an. Narrated by Dr. Huston Smith and filmed on location from India to Morocco, it investigates the whirling dervishes of Turkey and illuminates the Sufi way to God. (30 minutes) [Hartley/Insight]

Mosque
Emphasizing the monotheism common to Islam, Judaism, and Christianity, this program shows how Muslims integrate their faith and their lifestyles. It examines the functions of the mosque, and explains why it is the place of daily worship for Muslims. Focusing on Islam in Egypt, the video explains why worshippers remove their shoes before entering a mosque and shows the purification process they follow before entering the central area. It discusses the absence of pictorial representation, explains why Muslims face Mecca when they pray, and considers the role of religious leaders, the purpose of ritual slaughter, and the customs of Ramadan. The program also discusses the practice of Islam in the modern world. (29 minutes) [Insight]

Muslims in France
Shot mainly in Lyons, this program looks at the problems faced by the city's young Muslim population as they try to gain acceptance into French society. While adapting their religion to the modern world, they try not to break ties with North Africa and the Arabic world. A new kind of Islam is emerging. (30 minutes) [Religion]

Shiites, Followers of Ali
This program examines the break between the two major groups of Muslims, the Shiites and the Sunnis. It probes why Shiism was opposed to the authority of the Sunni caliphs and to power of any kind, how the Shiites split from the Sunnis, and how their practices have developed. (27 minutes) [Insight]

Sunnis and the Prohibited Mecca
Guardians of orthodoxy, the Sunnis of Arabia are also guardians of the Kaaba, the religious pole of Islam in Mecca. This video shows the yearly *haj* (pilgrimage) to Mecca, during which two million pilgrims walk in procession and perform a series of rituals. (27 minutes) [Insight]

Internet Resources

About Islam and Muslims
http://www.unn.ac.uk/societies/islamic/index.html

Academic Info: Islamic Studies
http://www.academicinfo.net/Islam.html

Al-Islam
http://www.al-islam.org

FIU Libraries Islam Internet Resources
http://www.fiu.edu/~library/internet/subjects/religion/relislam.html

Islamic Texts and Resources MetaPage
http://wings.buffalo.edu/sa/muslim/isl/isl.html

Resources on Islam
http://answering-islam.org.uk/L_islamic.html

Multiple-Choice Questions

1. The beginning of the Muslim calendar is the Western year
    a.   351 B.C.E.
    b.   63 B.C.E.
    c.   70 C.E.
   *d.   622 C.E.

2. Islam particularly stresses
   *a.   oneness of God.
    b.   having only one wife.
    c.   pilgrimage to Jerusalem once in a lifetime.
    d.   prayer twice each day.

3. Muhammad was born and raised in
    a.   Marrakesh.
    b.   Medina.
    c.   Mysore.
   *d.   Mecca.

4. *Islam* literally means
   *a.   submission.
    b.   tradition.
    c.   purity.
    d.   devotion.

5. Observant Muslims do not allow
    a.   interracial marriage.
   *b.   alcohol.
    c.   pilgrimage.
    d.   divorce.

6. Which of the following is NOT typical of Islam?
    a.   belief in an all-powerful God
    b.   giving to the poor
    c.   daily prayer
   *d.   belief in a Trinity

7. The phrase "Five Pillars of Islam" refers to
   a. the main mosque in Mecca.
   b. the first five books of the Qur'an.
   c. a book of Muslim architectural design.
   *d. essentials of Muslim belief and practice.

8. Islam and Judaism are similar in that they both
   a. forbid divorce.
   b. forbid alcohol.
   *c. make use of circumcision.
   d. use the same sacred book.

9. Muslims trace themselves back ultimately to what great patriarch?
   a. Paul
   *b. Abraham
   c. Moses
   d. Isaac

10. The Islamic month of fasting is called
   a. Lent.
   b. Hajj.
   *c. Ramadan.
   d. Nisan.

11. The year 1 of the Muslim calendar dates from what event in the life of Muhammad?
   *a. escape from Mecca to Medina
   b. birth of Muhammad
   c. death of Muhammad
   d. Muhammad's prophetic call by the Angel Gabriel

12. The sacred book of Islam, which gives the sermons of Muhammad, is called
   *a. Qur'an (Koran).
   b. Hijra.
   c. Sufi.
   d. Sunni.

13. The name given to Islamic mysticism is
   a. Solipcism.
   b. Shia.
   c. Sunna.
   *d. Sufism. `

14. The branch of Islam that is found primarily in Iran and Iraq is
   *a. Shiite.
   b. Sunni.
   c. Sufi.
   d. Druze.

15. Which country had a large Muslim population for almost 800 years?
   a. Italy
   b. Kenya
   c. Poland
   *d. Spain

16. The Shiite branch developed because
   a. the great size of the Muslim empire demanded that it be split into two parts for proper government.
   *b. of a disagreement over the line of succession from Muhammad.
   c. of a difference over the correct version of the Qur'an.
   d. one leader wanted to take power away from his son.

17. A memory of what Muhammad said or did is called
    a. caliph.
    *b. hadith.
    c. shia.
    d. hajj.

18. At first, before they were instructed to face Mecca for prayer, followers of Muhammad faced toward what city for prayer?
    a. Baghdad
    b. Alexandria
    *c. Jerusalem
    d. Jiddah

19. Muhammad's job was
    *a. caravan driver.
    b. stone mason and carpenter.
    c. tanner.
    d. watchman.

20. Regarding the afterlife, Muslims believe
    a. in reincarnation until one reaches perfection.
    *b. in heaven and hell.
    c. the soul ascends to the top of the universe.
    d. the individual dissolves into the divine essence.

21. One of the greatest examples of Islamic architecture is located in India and is called the
    a. al-Azhar mosque.
    b. Dome of the Rock.
    c. Sultan Ahmet mosque.
    *d. Taj Mahal.

22. The successor to Muhammad, for centuries a political as well as a religious figure, was called
    a. hadith.
    b. qiblah.
    *c. caliph.
    d. jihad.

23. Ramadan is the
    *a. name of the month in which Muhammad received revelation.
    b. celebration of the birthday of Muhammad.
    c. special feast that is held when a pilgrim returns from Mecca.
    b. Arabic name for the Muslim paradise.

24. The month-long fast that observant Muslims keep involves
    a. no drinking of alcohol until a new moon is sighted.
    *b. no eating or drinking of anything during the daylight hours.
    c. no eating at all, but drinking liquids is permitted at any time.
    d. eating and drinking only in the hour before sunrise.

25. The minaret is
    *a. a tower used to call Muslims to prayer.
    b. an indicator in a mosque of the direction of Mecca.
    c. the name for a chapter of the Qur'an.
    d. the name of the head covering worn by devout Muslim males.

26. Muhammad had his first revelations
    a. beside a river.
    b. on a mountaintop.
    c. while traveling to Syria.
    *d. in a cave.

27. During the pilgrimage, men must wear the robe of Abraham, which is
    a. a Sufi robe made of brown or gray wool.
    b. an orange robe worn with a piece of cloth over the shoulder.
    *c. a two-piece robe of white cloth.
    d. a blue robe that touches the ground, and a blue turban.

28. Part of the pilgrimage ritual involves
    *a. throwing stones at pillars.
    b. singing hymns in the valley outside Mecca.
    c. kneeling for an afternoon in silence.
    d. going without food during the days of the pilgrimage.

29. Muhammad and his followers escaped from Mecca to Yathrib (Medina). This event
    a. occurred in the tenth year of the Muslim calendar.
    *b. was the turning point, after which Muhammad gained success.
    c. caused Muhammad to suffer wounds from arrows as he was escaping.
    d. was foretold by Muhammad's last wife.

30. At the Kabah, what object is venerated?
    a. a copy of the Qur'an written by Ali
    b. a robe worn by the prophet Muhammad
    *c. a meteorite
    d. a cup that Muhammad gave to his daughter Fatima

Essay Topics

1. What kind of person was Muhammad? How was he viewed by his family, by his followers, and by those who opposed him?

2. Describe the type of belief and worship in Arabia at the time just before Muhammad's religious reform. What other religions were practiced there as well?

3. Describe as thoroughly as you can the elements in Islam that are shared with Judaism.

4. Describe as thoroughly as you can the elements in Islam that are shared with Christianity.

5. The Qur'an forbids wine. What has this meant regarding other types of intoxicants? How has this influenced Muslim cultures? How well is this prohibition actually kept in Muslim countries?

6. What are the roles of women in Islam? What kind of variation is there from country to country? What new developments can be expected?

7. Describe Sufism. How was Sufism initially thought of, and how did attitudes change? How did al-Ghazali change the perception of Sufism?

8. Who was al-Ghazali? Describe his life, his work, and his influence.

9. Describe the spread of Islam out of Arabia.

10. What is the Muslim notion of Paradise?

11. How has the Muslim notion of Paradise influenced art, architecture, and carpet design?

12. Islam prohibits the making of images of people and animals. How has this influenced the arts of Islam?

13. Describe the split between Sunni and Shiite Islam.

14. Describe the Qur'an.

15. Describe the pilgrimage to Mecca.

Chapter 11   Alternative Paths

Learning Objectives

After reading this chapter, the student should be able to

- discuss the reasons for the emergence of new religious movements.
- explain the difference between a cult and a sect.
- describe major examples of alternative religion.
- discuss the roles that new religious movements play.

Chapter Outline

First Encounter
Origins of New Religions
Neo-Paganism: Wicca and Druidism
Religions of the Yoruba Tradition: Santería, Voodoo, and Candomblé
Theosophy
Scientology
Falun Gong
Cao Dai
Rastafarianism
Baha'i
New Religious Movements: A Special Role
Personal Experience: Celebrating the Goddess
Religion beyond the Classroom
For Fuller Understanding
Related Readings
Key Terms

Lecture Supplements

The study of world religions brings students to a stage of learning in which they may appreciate many perspectives and ways of viewing the world. Students are ready at this point in the semester to recognize and distinguish key characteristics in religious systems, to examine critically the elements of religious movements, and to appreciate diverse and alternative religious worldviews. This chapter of Molloy introduces students to dynamic alternative religious movements and innovative interpretations of some of the religions already explored. Molloy demonstrates that a spectrum of new religions expresses the dynamic vitality of religious creativity that has historically exuded through the foundations of every culture. Contemporary religious expression draws upon religious movements and traditions in adapting to significant new aspects of our twenty-first century world. Students recognize their need for adapting to a pluralistic global culture and consider ways of adapting and forming well-rooted identities in this new cultural landscape.

The range of new religious movements is a response to contemporary issues and social conditions: expanding cultural diversity, alarming environmental issues, continuing political oppression, disturbing human rights issues, increasing anxieties and stress of modern life, revitalization of lost traditional identities, reformulation and reinvention of identities for new social contexts, confrontation of new science-based realities, and mixing of wisdom from other religions into local traditions. The need for adaptation to whatever historical conditions confront groups of humans has always inspired new interpretations and social formulations. Today the climate of change has accelerated these social reformulations, both in creative positive directions and in dangerous or destructive social ways. Molloy explores a number of religions in America, Latin America, Europe, and Asia. The spectrum of alternative religions represented might be categorized as syncretisms, metaphysical movements, and nature religions. *Syncretism* is the blending or mixing of religions, most noticeably the result of encounters between indigenous cultures and colonial religions; *metaphysical* represents those that are new ways of discussing the energies and concepts reemerging from encounters with science in new forms; and *nature religions* include both ecological mystical movements and socially engaged movements (see sections below). This chapter of Molloy's text provides an exciting opportunity for students to learn how to apply the study of religion to the actual contemporary social context of modern cultures. The alternative religions are redefining our pluralistic society with a range of spiritualities that apply to diverse circumstances and needs for transformation.

A. (Key words: syncretism, coexistence, revitalization)

Syncretism is a term that has been used widely to describe the blending and mixing of religions. However, the term should be problematized because of the broad spectrum of syncretistic possibilities. On the one hand are indigenous religions that tried to retain vestiges of their native religion when they adapted to compulsory evangelization by colonial religions. The example of Catholicism in Latin America is discussed by Molloy in the section on African "Yoruba religions" first brought to the Americas with the slaves, who preserved their origins, and missionized by Spanish, French, and Portuguese into their distinct adaptations. For an excellent introduction to Yoruba religions, the volume of essays by notable scholars, *Africa's Ogun: Old World and New,* edited by Sandra T. Barnes (Bloomington: Indiana University Press, 1997), surveys both precolonial Yoruba in Africa and the varieties of expression in the Americas. Syncretism may also be understood as the strategy of masking the indigenous culture's original religious world in order to "reclothe" its system with the appearance of the colonial religion in order to survive under the dominant religious institution. It is fascinating to observe the indigenous religions that are today examining their origins in revitalization movements and considering whether the colonial elements may be sorted out from the traditional culture to determine their own destinies as indigenous cultures.

Many indigenous religions found new freedom of religious expression during the late twentieth century, because of human rights campaigns, political liberation from oppressive colonial and military regimes, and the affirmation of international solidarity and intellectuals (for example, anthropologists and the emergence of scholarly approaches by indigenous leaders). Of course, these movements are the exception during a time when most of the world's indigenous religions face decline and even extinction, but the network of indigenous cultural activists is growing and challenging forces of globalization and oppression that cause degradation. This often involves "reinventing" themselves by exploring the religion of their ancestors and finding ways of practicing original ceremonies and worldviews without the colonial masks acquired to survive domination. The Yoruba religions in Molloy's text are an example of syncretized religions emerging from oppressive colonial environments. Other examples are the Pan-Mayan movements in Guatemala and Mexico (not used in the text), and the Rastafarian, Cao Dai, and Falun Gong movements that Molloy explores. These religions also serve to unify groups that must face political and economic realities that are oppressive or destructive of religion (e.g., Communism in Vietnam and China; military regimes in the Caribbean and Latin America).

It is important to recognize that often religions may coexist without really blending into an altogether new formulation. Many Native American cultures—for example, those of the American Southwest—may have continually practiced their precolonial religions while also practicing the colonial religion, particularly in Catholic communities. The Catholic missionaries, because of their sacramental and symbolic emphasis, often allowed indigenous religious expression as long as it included the Christian system, whereas many of those colonized by Protestant evangelical missionaries (e.g., in the United States) were forced into complete submission because their religions were considered idolatrous and in need of reeducation into the beliefs and biblical theologies of the missionaries. It would be fair to say that most religions in general are a synthesis of religious systems.

Molloy's examples of Cao Dai, Falun Gong, and Rastafarianism are good examples of ways that syncretic religions reformulate other traditions into their sociocultural framework and thus attract enough followers to legitimize their new movement and worldview into their society. While little complete research has been done on these movements, documents can be examined on-line for class discussions (see Hum Dac Bui, *Cao Dai: A Novel Religion* [Redlands, CA: Hum Dac Bui, 1992]; an American contact group is the Cao Dai Association of Washington DC Metro Area, 14611 Country Creek Lane, North Potomac, MD 20878. Telephone is (301) 424-3326; the Sydney Centre for Studies Caodaism maintains a home page at http://www.nla.gov.au/nla/pandora/caodaism.html; *Falun Gong* by Li Hongzhi: http://www.uidaho.edu/student_orgs/falun/eng/flg.htm; and Falun Dafa: http://www.falundafa.com/eng/index_en.htm).

B. (Key words: contemporary spirituality, cult, sect, denominationalism, metaphysics, problematize, pluralism, diversity, postmodernism)

Religion in America has diversified from the beginning, both in denominational and sectarian forms and in alternative religious freedom movements, utopian communities, cults of individuals, and experimental directions. Catherine Albanese, in "The Subtle Energies of Spirit: Explorations in Metaphysical and New Age Spirituality"

(*Journal of the American Academy of Religion* 67, no. 2 [June, 1999]: 305–325), introduces the historical sources of contemporary movements, navigating the various metaphysical and mystical movements that later reemerge in other forms as "New Age." Albanese, a significant scholar of nature religions and the diverse range of religions in America, writes: "Much, if not most, of contemporary metaphysics flies under the banner of the New Age. Here, in postmodern context, metaphysical religion may be read as a response to the nihilism of a nonreligious world at a time when biblically based traditions have trouble persuading and comforting many" (p. 315). Albanese argues that the work of Helena Blavatsky, as one example, reenters shrouded in the language of science and in theosophy, as a "spectrum" of energies or consciousness. This metaphysical framework inevitably focuses on the constancy of changes and movement of energies and therefore is always transforming "to combine all of the cultural currents that act as catalysts in our time" (p. 321). Examining the currents beneath these social movements demonstrates that religion, according to William Scott Green, has always been "at the core of American pluralism and grounds a rich American heritage of toleration." Alternative religions follow in the footsteps of earlier cultural catalysts, always creating and maintaining pluralism. "It therefore stands to reason that the study of religion can be and should be basic to an American education, " says Green ("The Difference Religion Makes," *Journal of the American Academy of Religion* 62, no. 4 [Winter, 1994]: 1191–1207).

C. (Key words: religion and ecology, Wicca, neo-paganism, Druidic, nature religions, environmentalism)

Given the dangers of the social devaluation of nature manifest in rampant environmental destruction and materialism, the alternative movements often navigate the way to hopeful visions of a more sustainable future, an ecological spirituality or sensory sacred sensibility that is socially transformative. The "nonmetaphysical" alternatives are much more about letting the real world of ordinary reality become our sacred experience. Roger Gottlieb, in "The Transcendence of Justice and the Justice of Transcendence: Mysticism, Deep Ecology, and Political Life" (*Journal of the American Academy of Religion* 67, no. 1 [March, 1999]: 149ff), explores the topic of mystical experiences that underlie wisdom traditions around the world. Gottlieb describes the mystical path of deep ecology as an antidote to the excesses and stress of our times, a spirituality that grounds the mystic in tangible multisensory nature. These "nonfundamentalist" currents also "synthesize spiritual insights across traditions" and as Gottlieb then says, they point the way to socially engaged spirituality. So, it may be that the spectrum of alternative religions falls somewhere between metaphysicality (the transcendent variety) on one end, and on the other end those that practice ecological and social connectedness either through syncretic practices and/or engaged activism. For an exemplary collection of significant materials to explore ecological religions, see *This Sacred Earth: Religion, Nature, Environment,* edited by Gottlieb (New York: Routledge, 1996).

Neopaganism, Wicca, and Druidism are another grouping of alternative religions that could be categorized as nature religions. Graham Harvey's *Contemporary Paganism: Listening to People, Speaking Earth* (New York: New York University Press, 1997) is an excellent scholarly source for introducing these movements. Graham is especially helpful in discussing the ways that modern movements find different sources in historical religious movements to legitimize a contemporary ecological interpretation that applies to present issues. The formation of earth-based religious movements in contemporary Europe and America synthesizes elements of pagan alternatives (often oppressed by institutionalized religions), indigenous religions (e.g., Native American, Celtic, and Druidic), and new encounters with scientific worldviews and ecological awareness. For a historical approach to Wicca, Ronald Hutton's *The Triumph of the Moon: A History of Modern Pagan Witchcraft* (New York: Oxford University Press, 1999) and Diane Purkiss, *The Witch in History* (London: Routledge, 1996), are both excellent resources.

New ecological religious movements also are significant in their approach to eco-activism. Many students might be aware, for example, of the "eco-saint" Julia "Butterfly" Hill who lived in a redwood tree in California for two years. Her embrace of her tree as a sacred being represents a deep religious engagement in symbolic acts that inspire new forms of religious eco-activism. For a study of some of these new movements, see Bron Taylor, ed., *Ecological Resistance Movements: The Global Emergence of Radical and Popular Environmentalism* (Albany: State University of New York Press, International Environmental Policy and Theory Series, 1995) and "Earth and Nature-Based Spirituality: From Deep Ecology to Scientific Paganism," *Religion* 30, no. 3 (2000). Bron Taylor's work in this field of nature religions is very instructive for exploring how this alternative religions category is especially contemporary in vision while embracing the values of bioregional indigenous religions. His examination of Earth First! as a religious system gives new perspectives on the ways that activists are religious. His article "Earth First!: From Primal Spirituality to Ecological Resistance" (in *This Sacred Earth: Religion, Nature, Environment,* ed. Roger Gottlieb [New York: Routledge, 1996]: 545–557) explores practices that are explicitly nonreligious in reference to prior religious systems, yet invent techniques comparable to other nature-based religions.

Notes on *For Fuller Understanding*

1. *Do research on the art, music, altar design, or ritual clothing of a Yoruba-based religion. Using books, recordings, or the Internet, find examples. Report on what you find.*

   Because the Yoruba-based religions are highly ritualistic, their arts are complex. Since drumming is an art form not developed in many religions, its study can be rewarding and of immense interest to students. Another fruitful avenue of research is comparison of the images of Santería or Voodoo with the traditional images of saints as found in Roman Catholicism. Stores in New York City, Miami, New Orleans, and Los Angeles might also be visited to discover altar implements and other religious objects connected with a Yoruba-based religion.

2. *Search for "Wicca" Web sites on the Internet. What Web sites did you find? What are the places of origination? What are some Wiccan names of the people who have posted the sites? What types of information and merchandise do they offer?*

   Most urban areas also have stores where Wiccan books and religious goods may be found. Such stores are often listed in the telephone directory yellow pages under "bookstores." People who work at the store can be good sources of information about local Wiccan practice.

3. *In your area, look for a center of Theosophy or of one of its offshoots (Anthroposophy, Krishnamurti Foundation). Attend a meeting or contact the center for information. Visit Web sites and do virtual tours.*

   Anthroposophical societies maintain libraries in some places, which may be consulted. The Krishnamurti Foundation operates a retreat and information center in Ojai, California, near Santa Barbara, about ninety miles north of Los Angeles. Videos of Krishnamurti in dialogue are available through the foundation and may be found in many libraries across the United States. The adjoining retreat center in Ojai may also be visited.

4. *Do research on the Waldorf schools. What is the philosophy behind them? How did they develop? Where are they located? If there is one in your area, visit it and investigate its curriculum. Report on your findings.*

   This is a good project for people interested in educational philosophy and practice. It might be interesting to interview a parent whose child attends a Waldorf school. What is different about the school from other schools? Why did the parent decide to make use of it? Another network of private schools is the network of Montessori schools. What similarities and differences exist between Waldorf schools and Montessori schools? How do they both differ from home-schooling?

5. *Using books and a variety of Web sites, do research on the Church of Scientology. Investigate the life and writings of L. Ron Hubbard. Evaluate the development of the church and public responses to it.*

   The Church of Scientology has aroused emotional reactions for and against its techniques. Students might want to research reactions in various countries. Connections between this church and Hollywood have been publicized, and these elements might be looked into. What movie stars have been practitioners, and what benefits do they think they have gained? What ideas of L. Ron Hubbard and Scientology can be seen in the film *Battlestar Earth*?

6. *If there is a Vietnamese community in your region, try to find out if Cao Dai is practiced there. Describe what you find.*

   This question also provides an opportunity for reading and for library research. Students can read about some of the saints of Cao Dai. The novels of Victor Hugo might be read, especially *Les Misérables* and *The Hunchback of Notre Dame*. (Students will also enjoy seeing film versions of *The Hunchback of Notre Dame* and the musical play *Les Misérables*.)

7. *Collect the lyrics of five or ten reggae songs. Analyze them for their ideas and language. List the main images. Try to find a few parallels for the images, ideas, and language in the Bible.*

   Biblical books of special importance will be Exodus, Psalms, Isaiah, and Revelation. Students can learn the structure of these books, their central images, and significant passages. Students enjoy sharing the lyrics and music in class and can do this with a portable CD player. Students might also enjoy writing lyrics and music for a reggae song of their own and then sharing it with the class.

8. *Create an imaginary religion dedicated to Bob Marley and based on reggae. What would be the sacred texts, the commandments, the images, the places of pilgrimage, the foods, the clothing, the holy days?*

Students can do research on the life and work of Bob Marley. They can study the lyrics of his songs, investigate his life and friendships, and find photos of his home in Jamaica. What would be a Rastafarian meal? What would be the ceremonies?

9. *With friends, attend a Baha'i service or meeting. Write a report that gives details about the participants, the meeting place, the texts that were read, and the announcements that were made.*

Baha'is do not aggressively convert non-Baha'is, but do welcome them warmly. Most meetings are in private homes, where the atmosphere is easygoing. Students who live in the Chicago area will enjoy visiting the Baha'i temple in Wilmette. It is a unique building that reminds one of Islamic and Gothic architecture, and it is surrounded by ponds and gardens. Students might enjoy trying to design on paper a Baha'i temple of their own or a temple that could be used for the services of several religions.

Video Resources

New Religious Movements
This video differentiates among churches, denominations, sects, and cults. It describes sect or cult formation in terms of "religious ecology" and explores social factors that determine whether a new religious movement is considered a sect or a cult. It then takes a closer look at the Baha'i faith and New Age religions. (60 minutes) [Insight Media]

Popular Religion: New Age
This video examines key themes in popular religion, including universalism, illuminism, and millennialism. It includes a clip of an eco-feminist, a Wiccan full-moon harvest ritual, and an interview with the group's spiritual leader. (60 minutes) [Insight Media]

Introduction to Women in Religion
This video introduces the history and contemporary position of women in some of the major world religions. It addresses the marginalization and exclusion many women face in the largely male-dominated religious world and focuses on women who are recovering an authentic spirituality that transcends the limitations of androcentric, patriarchal culture. (60 minutes) [Insight Media]

Cults
Cults serve as a refuge for those in search of meaning and/or freedom from the fetters of social convention. This video examines such ancient and modern cults as the Greek cult of Dionysus, early Christianity, the Church of Satan, the People's Temple, the Branch Davidians, Heaven's Gate, and the millennial cults. (50 minutes) [Insight Media]

Witches
This video explores the history of witchcraft, revealing how the male-dominated church transformed the benign image of the wise woman into the evil image of the witch. It shows how witches were blamed for the Black Death and burned as heretics. It also discusses the contemporary rebirth of witchcraft, or Wicca, in the practice of pre-Christian pagan rituals by more than 200,000 people in Europe and the United States. (50 minutes) [Insight Media]

History of Voodoo
This video examines Voodoo, its African origins, and its contemporary manifestations in the Caribbean and in the United States. It describes such techniques as the manipulation of representative dolls and the resurrection of the dead as zombies. It also discusses Voodoo rituals, animal sacrifice, spirit possession, and divination. (50 minutes) [Insight Media]

Public Vodun Ceremonies in Haiti
Vodun, an African-based, dynamic Haitian religion, emphasizes the family and the ancestor spirits. This video presents excerpts from three public ceremonies videotaped in Haiti in 1991 by a dance anthropologist, providing a context for understanding Vodun. (55 minutes) [Insight Media]

Internet Resources
Sites of general interest about new religious movements:
http://www.academicinfo.net/nrms.html
http://altreligion.about.com/religion/altreligion/index.htm

http://www.americanreligion.org/cultwtch/index.html
http://www.religiousmovements.org
http://www.religioustolerance.org/var_rel.htm
http://www.gtu.edu

Interreligious Spirituality
http://www.csp.org/

Scientology
http://www.scientology.org/home.html

Church Universal and Triumphant
http://www.tsl.org/

Wicca
http://www.bloomington.in.us/~pen
http://www.cog.org/

Yoruba-based religions
http://www.seanet.com/~efunmoyiwa/ochanet.html
http://www.nando.net/prof/caribe/caribbean.religions.html

Multiple-Choice Questions

1. One sign of a religious cult is that the movement
   a. performs no social services for the larger society.
   b. has a belief system that is syncretic.
   c. takes all its rules from a book that is considered authoritative.
   *d. strictly regulates contact between its members and nonmembers.

2. The word *pagan* comes from *pagus,* a Latin word that means
   a. nature.
   b. unbeliever.
   c. circle.
   *d. countryside.

3. The eight significant annual festivals of Wicca are called
   a. esbats.
   *b. sabbats.
   c. ovates.
   d. solstices.

4. A coven is
   a. an offering of salt and water made to the Goddess.
   b. a Wiccan name for walking around an altar in a circle.
   *c. a local group of Wiccan practitioners.
   d. a prayer made to one of the four directions.

5. A form of neo-paganism that is popular in England is
   a. Odinism.
   *b. Druidism.
   c. Gnosticism.
   d. Illuminism.

6. The Yoruba religion
   a. was appreciated and protected by European colonizers.
   b. did not mix with other religions.
   c. has many similarities with Buddhism.
   *d. exists in West Africa.

7. The gods of the Yoruba-derived religions are often called
    a. Ascended Masters.
    b. santeros.
    c. babalawos.
  *d. orishas.

8. Sometimes, when Santeriá practitioners are in trance,
  *a. they magically become a god, with some of the god's characteristics.
    b. they throw themselves on knives without being harmed.
    c. they draw sacred images on palm leaves, which are then burnt in the service.
    d. they see complex geometrical designs in their imaginations.

9. Literally, *Theosophy* means
    a. deep insight.
    b. internal theory.
    c. eternal philosophy.
  *d. divine wisdom.

10. Theosophy shows many similarities to
    a. Pure Land Buddhism.
    b. Sunni Islam.
  *c. Hindu Vedanta.
    d. Orthodox Judaism.

11. The founder of Theosophy was
  *a Helena Blavatsky.
    b. Jiddu Krishnamurti.
    c. Rudolf Steiner.
    d. Annie Besant.

12. Eurhythmy is the name in Theosophy for a spiritually oriented form of
    a. dress.
    b. singing.
  *c. dancing.
    d. community work.

13. The Church Universal and Triumphant combines elements of Theosophy and
    a. Cao Dai.
    b. Shinto.
    c. Islam.
  *d. Christianity.

14. The founder of Scientology was
    a. Charles Leadbeater.
  *b. L. Ron Hubbard.
    c. Jiddu Krishnamurti.
    d. Elizabeth Clare Prophet.

15. *The Bridge* is the name for
  *a. a diagram of stages of mental liberation.
    b. the founder of Scientology.
    c. the world center of Scientology.
    d. the offical journal of Scientology.

16. In Scientology, the state of full mental liberation is called
    a. Infinite.
    b. Open.
    c. Moksha.
  *d. Clear.

17. Literally, *Falun Gong* means
    a. deep-sight instrument.
    *b. law-wheel energy.
    c. spirit-vision way.
    d. cloud-mountain insight.

18. What is the name of the founder of Falun Gong?
    a. Kong Fuzi
    b. Ngo Van Chieu
    *c. Li Hongzhi
    d. Sun Yat Sen

19. The major practice of Falun Gong is
    *a. a series of five exercises, performed while standing and sitting.
    b. attendance at monthly martial arts sessions, held at the time of the full moon.
    c. daily chant at a home altar, using the mantra "Nam Myoho Renge Kyo."
    d. writing weekly in a journal of spiritual insights and self-examination.

20. In a vision, the founder of Cao Dai saw this:
    a. a church tower beginning to fall over
    b. a small tree, growing up into the sky and filling with birds
    *c. a large eye appearing in the air
    d. a dragon that had in its mouth a pearl, surrounded by flames

21. Cao Dai includes many beliefs that come from
    a. Islam.
    *b. Buddhism.
    c. Judaism.
    d. Shinto.

22. The organizational structure of Cao Dai is influenced strongly by
    *a. Roman Catholicism.
    b. Shinto.
    c. Methodism.
    d. Theosophy.

23. The majority of the followers of Cao Dai live in
    a. China.
    b. California.
    *c. Vietnam.
    d. the Caribbean.

24. The name *Rastafarianism*
    *a. comes from the name of a government leader.
    b. means "lion of Judah" in Amharic, the language of Ethiopia.
    c. presents the goal of the movement and means "self-pride" in Swahili, the language of East Africa.
    d. is a nickname given by its detractors.

25. The founder of Rastafarianism was
    a. Muhammad X.
    b. Elijah Muhammad.
    c. Ngo Van Chieu.
    *d. Marcus Garvey.

26. Rastafarianism makes frequent use of this book:
    a. Qur'an
    b. Science and Health with Key to the Scriptures
    *c. Christian Bible
    d. A Course in Miracles

27. A well-known representative of Rastafarianism was
    a. Margaret Thatcher.
    *b. Bob Marley.
    c. Ngo Van Chieu.
    d. Sun Yat Sen.

28. Reggae is
    *a. the type of music associated with Rastafarianism.
    b. the name for the special flag of Rastafarianism.
    c. the type of hairstyle common among Rastafarians.
    d. the name for a Rastafarian religious service.

29. Baha'i emerged from
    a. Christianity.
    b. Judaism.
    *c. Islam.
    d. Zoroastrianism.

30. The word *Bab* is the title given to the forerunner of the founder of Baha'i. The title means
    a. moon.
    b. star.
    c. light.
    *d. gate.

31. The founder of Baha'i was
    *a. Baha'u'llah
    b. the Bab.
    c. Ali.
    d. Hassan.

32. The religion of Baha'i is universalistic and even works for the establishment of
    a. a single world bank and an international storehouse of food that would be used to end starvation everywhere.
    b. a single television station beaming news to all continents.
    c. the conversion of the entire world to Baha'i.
    *d. a single world government.

33. The founder of Baha'i wrote
    *a. letters to major world leaders, including Queen Victoria.
    b. poetry in a secret code that is still not completely understood.
    c. plays that focus on the theme of world peace.
    d. music that is meant to accompany Sufi dancing.

34. The Baha'i religious calendar
    *a. has 19 months of 19 days.
    b. is a lunar calendar of 13 months.
    c. is the standard calendar of the West, with the addition of the birthdays of the Bab and of the founder.
    d. has 10 months of 36 days each, with 5 days added before the New Year, which begins in autumn.

35. The Baha'i faith is
    a. polytheistic.
    *b. monotheistic.
    c. agnostic.
    d. animistic.

Essay Questions

1. Explain three ways in which new religious movements arise.

2. What are two key differences between a sect and a cult?

3. What are three ideals or goals of neo-paganism? Please explain them.

4. List and explain the eight seasonal celebrations of Wicca.

5. Give four ways in which native African Yoruba religion and Roman Catholicism are similar; then explain how these similarities helped the Yoruba-based native religions from Africa blend with Roman Catholicism to create Santería and Voodoo.

6. Describe the beliefs and goals of Theosophy. How were these beliefs and goals modified by Anthroposophy and by Krishnamurti?

7. List and explain four beliefs of Scientology.

8. Give five special terms used in Scientology and explain what they mean.

9. Describe the origin, beliefs, and practices of Falun Gong. Why has it suffered recent persecution?

10. Describe the origin, beliefs, and practices of Cao Dai.

11. Discuss the role that these three figures played in the development and spread of Rastafarianism: (a) Marcus Garvey; (b) Haile Selassie; (c) Bob Marley.

12. Discuss the origins of Baha'i, with mention of major events in the life of Baha'u'llah.

13. Give and explain five beliefs of Baha'i. What similarities and differences do you see when comparing Baha'i with Islam?

14. Identify four elements that are frequently found in the new religious movements and explain how each element appears to satisfy contemporary needs.

Chapter 12   The Religious Search in the Modern World

Learning Objectives

After reading this chapter, the student should be able to

- describe profound changes in the modern world.
- discuss the impact of the women's movement, science, and secularism.
- explain the process of religious change and accommodation.
- discuss the phenomenon of fundamentalism.
- discuss the place that nature holds in religious thought.
- explain the features of eclectic spirituality.

Chapter Outline

First Encounter
Modern Influences on the Future of Religion
    The New World Order
    Multiculturalism and Interfaith Dialogue
    Women's Rights Movements
    Reassessment of Human Sexuality
    Science and Technology
    Secularism
    Environmental Challenges
The Recurring Challenge of Change
Naturism: A New Religious Phenomenon?
Eclectic Spirituality
    Interrelatedness
    Reverence and Respect
    Contemplative Practices
Personal Experience: *2001* and Beyond
Religion beyond the Classroom
For Fuller Understanding
Related Readings

Lecture Supplements

The final chapter portrays the horizon of modernity as a pilgrimage through all of the profoundly religious dimensions of contemporary culture. This includes the ironic twists that mix elements of many of the world's religions with the fragmented and often confusing fast-paced life of twenty-first-century civilization. When students are prepared to look at our own cultural realities with the same methodologies used in exploring other religions, they are struck by the many ways that events and cultural issues today are also religious phenomena, even in a materialist and globalized society.

Molloy presents the complexity of modern religious conceptualization and practice. Many different factors have defined the modern period and global context. Several issues addressed in Molloy are receiving attention in both journals and books. Such issues as women's roles and rights, the environment, and the globalization of the world's societies are all hot topics in media and academia. For the lecturer, there are several helpful articles for addressing the numerous issues. Peter Beyer discusses the process of globalization and its effect on religion in "The Religious System of Global Society: A Sociological Look at Contemporary Religion and Religions" (*Numen* 45, no. 1 [1998]: 1ff). In this article, Beyer discusses how the definitions of and conceptions of religion have been globalized. Arising out of Christian conceptualizations, the idea of what a religion is has affected the self-identity of many of the world's traditions, including Christianity, Hinduism, Islam, and Chinese religion.

A. (Key words: popular religion, contemporary material culture, world music)

Molloy demonstrates that contemporary music and media may be today's myth transmitters, and that computers are potential tools of religious activities and experience through the web of communities, imagery, and textuality of global communication. Molloy explores ways that contemporary popular culture has religious dimensions in similar ways to the religions we have studied in the course. David Chidester explores American society in this light in "The Church of Baseball, the Fetish of Coca-Cola, and the Potlach of Rock 'n' Roll: Theoretical Models for the Study of Religion in American Popular Culture" (*Journal of the American Academy of Religion* 64, no. 2 [Winter, 1996]), exploring how commodities have penetrated religious spheres in our lives and advertising has become the iconography of global civilization. As Chidester remarks: "The theoretical models of religions that we have considered allow some of the strangely religious forms of popular culture—baseball, Coca Cola, and rock 'n' roll— to become refamiliarized as if they were religion" (p. 759).

B. (Key words: environment, ecological philosophy, magic, language, religion, Naturism)

David Abram presents a straightforward explanation for the need of a modern ecological ethic. In *The Spell of the Sensuous: Perception and Language in a More-than-Human World* (New York: Pantheon Books, 1996), Abram presents a well-ordered discussion of the need to reconsider and reimagine the human relationship with the natural world. Abram stresses the participatory nature of perception and how this is always shaped by human experience of the sensuous earth: time, space, and earthly place define us as humans. Human thought and identity are indivisible from the natural world. Poetic and ethical in its concerns, the book presents how modern environmental issues are eternal and human at their core. He draws on the conceptions of magicians in Bali and Nepal and the importance of seeing the world as part of the human community, not as an object of exploitation. The work addresses and explicates the trends in Western religion and philosophy that have allowed modern peoples to lose touch with the environment. He also looks to various Native American traditions for a better model of land relationship and management. The work argues for a reorientation to the natural world that is philosophically grounded and humanly reasonable.

This popular work should inspire and excite all readers, both in acceptance and in criticism. It will be helpful to the lecturer and introductory student in several ways. In the course of the work, Abram deals with several important religious issues such as magic, animism, nature, and kinship. Eliade, Basso, and several other writers dealt with in this instructor's manual notes are discussed and evaluated in terms of ecology. Philosophic schools such as phenomenology are explained in terms easily accessible to the introductory student. What is useful for the student is that this book demonstrates or addresses many of the issues in Molloy's conclusion. The book is helpful in dealing with several religious topics in reference to Naturism. It is additionally a manifesto on Naturism. Thus it is both a research resource and a possible object of research as information on Naturism.

Other recent sources indicate that the greening of contemporary religion is already a unifying vision of a planetary paradigm shift in many cultures, with the sacred earth as common reference point. Roger S. Gottlieb, in "The Transcendence of Justice and the Justice of Transcendence: Mysticism, Deep Ecology, and Political Life" (*Journal of the American Academy of Religion* 67, no. 1 [March, 1999]), explains the present state of the relationship among society, environment, and spirituality. Gottlieb first introduces mysticism, deep ecology, and interconnectedness before applying them to social settings. He defines them not in philosophical terms but through personal spirituality and cites examples from numerous religions (see discussion on Alternative Religions).

C. (Key words: ecological approaches to religion, science and religion)

Although not identical to the emerging sense of modern environmentalism and nature religion, the analytical basis of ecological theories on the study of religion has asserted considerable influence. Herbert Burhenn, in "Ecological Approaches to the Study of Religion" (*Method & Theory in the Study of Religion* 9, no. 2 [1997]: 111–126), attempts to evaluate the concept of ecology and its appropriation by theorists for explaining and understanding religious behaviors. Originally employed by social scientists to map the role of culture and institutions in permitting humans to adapt to the nonhuman environment, these theories have recently been employed to develop naturalistic explanations of religion. Burhenn assesses these approaches according to a twofold division: one set of approaches traces out a monodirectional causation on religious beliefs and practices, while the other set attempts to display functional relationships connected by self-perpetuating feedback loops.

Such a study results in an appreciation of the necessity of a variety of explanatory techniques for understanding religion. It likewise connects the disconnected world of theory and academia to the lived-in world in which ecology has had profound effects both theoretically and behaviorally on religious behaviors and new interpretations of socioreligious movements such as environmentalism and Naturism. The article also demonstrates how many theories originating in the "hard" sciences (in this case, biology) have continually affected explanatory and interpretive strategies in the humanities and social sciences. Although this article is likely to be of greater interest to the scholar than to her or his students, it is helpful in providing some of the theoretical background for some of the movements and trends that dominate the contemporary scene.

D. (Key words: global culture, World Wide Web, religious interconnectivity)

Students learn from collaboration, exploration, research, discovery, and "epiphanies" that connect concepts. Stories, teaching, poetry, koans, contemplation, meditation, and instruction all have been the historical media traditionally associated with religions. In studying religions on the Web, is it possible that students may actually begin to feel again some connection with oral traditions behind our logocentric belief systems? Marshal McLuhan, in *The Medium Is the Message,* predicted that the technological age would bring a resurgence of image, orality, and simultaneous participation, conjuring up the collective psyche of earlier oral cultures. McLuhan predicted a "rediscovery of tribal, integral awareness that manifests itself in a complete shift in our sensory lives," according to Erik Davis. McLuhan described the emerging electronic society as "a resonating world akin to the old tribal echo chamber where magic will live again" (see Davis in *Techgnosis: Myth, Magic + Mysticism in the Age of Information* [New York: Three Rivers Press, 1998], p. 175. See also Erik Davis, *Corpus Cybermeticum: Digital Mysticism and the Religion of Technology* at http://www.levity.com/figment/corpus.html).

The World Wide Web has become a global cultural phenomenon and constitutes a field of material culture for religionists to study. A variety of religious perspectives on the Web are emerging, raising numerous issues about its usage, ethics, contents, and possibilities. Serious reflections and perceptions of the Web's religious phenomena have emerged, forming larger theoretical frameworks about its meaning and potential. Critical religious perspectives range from viewing the Web as a dangerous and insidious matrix of delusions to seeing it as evolutionary human consciousness arising. Ethical considerations include privacy issues, censorship, and morality issues, both as social dangers and as potential for humanity's coming of age.

The immense range of contents, community, freedom of expression, and artistic potentiality on the Web presents an opportunity to study the horizon of an emerging global civilization. This is a wave of communication technology that changes the way we teach and learn, whether viewed skeptically as the globalization process paving over the past, or as the emergence of a "planetary connectivity" communicating a new potential for collaboration. This emerging interwoven and networked system of intelligible symbols is hyperlinked to circles of teachers and students, religious practitioners, and cultural activists world-round. It constitutes an extraordinary educational paradigm shift and an emerging religious phenomenon.

A spectrum of pertinent issues, both practical and theoretical, emerges for consideration: How do we approach this revolution in communication with skillful means? Will students sense in new ways the transmission of teachings through digital-video, streaming-audio, cyber-shrines, and hyper-illuminated-texts? Will new technology give a new generation opportunity to observe a vast array of sacred art? Can we imagine creating the opportunity to explore analogous temples in virtual reality, like the Mind Palace of Kalachakra? I hasten to say "analogous" because what is emerging is unprecedented: a historical groundswell of awareness that our planet's ecology, the interconnectivity of its species, and the intercultural dialogue of humans, is remarkable and revolutionary. It is beyond "postmodern" and might participate in what Latin American philosopher Enrique Dussel calls "Transmodernity": the emergence of voices from the four quadrants of the Earth calling for mutual interdependence of resources and human rights, ecological justice, and a new collective consciousness. "The transmodern project achieves with modernity what it could not achieve by itself—a co-realization of solidarity, which is analectic, analogic, hybrid, and *mestizo,* and which bonds center to periphery, woman to man, race to race, ethnic group to ethnic group, class to class, humanity to earth, and occidental to Third World cultures. . . . This new project of transmodernity implies political, economic, ecological, erotic, pedagogic, and religious liberation" (*The Invention of the Americas: Eclipse of the Other and the Myth of Modernity* [New York: Continuum, 1995], p. 138). Enrique Dussel is a brilliant voice for bringing students provocative new ways of examining globalization with constructive critiques and resources from indigenous cultures and marginalized peoples. An excellent introduction to his vision is *Thinking from the Underside of History* by Linda Alcoff and Eduardo Mendieta, eds. (Lanham, MD: Rowman & Littlefield, 2000). Enrique Dussel's writings encompass theologies of liberation, discourse ethics, and philosophies of Levinas, Habermas, and others. Most original is his critique of Eurocentric teleologies (apocalyptic endings), his articulation of Amerindian *cosmovisiones,* an ethics of poverty, and rigorous Latin American philosophies from the margins of the colonial imperial borders. This anthology of essays on Dussel's thought provides analyses by scholars envisioning a sustainable new civilization, including feminist and liberationist perspectives, with an essay by Dussel in response.

Is the World Wide Web a way of embodying authentic representations of culture? We are beginning to ask new questions in taking seriously the challenge of this sudden surge of information. Will future scholars study the Cyber Sangha as material culture expressing a planetary vehicle of Buddhism? Will transmodern indigenous revitalization movements networking on the Web create new ways of solidarity and social change? Can one study and learn practices, such as meditation instruction, through the Web? Can isolated individuals join a community that feeds the spiritual mind through the senses touched by Web sites? Can the technological vehicle of the miraculous computer be used as a *vajra* (and *Dharmakaya*?) to reconnect communities and individuals wherever they are? The global sources of imagery and access to "sonic" texts (chants, dharma talks, interviews, lectures, music) and video sequences of imagery, ceremonial and ritual components, and master teachers are unprecedented. The impact of visual and sonic textuality changes how students think, and the time-honored notion of textual analysis is difficult to grasp for a generation growing up on visual information and sound power. The Web represents many challenges and opportunities for the study of world religions as a new form of textuality. The way we teach textuality and respect for the materials for learning religious studies will be shaped by scholars teaching students that "culture texts" are symbol systems of the sacred, if only they learn how to understand them.

Notes on *For Fuller Understanding*

1. *Visit a museum that has art of many centuries. What are the names of some artists who paint explicitly religious paintings? When do explicitly religious paintings seem to no longer be painted? What are the themes of modern painting? List any that you find to convey spiritual themes.*

   Among nineteenth-century artists, viewers should especially look for Van Gogh, Gauguin, Monet, Bierstadt, Inness, Church, and Cole. Among twentieth-century artists, they should look for Hartley, Dove, Rothko, O'Keeffe, Diebenkorn, and Frankenthaler. It's valuable to try to draw one or two paintings that the viewer particularly likes (even the quite abstract paintings!).

2. *Islam and Buddhism are spreading in North America. How do you think each religion will be changed by contact with the widespread behavior and values of the surrounding culture?*

   The most interesting information might come from people themselves. Look for Muslims and Buddhists in the community and in the college who would like to share their experiences. Also consult Muslim and Buddhist leaders in the community.

3. *How do you see feminism changing traditional religions in the next hundred years?*

   Try to find women among the clergy who will be willing to give their ideas about the future. Places to find them are among Protestant churches, Reform Judaism, and Buddhism. Male clergy and religious leaders will also have their opinions. It would be enlightening to ask this question of Catholic and Mormon bishops and leaders. Feminist theologians and other thinkers have been giving this topic much discussion in books and journals available in university libraries.

4. *Design a ritual that expresses human relationships with nature. What music might accompany it? Where would it occur? How frequently would it be celebrated?*

   Nature-based rituals that already exist could first be considered. Among them are Easter (eggs, rabbits, flowers, springtime colors) and Thanksgiving (harvest foods, autumn colors). It might also be good to consider appropriate buildings or shelters (if any), time of day for the ritual, and who would be the ritual specialists who would organize the ceremony.

5. *Write an imagined debate with a partner on the assertion that "religions have in human history done more harm than good and therefore should be banned." Include your partner's arguments, and thus show that you are aware of various stands on the proposition.*

   It is helpful to do brief research on some examples of religious mistreatment and cruelty. The topics might include the Inquisition, the Crusades, witch-hunting in the seventeenth century, the destruction of native religions, persecution of Baha'is in Iran, Hindu-Muslim conflicts in India and Pakistan, and so on. On the positive side, biographies of heroic people who have been inspired by religion should also be consulted.

Video Resources

A Conversation with Thomas Moore
Thomas Moore, author of the best-selling *Care of the Soul*, elaborates on how to find sacredness in everyday life. Moore, a former priest and therapist, opens with the observation that caring for the soul isn't one more thing to add to the "to do" list, like flossing teeth and exercising three times a week. Caring for the soul is all about the art of not doing so much in order to create the spaces where the soul can enter. So he recommends listening to music or washing dishes, anything that takes us a little bit out of ourselves so we can then truly hear ourselves. (60 minutes) [Palisades]

Merton: A Film Biography
Here is a comprehensive look at this remarkable twentieth-century religious philosopher who wrote more than sixty books on some of the most pressing social issues of our time, some of which are excerpted here. This film examines Merton's life and work through insightful interviews with those who knew him, including the Dalai Lama, poet Lawrence Ferlinghetti, Nicaragua's Minister of Culture Ernesto Cardenal, publisher Robert Giroux, musician Joan Baez, the monks he lived with, and the friends with whom he shared his deepest emotions. (57 minutes) [Palisades]

Quest: Discovering Your Human Potential
Deepak Chopra, Stephen Covey, Thomas Moore, Dr. Bernie Siegel, David Whyte, and Marianne Williamson, six of today's most influential leaders in the field of personal development, share their insights on the quest for spiritual harmony. (60 minutes) [Hartley]

Voices of a New Age
This PBS special brings today's foremost spiritual teachers together for the first time on a single program sharing their ideas about creating a better tomorrow. This wide-ranging program explores the frontiers in health, science, spirituality, and human consciousness. (60 minutes) [Hartley]

Internet Resources

Brother David's Library of Wisdom
http://www.estreet.com/users/brotherdavid/

Light!
http://www.cyberlight.org/

New Age Web Works
http://www.newageinfo.com/

Rastaology
http://members.tripod.com/~rastaology/

Rainbow Family of Living Light Unofficial Home Page
http://welcomehome.org/rainbow.html

Spirits Evolving
http://www.webcom.com/spirits/

University of the Seven Rays Home Page
http://www.sevenray.com/

Welcome Home to the Earth Channel!
http://www.earthchannel.com

Witches' Voice
http://www.witchvox.com

Multiple-Choice Questions

Note: The last chapter, of necessity, contains some speculative material. Testing on this chapter might best be done by projects and essays than by multiple-choice questions, although they can be used simply to review points made in the chapter.

1. The desire for separation of church and state came about as the result of
   *a. religious wars in Europe during the sixteenth and seventeenth centuries.
   b. greater travel as a result of mapmaking.
   c. contact between Europe and non-Western cultures.
   d. the thought of Chinese and Japanese philosophers.

2. One movement that might be considered a complete religion has been
   a. technology.
   b. consumerism.
   c. nationalism.
   *d. Marxist Communism.

3. Gender-neutral prayers
   *a. have come as a result of influence from the women's rights movement.
   b. have been well-received by most religious groups.
   c. were common a thousand years ago.
   d. are a literal translation of biblical prayers.

4. The Catholic Church has worked to accommodate itself to the modern world, as shown by
   *a. the Second Vatican Council.
   b. the Council of Trent.
   c. the refusal to ordain women as priests.
   d. the continued use of traditional clothing.

5. The Naturism movement is least strong in what regard?
   a. the prophetic, moral dimension
   *b. the sacramental, ritualistic dimension
   c. the mystical dimension
   d. the political dimension

6. A modern artist who has shown great sensitivity in the portrayal of flowers at very close range is
   a. Louise Nevelson.
   *b. Georgia O'Keeffe.
   c. Mark Rothko.
   d. Richard Diebenkorn.

7. Abraham Maslow was a psychologist interested in spirituality who talked about
   a. inner travel.
   b. dream insights.
   *c. peak experiences.
   d. environmental sensitivity.

8. Nirvana, used as the name of a former rock band, is an example of
   *a. intercultural influence.
   b. the influence of Buddhist missionary monks.
   c. a use of irony.
   d. a deliberate rejection of Christian ideals.

9. Applied science is
   a. scientific theory.
   *b. science used for practical purposes.
   c. the use of hypotheses to further scientific knowledge.
   d. the use of scientific theories by scientists of later centuries.

10. Living and thinking without reference to a religion is called
    a. rationalism.
    b. transcendentalism.
    c. ecotourism.
    *d. secularism.

11. T. H. Huxley, an English biologist, created what term?
    *a. agnosticism
    b. nontheism
    c. secularism
    d. pantheism

12. James Morton, dean emeritus of the Cathedral of Saint John the Divine, has said that *religion* is an old word for the reality of relationship, and that the new word for that reality is
    a. reverence.
    *b. ecology.
    c. recollection.
    d. tradition.

13. The artist who created a Japanese garden and spent more than forty years painting pictures of it was
    a. Vincent Van Gogh.
    *b. Claude Monet.
    c. Paul Cezanne.
    d. Pablo Picasso.

14. John Muir
    *a. worked to have Yosemite declared a national park.
    b. wrote books about using music for growth in spirituality.
    c. warned repeatedly about the use of pesticides.
    d. painted pictures of the Hudson River and its surrounding territory.

15. It is possible to see in the comic-book figure of Superman an underlying
    a. pessimism.
    b. cynicism.
    *c. messianism.
    d. multiculturalism.

16. The person who became famous for photographing Yosemite was
    *a. Ansel Adams.
    b. Diane Arbus.
    c. Dorothea Lange.
    d. Henri Cartier-Bresson.

17. French impressionist music, such as by Claude Debussy and Maurice Ravel, was often inspired by
    a. the rhythms of the machine age.
    b. the desire to express vitality and speed.
    c. a longing for the music of the Middle Ages.
    *d. the sounds and appearance of nature.

18. The yin-yang symbol is found as a commercial logo and also in the flag of
    a. Japan.
    b. Vietnam.
    *c. South Korea.
    d. Cambodia.

19. The first complete map of the world was created by
    *a. Mercator.
    b. Ptolemy.
    c. Columbus.
    d. Magellan.

20. The first World Parliament of Religions was held in 1893 in
    a. Calcutta.
    b. Geneva.
    c. Assisi.
    *d. Chicago.

Essay Topics

1. How does science view the universe, the earth, and human beings?

2. What challenges does science give to religion?

3. What challenges does religion give to science?

4. What would be examples of religious ideas and images that can be found in popular music?

5. How has the women's rights movement changed religion? Which religions seem to be the most changed, and which the least?

6. Describe the variety of religious attitudes toward human sexuality. What changes in religious attitudes about this topic during the past century can you list?

7. Some religions have looked at nature pessimistically, seeing it as dangerous to the spirit. List these religions and explain the reasoning behind their attitude toward nature.

8. Marxist Communism has shown a number of parallels with religions. Please explain.

9. What challenges does modern democratic capitalism bring to traditional religions?

10. Describe the change in attitude toward animals that seems to have been occurring in the past 150 years. How will this influence current religions?

1-1 Key Theorists of Religion

- **FRAZER—BELIEF IN SPIRITS WITHIN NATURE (ANIMISM)**

- **JAMES—BRINGS MEANING AND VITALITY**

- **FREUD—PROJECTION OF CHILDHOOD EXPERIENCE**

- **JUNG—INDIVIDUATION; PERSONAL DEVELOPMENT**

- **OTTO—SENSE OF THE HOLY**

Experiencing the World's Religions, Second Edition, Molloy, Copyright ©2002 The McGraw-Hill Companies, Inc.

- **SACRAMENTAL—EMPHASIZES RITUAL**

- **PROPHETIC—EMPHASIZES BELIEF AND MORALITY**

- **MYSTICAL—EMPHASIZES SENSE OF ONENESS WITH GOD OR THE UNIVERSE**

1-3 Varied Attitudes among Religions

- **SACRED REALITY—TRANSCENDENT OR IMMANENT**

- **UNIVERSE—CREATED OR ETERNAL**

- **NATURE—PERFECT OR IMPERFECT**

- **TIME—CYCLICAL OR LINEAR**

- **HUMAN BEINGS—CENTRAL OR PART OF NATURE AND SOCIETY**

- **WORDS AND SCRIPTURES—VALUABLE OR INADEQUATE**

- **EXCLUSIVENESS VS. INCLUSIVENESS**

Experiencing the World's Religions, Second Edition, Molloy, Copyright ©2002 The McGraw-Hill Companies, Inc.

- **POLYTHEISM—MANY GODS**

- **MONOTHEISM—ONE GOD**

- **PANTHEISM—ALL IS GOD**

- **ATHEISM—NO GOD OR GODS**

- **AGNOSTICISM—CANNOT KNOW EXISTENCE OF GOD**

- **TRANSCENDENT—SACRED IS BEYOND THIS WORLD**

- **IMMANENT—SACRED IS WITHIN THIS WORLD**

2-1 Key Terms

- **SHAMAN—VISIONARY PERSON WHO CONTACTS SPIRIT WORLD**

- **TABOO—SOCIAL PROHIBITION**

- **DIVINATION—SEEING INTO THE FUTURE OR PAST**

- **TOTEM—SYMBOLIC ANIMAL IMPORTANT TO A GROUP**

2-2 Life-Cycle Ceremonies

- **BIRTH**

- **NAMING**

- **"COMING OF AGE"**

- **MARRIAGE**

- **PASSING FROM LIFE (BECOMING AN ANCESTOR)**

2-3 Some Typical Patterns in Religions

- **RELATION—HUMAN RELATIONSHIPS WITH OTHER HUMAN BEINGS, WITH ANIMALS, AND WITH NATURE**

- **TIME—"ORDINARY" VS. "SACRED"**

- **SPACE—"ORDINARY" VS. "SACRED"**

- **CELEBRATION OF ORIGINS**

- **CELEBRATION OF GODS**

- **RITUALS OF RESPECT FOR ANCESTORS**

- **SACRIFICES TO NATURE GODS**

- **HEREDITARY PRIESTHOOD**

- **OUTDOOR FIRE ALTARS**

- **MEMORIZED VEDIC CHANTS**

- **OFFERINGS OF FOOD, DRINK, ANIMALS**

- **VEDAS**

- **UPANISHADS**

- **BHAGAVAD GITA**

- **RAMAYANA**

3-3 Important Concepts of the Upanishads

- **BRAHMAN**

- **ATMAN**

- **MAYA**

- **KARMA**

- **SAMSARA**

- **MOKSHA**

- **JNANA—KNOWLEDGE**

- **KARMA—SELFLESS ACTION**

- **BHAKTI—DEVOTION**

- **RAJA—MEDITATION**

- **HATHA—EXERCISES**

- **PRIEST (BRAHMIN)**

- **WARRIOR-NOBLE (KSHATRIYA)**

- **MERCHANT-CRAFTSMAN (VAISHYA)**

- **PEASANT (SHUDRA)**

- **UNTOUCHABLE (DALIT)**

4-1 Branches of Buddhism

- **THERAVADA—"WAY OF THE ELDERS"**
  "SOUTHERN SCHOOL"
  (SOUTHEAST ASIA)
  CONSERVATIVE
  MONASTIC FOCUS

- **MAHAYANA—"BIG VEHICLE"**
  "NORTHERN SCHOOL"
  (EAST ASIA)
  SPECULATIVE
  GREATER FOCUS ON
  LAYPERSON

- **VAJRAYANA—"DIAMOND VEHICLE"**
  TIBETAN BUDDHISM
  HIGHLY RITUALISTIC

4-1 Branches of Buddhism

Experiencing the World's Religions, Second Edition, Molloy, Copyright ©2002 The McGraw-Hill Companies, Inc.

- **SAMSARA—EVERYDAY WORLD OF CHANGE AND PAIN**

- **NIRVANA—RELEASE FROM SAMSARA; STATE OF BLISS**

- **DUKKHA—SUFFERING**

- **DHARMA—BUDDHIST TEACHING**

- **SANGHA—BUDDHIST COMMUNITY**

- **ARHAT—THE PERFECT PERSON IN THERAVADA**

- **BODHISATTVA—A PERSON OR DEITY OF COMPASSION IN MAHAYANA BUDDHISM**

- **DHYANA—MEDITATION**

- **TRIPITAKA—"THREE BASKETS" OF BUDDHIST SCRIPTURE**

- **SHUNYATA—"EMPTINESS"—THE INTERRELATED NATURE OF ALL REALITY**

- **TATHATA—"THUSNESS, SUCHNESS"**

4-3 Ritual Elements of Buddhism

- **MANTRA—SHORT SACRED CHANT**

- **MUDRA—HAND GESTURE**

- **MANDALA—RELIGIOUS DIAGRAM**

- **VAJRA—SHORT SCEPTER OR WAND**

- **STUPA—A CIRCULAR, DOMELIKE SHRINE**

5-1 Key Terms of Jainism

- **AHIMSA—NON-INJURY**

- **TIRTHANKARA—CROSSING-MAKER**

- **JIVA—SOUL, LIFE FORCE**

- **AJIVA—UNFEELING MATTER**

- **HYLOZOISM—BELIEF THAT ALL NATURE IS ALIVE**

- **SALLEKHANA—DEATH BY GENTLE SUICIDE**

5-2 Jain Ethical Recommendations

- **AHIMSA**

- **NONLYING**

- **NONSTEALING**

- **CHASTITY**

- **NONATTACHMENT**

5-3 Elements of Sikh Belief and Practice

- **TRUE NAME—GOD**

- **KARMA AND REINCARNATION**

- **SOUL AND BODY**

- **ADI GRANTH—SCRIPTURE**

- **LINE OF TEN HUMAN GURUS**

Experiencing the World's Religions, Second Edition, Molloy, Copyright ©2002 The McGraw-Hill Companies, Inc.

5-4 Five K's of the Sikh Khalsa

- **KESH—UNCUT HAIR**

- **KHANGA—COMB**

- **KACH—UNDERWEAR**

- **KIRPAN—SHORT SWORD**

- **KARA—STEEL BRACELET**

6-1 Taoist Virtues

- **WU-WEI ("NO ACTION")— SPONTANEITY**

- **QUIET**

- **HUMOR**

- **CLOSENESS TO NATURE**

- **SIMPLICITY**

6-2 The Five Great Relationships

- **FATHER-SON**

- **ELDER BROTHER-YOUNGER BROTHER**

- **HUSBAND-WIFE**

- **ELDER-YOUNGER OR FRIEND-FRIEND**

- **RULER-SUBJECT**

Experiencing the World's Religions, Second Edition, Molloy, Copyright ©2002 The McGraw-Hill Companies, Inc.

6-3 The Five Great Virtues

- **REN (JEN)—BENEVOLENCE**

- **LI—APPROPRIATENESS, PROPRIETY**

- **SHU—RECIPROCITY**

- **XIAO (HSIAO)—FAMILY DEVOTION, FILIAL PIETY**

- **WEN—CULTIVATION IN THE ARTS**

Experiencing the World's Religions, Second Edition, Molloy, Copyright ©2002 The McGraw-Hill Companies, Inc.

- **DUTY**

- **LOYALTY**

- **CONSENSUS**

- **MODERATION**

- **SELF-SACRIFICE**

- **THRIFT**

- **SELF-CONTROL**

7-1 Major Kami of Shinto

- **IZANAGI—PRIMEVAL FATHER**

- **IZANAMI—PRIMEVAL MOTHER**

- **AMATERASU—SUN GODDESS**

- **TSUKIYOMI—MOON GOD**

- **SUSANOWO—WIND GOD**

- **INARI—RICE GODDESS**

Experiencing the World's Religions, Second Edition, Molloy, Copyright ©2002 The McGraw-Hill Companies, Inc.

- **KAMI—SPIRIT**

- **JINJA—SHRINE**

- **TSUMI—POLLUTION**

- **HARAI—PURIFICATION**

- **GAGAKU—MUSIC**

- **KADOMATSU—ARRANGEMENT OF PINE AND BAMBOO AT DOOR**

- **SHIMENAWA—TWISTED ROPE AROUND A SACRED TREE OR SITE**

- **KAMIDAN—HOME ALTAR**

- **MATSURI—FESTIVAL**

7-3 Offshoots of Shinto

- **TENRIKYO**

- **OMOTOKYO**

- **P. L. KYODAN**

- **SEICHO-NO-IE**

- **HONMICHI**

8-1 Categories of the Hebrew Bible

- **TORAH (PENTATEUCH)**

- **PROPHETS—FORMER AND LATTER**

- **WRITINGS**

8-2 Major Festivals of Judaism

- **ROSH HASHANAH—NEW YEAR—AUTUMN**

- **YOM KIPPUR—DAY OF ATONEMENT—AUTUMN**

- **SUKKOT—HARVEST FESTIVAL—AUTUMN**

- **HANUKKAH—REDEDICATION OF THE SECOND TEMPLE—WINTER**

- **PURIM—WINTER**

- **PESACH—PASSOVER—SPRING**

- **SHAVUOT—SUMMER**

8-3 Branches of Contemporary Judaism

- **ORTHODOX**

- **CONSERVATIVE**

- **REFORM**

- **RECONSTRUCTIONIST**

- **NO PORK**

- **NO SHELLFISH**

- **SEPARATION OF MEAT AND DAIRY PRODUCTS**

- **MEAT MUST HAVE ALL BLOOD REMOVED AND HAVE BEEN PREPARED UNDER APPROVED RABBINIC SUPERVISION**

9-1 Categories of the New Testament

- **GOSPELS—FOUR ACCOUNTS OF THE LIFE OF JESUS**

- **ACTS OF THE APOSTLES— EARLY CHRISTIAN HISTORY**

- **EPISTLES—LETTERS BY PAUL AND OTHERS**

- **REVELATION—SYMBOLIC PROPHECY**

Experiencing the World's Religions, Second Edition, Molloy, Copyright ©2002 The McGraw-Hill Companies, Inc.

9-2 Important Early Christian Figures

- **PETER**

- **PAUL**

- **CONSTANTINE**

- **AUGUSTINE**

- **BASIL**

- **BENEDICT**

9-3 Important Christian Figures of the Middle Ages

- **FRANCIS OF ASSISI**

- **DOMINIC**

- **HILDEGARD OF BINGEN**

- **JULIANA OF NORWICH**

- **THOMAS AQUINAS**

- **MEISTER ECKHART**

- **KYRIE—LORD HAVE MERCY**

- **GLORIA—GLORY TO GOD IN THE HIGHEST**

- **CREDO—I BELIEVE IN ONE GOD**

- **SANCTUS—HOLY, HOLY, HOLY**

- **AGNUS DEI—LAMB OF GOD**

9-5 Traditional Subjects of Christian Art

- **NATIVITY—BIRTH OF CHRIST**
- **BAPTISM OF JESUS**
- **WEDDING FEAST OF CANA**
- **THE RAISING OF LAZARUS**
- **MIRACLE OF LOAVES AND FISHES**
- **TRANSFIGURATION**
- **LAST SUPPER**
- **CRUCIFIXION**
- **RESURRECTION**
- **ASCENSION OF JESUS**
- **PENTECOST**
- **DORMITION—DEATH OF MARY**
- **APOSTLES AND SAINTS**
- **LAST JUDGMENT**
- **HEAVEN AND HELL**

Experiencing the World's Religions, Second Edition, Molloy, Copyright ©2002 The McGraw-Hill Companies, Inc.

- **WHITE—JOY**

- **RED—LOVE, BLOOD, AND MARTYRDOM**

- **PURPLE—PENITENCE, LENT**

- **GREEN—HOPE, GROWTH IN CHRISTIAN LIFE**

- **BLACK—DEATH**

- **BLUE—ADVENT, MARY**

- ## MARTIN LUTHER—LUTHERANISM

- ## JOHN CALVIN—CALVINISM

- ## HENRY VIII—CHURCH OF ENGLAND (ANGLICANISM)

- ## GEORGE FOX—SOCIETY OF FRIENDS (QUAKERS)

- ## JOHN AND CHARLES WESLEY— METHODISM

- ## MOTHER ANN LEE—SHAKERS

9-8 Important Styles of Church Architecture

- **ROMANESQUE**

- **GOTHIC**

- **BAROQUE**

- **NEOCLASSICAL**

Experiencing the World's Religions, Second Edition, Molloy, Copyright ©2002 The McGraw-Hill Companies, Inc.

- **MASS**

- **MOTET**

- **ORATORIO**

- **PASSION**

- **HYMN**

10-1 The Five Pillars of Islam

- **CREED: ONE GOD; MUHAMMAD IS GOD'S MESSENGER**

- **PRAYER FIVE TIMES A DAY**

- **CHARITY TO THE POOR**

- **FASTING DURING RAMADAN**

- **PILGRIMAGE TO MECCA**

10-2 Branches of Islam

- **SUNNI**

- **SHIITE**
  - **—TWELVERS**
  - **—SEVENERS**
  - **—OTHERS**

10-3 Practices and Prohibitions of Islam

- **NO ALCOHOL**

- **NO PORK**

- **NO GAMBLING**

- **NO IMAGES OF HUMAN BEINGS OR ANIMALS**

- **MALE CIRCUMCISION**

- **FOUR WIVES ALLOWED**

- **MODESTY IN CLOTHING**

- **SPECIAL PROTECTION OF WOMEN**

Experiencing the World's Religions, Second Edition, Molloy, Copyright ©2002 The McGraw-Hill Companies, Inc.

11-1 Possible Origins of a New Religious Movement

- **DIVISIONS EMERGE IN AN OLDER RELIGION**

- **AN OLDER RELIGION MOVES INTO A NEW CULTURE AND IS CHANGED**

- **TWO OR MORE RELIGIONS BLEND**

- **AN INDIVIDUAL BEGINS A NEW RELIGION AS THE RESULT OF A REVELATION**

Experiencing the World's Religions, Second Edition, Molloy, Copyright ©2002 The McGraw-Hill Companies, Inc.

SECT:

- **OFTEN IS A LARGE MOVEMENT THAT EMERGES FROM AN ESTABLISHED RELIGION**

- **CAN HAVE MANY MEMBERS**

- **FAIRLY LOOSE STRUCTURE**

- **MILD CONTROL OVER INDIVIDUALS**

CULT:

- **OFTEN EMERGES INDEPENDENTLY**

- **SMALL NUMBER OF FOLLOWERS**

- **SOCIALLY ISOLATED**

- **OFTEN UNDER THE CONTROL OF A CHARISMATIC OR DICTATORIAL LEADER**

Experiencing the World's Religions, Second Edition, Molloy, Copyright ©2002 The McGraw-Hill Companies, Inc.

11-3 Similarities between Yoruba Religion and Catholicism

- **BELIEF IN ONE "HIGH GOD"**

- **DEVOTION TO HELPFUL DEITIES OR SAINTS**

- **IMPORTANCE OF RITUAL**

- **EMPHASIS ON REAL OR SYMBOLIC SACRIFICE**

- **ANTHROPOSOPHY**

- **KRISHNAMURTI**

- **CHURCH UNIVERSAL AND TRIUMPHANT**

- **THETAN—THE INDIVIDUAL SOUL**

- **PRE-CLEAR—AN UNLIBERATED PERSON**

- **ENGRAM—A BLOCKAGE TO PERSONAL GROWTH, ACQUIRED PREVIOUSLY IN THIS LIFE OR IN AN EARLIER LIFE**

- **PROCESS—A TECHNIQUE FOR UNDERSTANDING BLOCKAGES TO PERSONAL GROWTH**

- **AUDITOR—A COUNSELOR WHO ASSISTS IN DISCOVERING AND DISSOLVING BLOCKAGES, OFTEN THROUGH A SERIES OF QUESTIONS**

11-6 Important Individuals in the Development and Spread of Rastafarianism

- **MARCUS GARVEY**

- **HAILE SELASSIE (RAS TAFARI)**

- **BOB MARLEY**

- **EMERGENCE FROM SHIITE ISLAM IN IRAN**

- **MAJOR FIGURES:**

  —**THE BAB**

  —**BAHA'U'LLAH**

  —**SHOGI EFFENDI**

- **ONE GOD**

- **REGULAR REVELATION FROM GOD**

- **BELIEF IN SOUL AND AFTERLIFE**

- **UNITY OF ALL RELIGIONS**

- **EQUALITY OF ALL HUMAN BEINGS**

- **EQUAL OPPORTUNITY FOR FEMALES**

- **NEED FOR A SINGLE WORLD GOVERNMENT**

- **IMPORTANCE OF EDUCATION**

11-9 Important Elements of New Religious Movements

- **SMALL GROUPS, CLOSENESS OF MEMBERS**

- **IMPORTANCE OF WOMEN AS LEADERS AND IDEALS**

- **ACTIVE DEVOTIONAL LIFE, FREQUENTLY MYSTICAL**

- **CLEAR PRACTICES FOR SELF-CULTIVATION**

Experiencing the World's Religions, Second Edition, Molloy, Copyright ©2002 The McGraw-Hill Companies, Inc.

12-1 Modern Influences on Religion

- **THE NEW GLOBAL WORLD ORDER**

- **MULTICULTURALISM**

- **INTERFAITH DIALOGUE**

- **WOMEN'S RIGHTS MOVEMENTS**

- **SCIENCE AND TECHNOLOGY**

- **SECULARISM**

- **ENVIRONMENTALISM**

Experiencing the World's Religions, Second Edition, Molloy, Copyright ©2002 The McGraw-Hill Companies, Inc.

- **SENSE OF THE SACRED IN NATURE**

- **SACRED PLACES**

- **PILGRIMAGE SITES**

- **SACRED LITERATURE**

- **SEASONAL FESTIVALS**

- **COMMANDMENTS**

- **DIETARY LAWS**

12-3 Elements of Modern Eclectic Spirituality

- **INTERRELATEDNESS**

- **REVERENCE AND RESPECT**

- **CONTEMPLATIVE PRACTICES**

- **LYRICS OF POPULAR MUSIC**

- **ROCK CONCERTS—RELIGIOUS SERVICES**

- **ROCK VIDEOS—RELIGIOUS IMAGES**

- **COMICS—RELIGIOUS IMAGES AND QUESTIONS**

- **SUPERMAN—MESSIAH FIGURE**

- **"PRESLEYANITY"—CULT OF ELVIS**

- **VENERATION OF BOB MARLEY**

Experiencing the World's Religions, Second Edition, Molloy, Copyright ©2002 The McGraw-Hill Companies, Inc.